Socio-Economic Empowerment

Pratap Pinjani
Department of Sociology
Government College
Ajmer – 305 001

•

Executive Editor
J N Govil

2018

Studium Press (India) Pvt. Ltd.

Socio-Economic Empowerment

ISBN: 978-93-85046-18-6

Published by:

Studium Press (India) Pvt. Ltd.
4735/22, 2nd Floor, Prakash Deep Building
(Near Delhi Medical Association),
Ansari Road, Darya Ganj, New Delhi-110 002
Tel.: + 91-11-43240200-15 (15 lines); Fax: 91-11-43240215
E-mail: studiumpress@gmail.com

Printed at India

About the Author(s)

Dr. Pratap Pinjani (b.1965) holds Ph.D. degree in Sociology from MDS University, Ajmer and has been recipient of Governor Chancellor Medal (2015). He has a number of publications of articles and papers to his credit in journals and periodicals of repute. He has presented 40 papers in seminars and conferences at national and international levels. Attended seminars at Yokohoma (Japan) and Vienna (Austria), for which he received a travel grant from UGC (2014) AND ICSSR. (2016) and completed three minor research projects funded by UGC. Presently he is the Head, Department of Sociology, Govt. College, Ajmer since 2014 and teaching Sociology in various institutions from 1991 and engaged in guiding 9 Ph.D. scholars and M.Phil. Students, 8 students were awarded Ph.D. degree and 33 students were awarded M.Phil. degrees under his guidance. He is a life member of International Sociological Association, Indian Sociological Society and various professional bodies.

Dr. J.N. Govil *(b. 1945)*: Obtained his Master's and Doctorate degrees from Agra University, Agra, India. In his career span of 41 years research experience at the Indian Agricultural Research Institute, New Delhi, Dr. Govil has been involved in the breeding of cross-pollinated, often cross-pollinated, and self-pollinated crops. His research was mainly focused on breeding for better quality, disease resistance, and for higher productivity in *Pennisetum, Sorghum,* maize, chickpea, and pigeonpea. During these years at IARI, he has released nine varieties of early pigeonpea in arhar-wheat rotation. Dr. Govil has been well exposed to the international scientific community through various programmes at UK, Denmark and Thailand. He also participated in various international seminars and conferences. Dr. Govil is credited with more than ninety research papers in various journals of national and international repute in various aspects of genetics, crop breeding, and topics on general agriculture. He has also guided more than a dozen post-graduate students. Dr. Govil is recipient of no. of Awards and Honor presented by ICAR and Agricultural Societies. He has written and edited a number of books on Medicinal Plants and other books with international authors. A new series **"Recent Progress in Medicinal Plants"** has been published by *Studium Press, LLC, USA* in 46 volumes under Dr. Govil's Chief Editorship. Dr. Govil has been the main resource person as Executive Editor in Execution, Co-ordination and Completion of Projects in bringing 12 Vols Set each on ***Nanotechnology, Biotechnology, Energy Science and Technology,*** and ***Environmental Science and Engineering and other books on Social Sciences and Humanities***. Simultaneously, Dr. Govil has brought four volumes set of Chemical Technology Series comprising 2 vols each on ***Advances in Fertilizer Technology*** as well as on ***Petroleum Engineering*** under the capacity of Acquisition Editor of the Series. Dr. Govil retired from ICAR service during the year 2007. Presently, he is working as Publishing Director and Managing Editor with Studium Press LLC, USA (Camped at New Delhi, India) and has brought out nearly 310 scientific books publication during last eight years. *E-mail: jngovil@gmail.com; jngovil@hotmail.com*

Preface

Development is defined as a state in which things are improving. But it is defined in different ways in various contexts, social, political, biological, science and technology, language and literature. In the socio-economic context, development means the improvement of people's life styles through improved education, incomes, skill development and employment. It is the process of economic and social transformation based on cultural and environmental factors.

An edited volume of essays/articles is like Vitamin B complex. The hallmark of such a book has its broad spectrum with intensive focussing on various aspects of the umbrella theme. The present venture seems to justify it in toto.

The yardstick to measure the progress and growth of a nation usually pertains to the socio-economic paradigms. It is with this intent that present collections of articles have been proposed. And, therefore almost all the articles contained herein share a common focus on current socio economic growth. An ancient country with huge legacy of cultural importance, India is on its heels and toes to compete with the developed nations of occidental world. At this juncture the demand of the hour is to keep an adequate balance between has-been and an envisioned will be. The present volume aims not only as a post mortem of the current socio-economic scenario but also at skilled surgery with a hope to provide a vector to the prospect of a better future for India and the humanity at large.

The value orientation of empowerment suggests goals, aims and strategies for implementing changes. Empowerment theory provides principles and a framework for organizing our knowledge.

The present book is the compilation of 14 articles on various aspects of socio economic empowerment. The present volume also reflects the view on such important issues which directly reflect the society at large.

In the first article Mehdi Monadjemi and John Lodwijks discussed about an unrestricted capital flows that have financial crises and affected the daily lives of people throughout the world appreciate monetary should be follow by the control banks to overcome the financial crises.

Tsertseil Juliya in his article discussed about the matters of economic development of regions on the basis of clusters. M. Porter proposed the Model of regional cluster, which is characterized by multiplier effect focused on improving competitiveness of the region.

The third article of Ali Ghahremanlou is related with different schemes introduced by India to enhance the quality of electricity supply because the power outages are still occurring.

The fourth article of Nejia Zaoulai is based on Theoretical External Transport pricing as transport place an important role in our economic, political, and cultural life. Many actions taken by the government in recent years to improve the efficiency of transport by managing congestion and decreased number of accidents which impact the transport environment.

The fifth article of M. Kunhaman is focused on issues of development and discussed relevance and role of state in the development.

The article of Syarifuddin and Eatna Ayu Damayanti discussed about the strategy of 'change' and explaining about the budget policy in Accounting. It also laid emphasis on case study of Bate in Jembeana Regency. The objective of this article is to describe how local government that is massively complex and not simple.

The seventh article of Qihui Chen stress on causal inference methods in social science research, basically it is devoted to an in depth introduction of empirical methods that are used in the fields of demography economics, education and sociology.

The eighth article of Elena Kalcheva, Ahmad Taki and Yuri Hadi is closely related the quality and characteristics of the infrastructure in several high-rise states in Sofia and Bulgaria and evaluates to which extend its serve the resident in the tall building and discuss how the following need to be implemented: new layouts a the streets introduction at viable public spaces with strong sense of place.

The ninth article of Jubril Atanda discussed about the current situation of the world to understand phenomenological character of a city. Nicosia (North-Cyprus).

The tenth article of Rafael Gustavo De Lima, Elisete Dahmer Pfitscher and Vittor Soares Rocha discussed the study creates and applies a sustainability assessment model for ICT's (SIAS/ICT) in southern of Brazil combining with the GRI (Global Reporting Initiative), the (A3P) (Environmental agenda in Public Administration) and ISCN (International sustainable campus network).

The eleventh article of Fusun Yildizba basically describes the connection between human rights and democracy is examined. Basic concepts of the children's right are analysed within the framework of historical development.

The twelfth article of Nazia Jamal and Farhana Jamal discussed about the women empowerment and the concept of microfinance is described by F.A.J. Bouman's in his book, 'Small short and Unsecured'

In the thirteenth article Nazia Jamal talked about economic reforms and the processes of restructuring Indian economy and eradicates the poverty from India by restructuring Indian economy through economic reforms.

Rohini Ruhil in his article emphasized on Gender and Tobacco used in India. The paper concludes with a need to empower and educate women and to support women representation in tobacco control initiatives especially in leadership roles.

The book has contributions from India, China, Cyprus, Russian, Tunisia and U.K.

It is my great pleasure to record my special debt of gratitude to all the distinguished authors who have contributed to the making of this volume, for their timely response and generosity in accepting the invitation and for their efforts in completing this book. It is the quality of their contributors that has made this book extremely valuable. I am extremely thankful to them all.

I highly appreciate the all round cooperation and support of Dr. J.N. Govil for its execution, printing and publish the book with patience, care and interest. Constructive suggestions for improvement of the book will be gratefully acknowledged. Academicians and professionals both will be find this book most informative and useful.

(Dr. Pratap Pinjani)

Table of Contents

1

Monetary Policy and Macroeconomic Stabilization

MEHDI MONADJEMI[1]* AND JOHN LODEWIJKS[1]

ABSTRACT

There is now considerable disquiet about the appropriate monetary strategy that central banks should follow in the aftermath of the global financial crisis. Before the Global Financial Crisis Central Bank Independence was a popular topic among those who favoured price stability. A conservative central banker, without being influenced by the economic policies of the government, could maintain as its primary priority the maintenance of price stability. The response of central bankers to the financial crises seems to indicate a very different approach now to macroeconomic targeting. Central banks are directing monetary policy towards output and employment. Furthermore, speculative capital flows, asset price bubbles and unsettled currency unions are adding further complexity to the role of central bankers around the world.

***Key words*:** Monetary policy, Central banks, Capital mobility, Instability

1. INTRODUCTION

International financial developments have become an important factor affecting the daily lives of people throughout the world. Unrestricted capital flows have created financial crises that have caused falling output and living standards in the affected countries and have proved contagious for other places in the world. Interconnected and integrated

[1]University of NSW and S P Jain School of Global Management, 5 Figtree Drive, Sydney Olympic Park, NSW, 2127, Australia.

**Corresponding author*: E-mail: M.Monadjemi@unsw.edu.au, John.Lodewijks@spjain.edu.au

global financial markets now mean that no country is safe from economic crises that originate far from its own borders. The proliferation of financial crises is often viewed as one of the defining aspects of the intensification of financial globalization over the last few decades. Public sector bailouts of troubled financial institutions (and countries) has led to rising government indebtedness where in a worse-case scenario budgets are consumed entirely by interest payments on debt.

In this context we look specifically at what central banks have done and are doing to achieve macroeconomic stabilization. We focus on the evolution of monetary policy and the challenge to inflation targeting in the midst of lack-lustre economic growth and economic stagnation. Internationally mobile capital flows can add another ingredient to economic instability while eurosclerosis seems now to have another dimension; sovereign debt defaults are a distinct possibility. It is these issues we now discuss.

2. THE EVOLUTION OF MONETARY POLICY

Monetary policy is designed to influence prices, output and employment and the exchange rate. This policy is conducted by the central bank though variation of the quantity of money in circulation or interest rates. The effects of monetary policy on output and the price level has been the subject of extensive debate in economics. Classical economists such as Adam Smith, David Ricardo and David Hume believed that in a free market system wage, price and interest rate flexibility moves the economy towards full employment. Economic instabilities are temporary, and hence there was no role for discretionary monetary and fiscal policy.

The Great Depression of 1930s proved that the labour mark can suffer from unemployment for a long period of time. In 1936 John Maynard Keynes in the *General Theory of Employment Interest and Money* argued that government intervention is required to compensate for the fall in aggregate demand. Keynes emphasized the use of fiscal rather than monetary policy in recession. He showed that in deep recession when interest rates are very low, monetary policy cannot stimulate aggregate demand. He reasoned that at the liquidity trap which occurs at a very low rate of interest, people prefer to hold liquidity. In this situation, any expansion of the money supply will be held rather than being spent to purchase goods and services. Furthermore, Keynes argued that in addition to the existence of the liquidity trap, the interest elasticity of investment demand is low. Accordingly, in deep recession monetary policy is incapable of increasing production and employment.

Fiscal policy was used to promote growth and reduce unemployment in 1940s, 1950s and the 1960s when inflation was not a serious problem. Monetary policy was accommodating to the fiscal policy stance. Significant oil price increase by OPEC in the 1970s, from 2 dollars per barrel to 11 dollars, led to double-digit rates of inflation and unemployment in industrial countries. Fiscal policy proved ineffective when there was unemployment and inflation simultaneously.

During the 1960s there was an extensive debate between Monetarists and Keynesians over implementation of monetary and fiscal policy. Friedman (1968) argued that discretionary monetary policy, instead of eliminating macroeconomic instability, increased the fluctuations. Friedman believed that monetary policy influences the economy with long and variable lags. The central banks do not have perfect knowledge about the timing of these lags. When they conduct discretionary policy they may generate a cycle rather than eliminating the existing ones. Friedman preferred rules over discretion. For instance, a constant growth of the money supply that is in line with the rate of growth of the economy.

Milton Friedman was very influential in emphasising the importance of monetary policy for macro-economic stabilization. Friedman and Schwartz (1963) demonstrated a high correlation between money and prices in the United States for 100 years.

Monetary targeting was exercised by many countries including US, UK, Canada, Australia and New Zealand to control inflation. This monetary strategy was successful to reduce inflation in the above mentioned countries at the expense of increasing unemployment. Friedman (1968) and Phelps (1968), in the context of adaptive expectations, showed that an expansionary monetary policy is effective only in the short run to reduce unemployment but increases inflation. In the long run unemployment adjusts to the natural rate and inflation remains high. This message encouraged politicians to adopt monetary targeting to successfully reduce inflation.

Those that used rational rather than adaptive expectations claimed that the private sector can fully anticipate the outcome of government policies and acts to offset the effects of policies. Only unanticipated policies can influence output and employment. For example, the government may attempt to increase the money supply to expand the economy. The private sector anticipates that, as a result of that policy, prices will rise. Workers demand higher money wages causing real wages and employment to remain constant. Under rational expectations, discretionary monetary policy is completely ineffective.

Kydland and Prescott (1977) considered the choice between policy discretion and rules under the assumption of rational expectations. Their study demonstrated that exercising monetary policy with a rule leaves the society at the optimum level of unemployment and inflation, whereas, a discretionary policy increases inflation leaving unemployment unchanged. This suggestion is similar to Phelps (1968) and Friedman (1968) where in the long run a discretionary increase in the money supply policy raises inflation without reducing unemployment. The difference between the two studies is that the Kydland and Prescott's research suggests that monetary policy based on a rule leaves both unemployment and inflation at zero percent.

Monetary targeting created several problems for those countries that conducted monetary policy based on this strategy. This procedure requires setting a range for the central bank in terms of their tolerance with inflation, for example, a 2 to 3 percent range. If the actual inflation exceeds this range, monetary authorities increase interest rates in order to reduce aggregate demand and maintain the inflation in the target range. However, deregulation and financial innovation caused instability in the relationship between money and economic activity. As a result monetary aggregates started giving misleading signals about the state of the economy. Hence, monetary authorities were not able to predict the effects of their policy on prices and output.

3. THE ROLE OF THE CENTRAL BANK

Monetary policy is conducted by the central bank. In addition to the implementation of monetary policy, central banks also perform the following functions: Custodian of nation's gold and foreign exchange reserves; Banker of the government; Holding banks' reserves; and the Issue of notes in circulation. One of the most important roles of the central bank is implementation of monetary policy through changing monetary base or setting interest rates.

The following discussion shows the relationship between money and monetary base (currency in circulation and reserves of banks with the central bank) (Monadjemi and Lodewijks, 2015).

$$MB = C + BR \tag{1}$$

Where MB, C and BR are monetary base, cash in circulation and banks' reserves respectively

$$r_d = BR/D \text{ or } BR = r_d \times D \tag{2}$$

In (2) D is banks' deposits and r_d is reserve requirement ratio (percentage of deposits banks are legally obligated to hold in reserves) respectively.

$$MS = C + D \tag{3}$$

In (3) money supply is cash in circulation plus bank deposits. Assume that cash deposit ratio c = C/D, which is less than unity, 0 < c < 1.

$$MS/MB = C + D/C + BR = (C/D + D/D)/C/D + BR/D \tag{4}$$

$$MS = MB\ (c + 1)/(c + r_d) \tag{5}$$

The ratio $(c + 1)/(c + r_d)$ in (5) is greater than 1 since c and r_d are less than 1. This ratio is called the money multiplier and shows that every one-dollar change in MB leads to a larger change in the supply of money.

The following simplified balance sheet of the central bank shows the sources of change in MB and MS.

Table 1: Simplified balance sheet of the central bank

Assets	***Liabilities***
Gold and foreign exchange reserves (GFX)	Currency (notes) in circulation (C)
Government security (GS)	Commercial banks' reserves (BR)
Bank loans (BL)	Government account (GA)
Other assets (OA)	Other liabilities (OL)
	Net worth (NW)

Two sides of the balance sheet must be equal. Accordingly, identity 1 can be written:

$$GFX + GB + BL \in C + BR + GA + (OL - OA + NW) \tag{6}$$

Or

$$C + BR \in GFX + GB + BL - GA \tag*{(6)'}$$

For our purpose OL – OA + NW are not important and usually they are not large. For this reason the sum has been dropped from identity 6'. In 6' C + BR is monetary base (MB) or high powered money. Changes in the items on the right hand side of 6' cause changes in MB.

MB and MS can change through central bank open market operations (purchase or sales of government securities GS), central bank intervention in the foreign exchange market (GFX), financing of government budget deficits by borrowing from the central bank (GA) and bank loans (BL).

The central bank cannot target both money supply and interest rates together. They have to choose between monetary targeting and interest rate targeting. Poole (1970) showed that if the objective of the central bank is to minimize deviation of output, monetary targeting is optimal when shocks originate from the real sector and interest rate targeting is preferable when there are financial disturbances.

Monadjemi and Lodewijks (2014) argued that inflation targeting was a popular strategy for monetary policy in developed countries during the decade of 1990s. The strategy for implementing monetary policy in the 1970s, 1980s and the 1990s respectively changed from monetary targeting, exchange rate targeting and inflation targeting and central bank independence. It is interesting to note that the change in the strategy occurred at the same time for the countries that followed the above monetary policy strategies. After the breakdown of monetary targeting in late 1970s, several countries adopted exchange rate targeting. Stability of the exchange rate is vital for open economies with significant international trade. The most well-known exchange rate targeting is the European Monetary system. Under this system eight European counties agreed to keep their exchange rate fixed against the German Mark. This arrangement was successful to maintain the inflation of member countries at a very low level in line with Germany's inflation rate.

Monadjemi *et al.* (2013) argued that during the decade of 1990s, several countries, such as Australia, Brazil, Britain, Canada, Chile, Norway, South Africa, Korea, and New Zealand, used inflation targeting for conducting monetary policy. With inflation targeting, the central bank conducts monetary policy for keeping the expected rate of inflation within a target range. Countries that exercised inflation targeting were successful in keeping their rate of inflation within the targeted range.

The preference of price stability against growth and employment was suggested in Rogoff (1985). Rogoff argued that the society is better-off if the central bank and society have different objective functions. In other words, the monetary authorities need to be conservative with an objective function that weights the price stability more than employment. Monetary decisions made by a conservative central bank should be independent of government policies for expanding output and employment.

Monadjemi *et al.* (2013) maintained that an independent central bank will not conduct monetary policy based on the economic policy of the government, which may have been influenced by political considerations. Germany (before introduction of the euro), Japan and Switzerland have the most independent central banks and their respective inflation rates are the lowest in the world. New Zealand is the classic example of the relationship between central bank independence and inflation control. During 1955–1988 when the annual average rate of inflation in New Zealand was 7.6 percent, monetary policy was conducted based on the economic priorities of the government. In 1988, legislations were introduced that supported the independence of the central bank and maintenance of low inflation. The average rate of inflation in New Zealand during 1989–2000 declined to 2.7 percent per year.

Some authors distinguished between political independence and economic independence. Political independence was defined as the ability of the central bank to conduct monetary policy without government consultation. Economic independence is referred to as the ability of the government to borrow from the central bank. The ability of the government to borrow from the central bank affects the monetary base and reduces control of the central bank over price stability. There appears to be a negative relationship between inflation rate and the index of central bank independence. However, there does not seem to be a specific relationship between growth, employment and the central bank independence.

The independence of the central bank contributes to the control of inflation because governments generally attempt to expand output and employment by borrowing from the central bank (printing money) which may cause inflation. Accordingly, a conservative central banker, without being influenced by the economic policies of the government, can control inflation.

4. THE GLOBAL FINANCIAL CRISIS (GFC) AND THEREAFTER

Before the financial crises of 2007–2008, several developed countries conducted monetary policy by setting interest rate based on inflation targeting. The financial crisis occurred in the financially advanced economies and caused severe recession in the affected countries. Output and employment in those countries declined significantly. The interest rates in the affected counties declined to near zero. However, output and employment did not increase and remained low. The situation was similar to the liquidity trap which was introduced by Keynes regarding the ineffectiveness of conventional monetary policy at the very low rate of interest. Japan's economy went through the same developments in the 1990s. With interest rates near zero the Bank of Japan conducted unconventional approaches to monetary policy that would be replicated in response to the global financial crisis.

The unconventional monetary policy is divided into two broad categories of asset purchases and forward guidance. Asset Purchases is similar to the conventional open market operations where the central bank purchases or sells short term government securities. However, under Asset Purchases the central bank attempts to reduce the long term interest rate by purchasing long-term government bonds and mortgage-backed securities. Under the quantitative easing the central bank prints money to purchase assets. Most of the central banks of affected countries exercised quantitative easing during financial crises of 2007–2008. It appears that quantitative easing was effective in reducing the long term rate of interest in the affected countries.

Forward guidance is related to the transparency of the future policies of the central bank. Through Forward Guidance the Bank of Japan in the late 1990s, the Federal Reserve Bank of the US and the Bank of England during the financial crises in 2008, attempted to persuade the markets that as long as there is no fear of inflation, they will keep the rate of interest at very low levels. In the case of some countries official interest rates have even been set at negative levels.

The actions of the U.S Federal Reserve were unprecedented. In 2009 with interest rates close to zero, the Federal Reserve engaged in very unorthodox monetary measures involving quantitative easing, capital injections, and central bank swap lines that were described as having "revolutionized monetary policy". A stunning series of unprecedented interventions into the financial system rescued both illiquid and insolvent financial institutions and even involved swapping safe government bonds for toxic assets.

In the U.S. 40 percent of conventional deposits were uninsured and the government was forced to provide a blanket guarantee–the equivalent of deposit insurance–to all existing money market funds. They guaranteed bank debt irrespective of how prudent or otherwise these institutions had been. The Federal Reserve made loans directly to ailing financial institutions, including non-depository institutions, and bought up long terms government debt and mortgage-backed securities, credit card debt and auto loans. The central bank became lender of first, last and only resort marshalling a massive expansion of government support for the financial system. The Government became effective owners of a large part of the financial system as it bought shares and injected capital to prevent foreclosures. The nature of the intervention was so extensive that the distinction between monetary and fiscal policy is now not at all clear as the monetary interventions have clear spending and tax implications. The subsidization of the financial system - subsidizing the 'bad' investment decisions of the banks and non-banks with taxpayer money – and the purchase of risky asset-backed securities, will all leave a burden that will eventually fall on taxpayers.

5. INTERNATIONAL CAPITAL MOBILITY

International capital mobility has become an attractive topic of study since deregulation of financial market and larger and faster mobility of capital internationally (Monadjemi and Lodewijks, 2015). Several economists argue that greater linkage of international capital markets has contributed significantly to the global financial crises in 2007–2009. Accordingly, measurement of capital mobility is important since it may indicate the extent of global financial crises.

There are several measures for testing international capital mobility. In a closed economy saving and investment are perfectly correlated. In an open economy with capital inflow, the correlation between saving and investment declines. In conditions of perfect capital mobility, domestic and foreign interest rates are equal. In this case, given interest parity condition (ICP)[1], the expected change in the exchange rate is equal to zero. Several studies have attempted to test the degree of international capital mobility directly, by examining the difference between domestic and foreign interest rates. Most studies found significant differences between US interest rates and foreign rates due to the differences between risk of bankruptcy, inflation and liquidity. Interest rates of advanced economies such as US and Western Europe were much closer moving in the same direction.

---

[1]Assume that the only risk of holding foreign currency assets is the risk of change in the exchange rate. The return on 1 dollar invested in foreign currency is the interest rate plus the expected change in exchange rate which can be positive or negative that is;
$r^* + E\Delta e$. The return of 1 dollar invested in domestic currency is r, the rate of interest.
Inflow occurs when $r > r^* + E\Delta$Capital e that is return in domestic currency is greater than the return in foreign currency. Capital outflow takes place when $r < r^* + E\Delta e$. IPC holds when $r = r^* + E\Delta e$. When IPC holds the capital market is in equilibrium and there is no incentive for capital movement.

The following equation is suggested for testing the degree of capital mobility:

$r - r^* = (e^e - e)/e + \rho$ where ρ, r, r^*, e^e and e are all of the risk associated with the domestic currency assets, domestic rate of interest, foreign interest rate, expected change in the exchange rate and the exchange rate respectively. In this form, domestic interest rates have to compensate for expected depreciation of domestic currency as well as other risk associated with holding home county assets.

Since most of the borrowings and lending transactions continue in the future, expected inflation has to be taken into consideration. Accordingly, real rather than nominal interest rates are more appropriate in financial transactions. Real interest rates are nominal rates less expected inflation;

$$R = r - \pi^e \quad (7)$$

In (7) R and π^e are real interest rate and expected inflation respectively. The difference between domestic and foreign real interest rate is:

$$R - R^* = (r - \pi^e) - (r^* - \pi^{e*}) \quad (8)$$

In (8) those with * represent foreign variables. The real interest parity condition (RIPC) is presented in (9).

$$R - R^* = E\Delta Re \quad (9)$$

Where *Re* is the real exchange rate. The following equations show how (9) is derived from a combination of (9) and the expected change in real exchange rate.

$$RE = \mathrm{e}P^* / P$$

$$E\Delta Re = E\Delta e - (\pi^e - \pi^{*e})$$

If IPC holds $r - r^e = E\Delta e$ then

$$E\Delta Re = (r - \pi^e) - (r^* - \pi^{e*}) = R - R^*$$

Some researchers argue that RIPC is used as a criterion for international capital mobility. That is, international investors consider RIPC as a signal for capital movement. This is a debatable issue as IPC and RIPC ignore other political and economic risks between countries except the risk of foreign exchange rate fluctuations.

Other researchers are far more concerned with the effects of capital mobility. Since the late 1980s many Asian developing economies had experienced surges in capital inflows and the surges were largest in the countries that later experienced the strongest effects of the crisis. Only a small fraction of this inflow came in the form of direct foreign investment, the remainder was portfolio investment or investment mediated through the banking sector. This private capital inflow was driven by the speculative tendencies of investors, particularly in commercial real estate, and resulted in a rampant increase in domestic asset prices. The rise in asset prices induced further capital inflows. Much of the collateral the banks accepted for foreign loans was real estate and equities, assets whose prices contained a large "bubble" element. As much of the capital inflow was short term, the banks were borrowing short and lending long.

The Asian financial institutions of affected countries were ill equipped to deal with globalisation's sudden surges of capital inflows. The banks were poorly regulated and standards of loan appraisal were generally inadequate. When the bubble burst, the foreign capital departed as quickly as it had come in, leaving plunging currencies and unsustainable debt to equity ratios as asset prices collapsed. Some observers say that the principal cause of the ensuing crises was domestic financial sector weakness which permitted overinvestment in the property sector of these Asian economies through excessive foreign borrowing at short maturities. Others point to internationally mobile capital and the need to control it in some way to prevent future crises. Their concerns relate to the development of derivatives and other highly levered financial intermediaries, such as hedge funds and bank proprietary trading departments, which are programmed to move large pools of capital quickly between different financial markets.

It is interesting to note that the countries that escaped the crisis either had enormous international reserves like Singapore and Hong Kong or capital controls. Singapore had both, with a set of rules on capital transactions, for example, non-residents cannot borrow in Singapore dollars. The experience of China shows that controls are strictly applied over capital flows and this has insulated the economy from financial shocks. In India capital accounts have not been liberalized with limits on large-scale capital transfers within short periods of time. Vietnam has stringent controls over both the capital and the current accounts. In Chile 30% of all non-equity capital flowing into the country must be deposited interest-free at the central bank for one year. Any foreign money entering into Chile must stay in the country for at least one year and Chilean banks and firms can only borrow from the international capital markets if the borrowing quality is rated as high as Chile's government bonds. These control mechanisms reflect the feeling that the net benefit of short-term capital is small or even negative.

The Asian Financial Crisis brought into question the suitability and practicality of the basic financial liberalization-globalization model that has been promoted widely in both developed and developing countries over the previous 20 years. A number of commentators argue that the financial crisis in Asia was caused by the unpredictability and instability of large flows of loan, portfolio and other non-equity capital.

A related concern is the fragility of domestic financial markets and the need for stronger prudential supervision. Observers have noted that banks generally appear to take risks in excess of those taken by other firms, for example, US banks are ten times as highly geared as manufacturing companies. This then suggests the need to raise bank capital to asset ratios. A more general concern relates to the sequencing of economic liberalization in many of these countries. In general, trade liberalization should precede financial liberalization, domestic financial liberalization should precede external financial liberalization, and direct investment liberalization should precede portfolio and bank loan liberalization (capital account liberalization).

What stands out are the unexpectedly large adverse effects on real variables (output, employment and firm insolvency) that can occur when a fragile under-regulated financial sector with inadequate prudential supervision is exposed to volatile and large capital injections. Asset prices can exhibit bubble behaviour and crash quite precipitously and the contagion impacts on countries far from the source of the initial financial instability.

6. MACROECONOMIC STABILIZATION IN EUROPEAN MONETARY UNION

Monadjemi and Lodewijks (2014) argued that the Global Financial Crisis had a devastating impact on many European Monetary Union member countries and resulted in growing public and private sector indebtedness, the collapse of economic activity, high levels of unemployment, particularly for youth, and the threat of deflation. The European Central Bank's decision to reduce its main refinancing rate in June 2014 from 0.25% to 0.15% was accompanied by the deposit rate on excess reserves also being reduced by 0.10% (from 0% to –0.10%). The tax on excess reserves represents an attempt to avoid deflation in the eurozone by promoting bank lending.

Furthermore, as austerity measures were implemented in the UK, Ireland, Spain, Italy, Greece, Portugal and France, the results have been associated with high unemployment and rising social tensions.

The strategy of internal devaluation has been employed as the traditional approach of restoring competiveness through currency devaluation is no longer available. Currency devaluations cut the purchasing power of consumers by making the national currency weaker and thus foreign goods more expensive. This has the virtue of increasing consumption of domestically produced goods, while making exports cheaper. This option is no longer available as national currencies have disappeared. So they are left with internal devaluations by cutting wages across the board. While internal devaluations have contributed to reduced current account deficits this has resulted from repressed domestic demand, due to wage cuts and increased unemployment, which has led to a collapse in import spending. Further, an internal devaluation exacerbates the burdens of servicing private debt and further dampens any hope of a recovery in private demand as the income of consumers has been reduced.

Not surprisingly, the design of the European Monetary Union has been subject to intense scrutiny. The chief challenge to such a monetary union was the different levels of productivity between the higher productivity of the older member states of the West and the newer, lower productivity members from the East. The presence of asymmetric shocks was also a key problem. Furthermore, within the eurozone, the centralisation of monetary policy condoned housing bubbles in Spain and Ireland prior to the Global Financial Crisis. The strategy of internal devaluation, combined with budgetary austerity, has had a strong negative impact in terms of growth and employment throughout Europe and led to the near collapse of Europe's 'Social Model' (balancing unrestrained market forces by a 'social dimension') with social safety nets disappearing or severely reduced.

Increased doubts are being expressed about the conventional view of a low inflation strategy. Higher average inflation and higher nominal interest rates to start with, would have helped to lower interest rates more, thereby most likely reducing the decline in output and deterioration of fiscal positions in the aftermath of global crisis. This reservation against the low inflation strategy has been shared by leading economists such as Kenneth Rogoff, Greg Mankiw, Paul Krugman and Brad DeLong.

Some observers are even suggesting that countries need to restore their policy sovereignty. This inevitably involves exiting the European Monetary Union and reinstating a fiat (non-convertible) currency, a flexible exchange rate regime and monetary independence. Whether such a radical strategy ensues, it does suggest quite clearly that a monetary union with a singular focus on inflation targeting can achieve inflation control but this is clearly not a sufficient condition for macroeconomic stabilization.

7. CONCLUSIONS

In a well-functioning market economy, markets are supposed to provide the incentives that lead individuals to do what is in society's interest. Financial markets have the responsibility of performing the essential societal functions of managing risk, allocating capital and mobilizing saving while keeping transaction costs low. Financial markets should allocate capital to its most productive use where the returns to society were highest. Unfortunately there have been episodes where financial markets have misallocated capital, engaged in excessive risk-taking and lending to those that could not repay, leading to a situation where private rewards were unrelated to social returns. Indeed, banks can perform so poorly at credit assessment and mortgage design that they put the entire economy at risk.

These episodes have imposed new challenges on central banks and on the operation of monetary policy. This chapter has outlined some of these challenges and some of the responses but it is a very fluid situation and we can expect far more unconventional monetary policy and prudential supervision of financial institutions in the future.

REFERENCES

Friedman, M. (1968). The role of monetary policy. *American Economic Review*, 58(1): 1–17.

Friedman, M. and Schwartz, A.A. (1963). Monetary History of the United States 1867–1960. Princeton University Press, Princeton.

Kydland, F. and Prescott, E. (1977). Rules rather than discretion: The inconsistency of optimal plans. *Journal of Political Economy*, 85: 473–491.

Monadjemi, M. and Lodewijks, J. (2014). Inflation targeting and macroeconomic stabilization. *Research in World Economy*, 5(2): 93–98.

Monadjemi, M. and Lodewijks, J. (2015). *Money and Monetary Policy in an Open Economy*. Book boon, London.

Monadjemi, M., Yoon, K. and Lodewijks, J. (2013). Central bank behaviour before and after the great recession. *Economics*, 2(5): 55–61.

Phelps, E. (1968). Money wage dynamics and labour market equilibrium. *Journal of Political Economy*, 76(4): 678–711.

Poole, W. (1970). Optimal choice of monetary instruments in a simple stochastic macro model. *Quarterly Journal of Economics*, 84: 197–216.

Rogoff, K. (1985). The optimal degree of commitment to an intermediate monetary target. *Quarterly Journal of Economics,* 100: 1169–1189.

2

Economic Development of Regions on the Basis of Clusters

TSERTSEIL JULIYA[1]*

ABSTRACT

This section highlights matters of economic development of regions using the cluster approach; petrochemical cluster of one of the Russian Federation regions – Republic of Tatarstan – is provided for illustrative purposes. Model of this regional cluster has been developed based on the approach proposed by M. Porter. At the present time key attention is paid to economic development of regions; special emphasis is laid on innovative development of regions to receive additional competitive advantages in the age of globalization of world economic relations.

***Key words*:** Cluster, Region, Development, R&D

INTRODUCTION

Development of regional economy within clusters is considered in the age of globalization of world economic relations and strengthening of competitive fighting as principal direction of economic development of the country in whole. Regional cluster is considered as an instrument of innovation-based economy which is characterized by multiplier effect focused on improving competitiveness of the region. The result of networking cooperation of enterprises and organizations – participants of a cluster – is acceleration of innovation process that determines improvement of strategic advantages (Porter, 2000). Process of clusters development is most intensely performed in the regions which actively

[1]Russian Economic University named after Plekhanov G.V., 119019 Nikitsky Boulvar, 17–81, Moscow, Russian Federation

**Corresponding author*: E-mail: zerzeo18811@mail.ru

create innovative infrastructure to support industrial capacity with scientific-innovation and educational potentials (Porter, 2003). In the meantime, existence of a cluster in the region itself, particularly support of its development by state not always preconditions growth of innovative development in the region.

Some authors, M. Muro and B. Katz, hold to an opinion that Federal Government should support and stimulate development of spontaneous "natural" clusters in the territory of regions (Muro and Katz, 2010). Only in this case investments will be reasonable and will be accompanied by innovation growth of regional economy. M. Porter determines regional innovative (or industrial) cluster in his articles as geographical concentration of disengaged business units, suppliers of services, raw materials and materials, coordinating centers, associations of institutes of specialized fields and spheres (Porter, 1990).

The authors consider concept of regional economy development based on clusters; this concept provides for consistent cooperation of state and commercial economic sectors that results in increase of population income, creation of new work places within a region, increase of tax revenues in value terms for the treasury of all levels of governance, constant qualitative growth of domain experts in various economic sectors.

Stable development of a cluster is determined by following groups of factors:

- External environment and composition of participants;
- Consistency of communications and self-organization level;
- Strategic commitment to innovations of companies and universities included in a cluster.

Peculiarities of substantiation and implementation of cluster policy within the Russian Federation are the following fundamental preconditions:

- Creation of territorial production complexes within regions to stimulated their economic development in main sectors of economy: extraction industry and processing industry (territorial production complex) before 1990th;
- Existence of federal special-purpose programs at the present moment aimed at support and development of main sectors of economy using such instruments as construction of infrastructural assets in the territory of clusters;

Table 1: Comparative analysis of economic model of development within traditional approach and economic model of development based on clusters

Key factors	*Traditional economic development*	*Economic development based on clusters*
Theoretical background	Neoclassical theory and its presentatives: R. Solow, P. Douglas, Cobb (Antras, 2004), A. Marshall (Van de Ven, 1995), Arthur Pigou, J.B. Clark, C. Menger, E. Bem-Bawerk, J. Buchanan, F, J. Tobin (Solow, 1956).	Innovative and institutional theories and their representatives: T. Veblen, W.C. Mitchell, J.M. Clark, J. Commons, R. Coase, O. Williamson, D. North, R. Nelson, S. Winter, J. Hodgson, (Dunn, 2011) at the present time – M. Porter (Porter, 1998), A. Auzan (Lowenberg, 1990), (Barro and Sala-i-Martin, 2004).
Key participa-nts of mutual relations	Individual economic entities	Associations of economic entities which form entrepreneurial chains on the based on human capital (Goldin, 2014), (Flamholtz, 1999).
Economic deve-lopment incent-ive mechanisms	Decrease of taxation load, in-vestments in design and deve-lopment works, government-sponsored development pro-grams at macro-level	Entrepreneurial chains (Keiser and Ringlstetter, 2011), associa-tions of institutes within suppor-ting government-sponsored deve-lopment programs, special pur-pose financing from budget funds of all levels: federal, regional, local
Key processes, actions	Concentration of capital and efficiency increase labor	Arising regional formations (clu-sters) stimulate innovative acti-vity of companies, organizations, enterprises, financial institu-tions, institutes and universities based on synergy positive effect (Porter, 1990, 1998, 2000, 2003)
Role of state	Macroeconomic process man-agement and provision for inflow of physical resources	Informational assistance, provi-sion of private-public partnership, stimulation of processes when creating intangible assets (Ketels and Memedovic, 2008)

(*Source*: Prepared by the author)

- Formation of free economic zones within regional clusters that provide for decrease of transaction expenses of enterprises – participants of a cluster;
- Innovative course of development of enterprises – participants of clusters of chemical, pharmaceutical industries and machine building;

- A wide range of research and design institutes within military-industrial complexes which at the present moment are specialized in aviation, petrochemical and military-industrial production.

Modern enterprises in the Russian Federation regions when increasing their competitive ability faced the following problems to be solved:

- Optimization of enterprise balance structure;
- Correlation of rates of growth of main financial results of activity with rates of growth of main balance sheet items of the enterprise;
- Increase of share of intangible assets in the structure of non-current assets of the enterprise;
- Balance of shares of equity capital and debt capital taking into consideration expenses for attracted capital;
- Reveal of non-financial factors of the environment which influence cost of debt capital;
- Decrease of level of market concentration to increase intensity of competitive relations;
- Increase of finished product share in the marketable products;
- Improvement of corporate management system of the enterprise;
- Substantiation of forecasting rates of growth taking into consideration factors of external and internal environment.

Creation and development of these clusters in the region make it possible to solve this problem. Due to competitive struggle between enterprises and organizations of allied industries as well as cooperation in the accompanying industries one can achieve quantum growth in the above mentioned projections. Factors which provide for formation of innovative-sectoral clusters can include the following:

- Increased competition that causes formation of stable long-term cooperation ties;
- Modification of economic environment that increase functioning efficiency of associations of enterprises;
- External pressure on economic sector that requires joining efforts to successfully withstand pressure;
- Emerging of new technologies;
- Necessity of scientific and technical cooperation in the high-technology economic sectors.

Cluster approach for formation of corporate strategies of a company provides for implementation of creation and development of cluster formations within the region to increase market price of enterprises – participants of a cluster.

The regression analysis given by the author is shown in Fig. 1 (Tsertseil and Ordov, 2016) was to evaluate functional relationship of the effective index conditional average (the share of sold innovation products in the total volume of revenue) and the factorial index (the share of R&D organizations in the total quantity of enterprises) on the territories of innovation clusters in the Russian Federation.

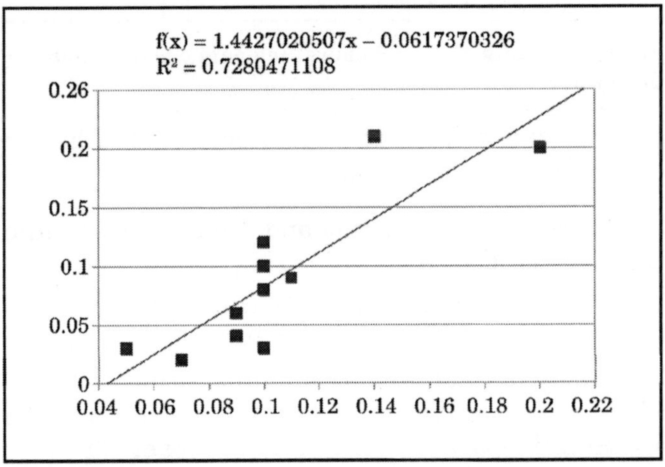

Fig. 1: R&D organizations and volume of innovation products produced on the innovation cluster's territories in Russian Federation. (*Source*: Tsertseil and Ordov, 2016)

Innovation shall mean a final result of innovation implementation to change object of management and receive economic, social, ecological, scientific-technical or other type of effect.

On the one hand, innovation cluster is the aggregate of geographically separated enterprises and organizations having common scientific base and forming technological, logistic and infrastructure chains that is based on use of advantages of simultaneous action of different market mechanisms (cooperation and competition) which enable to produce and quickly distribute new knowledge and technologies. On the other hand, regional innovative-based economic clusters act as an important instrument to implement economic policy which combines activation of market mechanisms and use of potential effects of state participation in implementation of complex social-economic relations.

Supportive sector	**The chemical industry in the region**	**Competing sectors**
Technopolis Khimgrad Business-incubator Ideya Free economic zone Alabuga Specialized regional and federal institutes in the sphere of Research and Development	Key vertical integrated enterprises: Petrol desired fraction Ethylene glycol Polyethylene Truck tires	Technoparks, regional technopolises and business incubators within Russian Federation, chemical enterprises of Central and Northwestern Federal Districts

Fig. 2: Key participants of petrochemical regional cluster (*Source*: Prepared by the author)

Main enterprises of petrochemical cluster located within the Republic of Tatarstan include the following:

- In the sphere of oil extraction and processing – "Tatneft" OJSC, "TANEKO" OJSC, "TAIF-NK" OJSC;
- In the sphere of petrochemistry – "Nizhnekamskneftekhim" OJSC, "Kazanorgsintez" OJSC, "Kazan Synthetic Rubber Plant" OJSC;
- In the sphere of final product manufacturing – "Nefiscosmetics" OJSC, "KVART" CJSC, enterprises – participants of industrial parks "Kamskiepolyany", "Ì-7" and technopark "Khimgrad";
- In the sphere of inorganic chemistry – "L. Ya. Karpov Chemical Plant" OJSC, "Mendeleevsk Chemical Plant" LLC.

According to branching-off groups, the following enterprises can be referred to the related business: "Kazan Synthetic Rubber Plant" OJSC, "Nizhnekamskneftekhim" OJSC, "Nizhnekamskshina" OJSC, "L. Ya. Karpov Chemical Plant" OJSC as well as plants located outside the Republic of Tatarstan, particularly "Starolen" LLC in Budyonnovsk (polyethylene production), Yaroslavl Synthetic Rubber Plant, Tomsk Synthetic Rubber Plant.

As can be seen from the above, innovation regional cluster features a combination of economic entities – participants of a cluster (industrial enterprises, service organizations, scientific-and-research institutes) located within the same territory – territory of a cluster which are characterized by the following key features:

- Combination of all stages of production (technological) process that includes scientific-research as well as development activity (R&D),

Table 2: Participants of petrochemical cluster of the Republic of Tatarstan

Group	*Cluster participants*	*Industry sector*
1	Anchor enterprises of chemical industry	Extractive and processing industry
2	Research and design institutes	Service sector
3	Technopolises, technoparks, free economic zones	Infrastructure
4	State authorities	Legal and regulatory framework

(*Source*: Prepared by the author)

Table 3: The types of final manufacturing product of enterprises – participants of regional chemical cluster within Republic of Tatarstan

Product name	*Industry where this product will be used*
Polycarbonate	Electronics, optics, automobile manufacturing, construction
HPP high-pressure polyethylene	Production of plastic food and technical wraps, insulating materials.
Plastic articles	Irrigation systems, gas supply, process piping systems.
Organic products	Oil and gas industry, perfumery products, heat-exchange apparatus, internal-combustion engines.
Phenol	Production of medical drugs, synthetic resins, herbicides, lubrication oils.
Ethyl acetate	Coating materials, solvents.
Bisphenol	Resins, varnish, glue.
Isoprene rubber	Defence industry, automobile manufacturing
Butyl rubber	Automobile manufacturing
Halobutyl rubber	Automobile manufacturing
Butadiene rubber	Tire industry
Styrene, polystyrene	Latex industry
Neonol	Production of synthetic detergents
Ethylene glycol	Raw material for polyethylene production

(*Source*: Tsertseil, 2015)

Table 4: The enterprises used the products of key chemical enterprises - participant petrochemical cluster in the Republic of Tatarstan.

Sl. no.	*The name of enterprises used the products of OJSC «Nizhnekamskneftekhim» (NNKh)*	*The types of chemical products*	*Output per year, th./rub.*	*The sector of industry used the made production*	*Location*
1	The industrial park "Kamsk's glade"	Polymeric products: • Propilenovy thread	92 thousand tons	Construction branch	Nizhnekamsk city, Republic of Tatarstan
2	OJSC "Polymatize"	Nonwoven fabrics	20 thousand tons	Construction branch, agriculture	Elabuga city, Republic of Tatarstan

Table 4: (*Contd...*)

Table 4: (*Contd...*)

Sl. no.	*The name of enterprises used the products of OJSC «Nizhnekamskneftekhim» (NNKh)*	*The types of chemical products*	*Output per year, th./rub.*	*The sector of industry used the made production*	*Location*
3	LLC "Polimercoldness technique"	Polymeric sprinklers and water catchers	30 thousand tons	Construction branch, chemical industry	Nizhnekamsk city, Republic of Tatarstan
4	OJSC "Chemical plant named Carpov L.Y."	Product of the inorganic chemical industry: plates from expanded polystyrene; reactants; reagents for water processing; innovative inhibitors	110 thousand tons	Construction branch, chemical industry	Mendeleevsk city, Republic of Tatarstan
5	OJSC "Kamsk's plant of polymer materials"	Concentrate of technical carbon; polymeric composites; polystyrene	66 thousand tons	Petrochemical, automobile, construction, packing branches.	Nizhnekamsk city, Republic of Tatarstan
6	LLC "Agricultural plant"	Polymeric products for construction of agricultural industry: polyethylene pipes for water supply; pipes the corrugated polypropylene	30 thousand tons	Agricultural industry	Naberezhnye Chelny city, Republic of Tatarstan
7	LLC "Betar"	Metering devices of water and gas; components for systems of water supply	40 thousand tons	Agricultural industry, construction branch	Naberezhnye Chelny city, Republic of Tatarstan
8	LLC "Kamsk's plastic"	Plastic products	35 thousand tons	Automobile, construction	Nizhnekamsk city, Republic of Tatarstan
9	Technopolis Chimgrad	Chemistry and pharmaceutics products	11 billion rubbles	Aviatsionny industry, construction	Kazan city, Republic of Tatarstan
10	Technology park "Idea"	Composite materials of biotechnology	4,2 billion rubbles	Services sector, education	Kazan city, Republic of Tatarstan

(*Source*: Tsertseil, 2015)

enterprises – participants of a cluster within the same or several economic industries;

- Constant widening of cooperation and coordination ties between enterprises – participants of a cluster;
- Availability of positive synergy effect due to high level of cooperation and competitive relations among enterprises – participants of a cluster;
- Creation of innovative product (goods, works or services) which provide a high level of profitability of enterprises – participant of innovative cluster;
- Increase of share of intangible assets in the structure of assets of enterprises – participants of a cluster;
- Increase of share of innovative products, works and services in total receipt from sales of enterprises – participants of a cluster;
- Increase of gross margin from sales in the total receipt of enterprises – participants of a cluster due to implementation of R&D results into production process;
- Increase of share of organizations in the sphere of R&D among total amount of innovative cluster participants.

Availability of a cluster in the region promotes increase of research activity intensity where there are supporting government-sponsored development programs. As we see in Fig. 3, when considering intensity of innovative activity within territory of some regions of Central and Northwestern Federal Districts: Bryansk region, Voronezh region, Ivanovo region, Kaluga region, Kostroma region, Oryol region, Smolensk region, Tambov region, Tver region, Tula region, Yaroslavl region, the Republic of Karelia, the Komi Republic, Arkhangelsk region, Murmansk region, Novgorod region the following correlation has been formed:

All above mentioned processes of cooperation in the sphere of petrochemistry of the Republic of Tatarstan in the best possible way demonstrate mechanism for creation and development of cluster formation in the region since clusters better than industry sectors use important ties, complementarity of sectors, distribution of technology, experience, information, marketing as well as realization of customer needs which penetrate through companies and economic sectors. Such ties are the basis for competitive fighting, production capacity increase and, particularly, for determination of directions and intensity of organization of new business and innovation implementation. Major part of cluster participants does not directly compete with each other and they just service different segment of a sector. However, they have

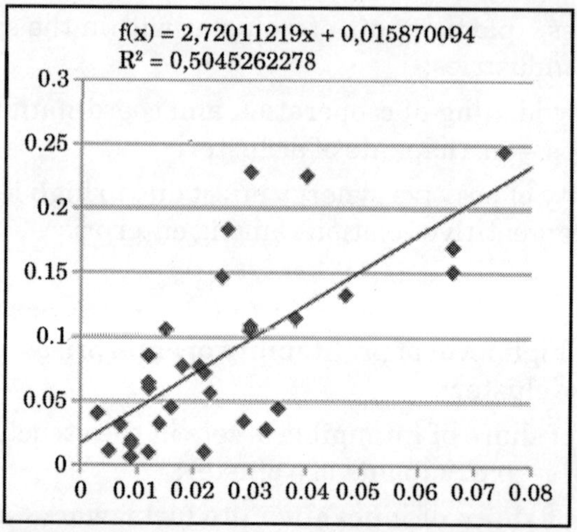

Fig. 3: The relationship between the share of the innovation produce expenditures in the overall volume of expenses (x) and the share of innovation product sales proceeds in the total volume of revenue (y) on Central and Volga-region Federal Districts, 2014. (*Source*: Tsertseil and Ordov, 2016)

a lot of equal demands and capabilities; they meet a lot of equal restrictions and hindrances on the way of improvement in the productivity. Consideration of a group of companies and organizations as a cluster enables to reveal favorable opportunities to coordinate actions and beneficially mutually interact in the spheres of common interests without the danger to distort competition or restrict contest intensity. Cluster provides for capability to lead meaningful and efficient dialogue between related companies and their suppliers, with government as well as with other involved institutions. State and private investments aimed at improvement of functioning conditions of a cluster is enable to increase in future the efficiency of activity of enterprises and companies – participants of a regional cluster.

REFERENCES

Antras, P. (2004). Is the U.S. aggregate production function Cobb-Douglas? New estimates of the elasticity of substitution. The Berkeley electronic press [Internet]. 4(1). Available from: *http://www.scholar.harvard.edu/files/antras/files/cespublished.pdf*

Barro, R.J. and Sala-i-Martin, X. (2004). Economic growth. 2th ed. MIT Press.

Dunn, S.P. (2011). The Economics of John Kenneth Galbraith. Introduction, persuasion and rehabilitation. Cambridge University Press.

Flamholtz, E.G. (1999). Human resource accounting: Advances in concepts, methods and applications. 3th ed. Kluwer Academic Publishers.

Goldin, C. (2014). Human capital. Harvard University. Springer [Internet]. Available from *http://scholar.harvard.edu*

Hofman, E., Maucher, D., Hornstein, J. and Ouden, Den R. (2012). Capital equipment purchasing. Optimizing the total cost of Capex sourcing. Professional Supply Management.

Keiser, S. and Ringlstetter, M. (2011). Strategic management of professional service firms. Theory and practice. Springer [Internet]. Available from *http://scholar.harvard.edu*

Ketels, H.M. and Memedovic, O. (2008). From clusters to cluster-based economic development. *Int. J. Technological Learning, Innovation and Development*, 1(3): 375–393.

Lowenberg, A.D. (1990). *Neoclassical Economics as a Theory of Politics and Institutions*, 9(3): 619–640. Available from *http://object.cato.org*

Muro, M. and Katz, B. (2010). The new "cluster moment": How regional innovation clusters can foster the next economy. Metropolitan Policy Program, pp. 57–59.

Porter, M.E. (1998). Clusters and the new economics competition. Harvard Business Review.

Porter, M.E. (1998). Frameworks and key concepts. Harvard Business School. Institute for Strategy and Competitiveness.

Porter, M.E. (2008). On competition, updated and expanded edition. Harvard Business Publishing.

Porter, M.E. (1990). The competitive advantage of nations. New-York Free Press.

Porter, M.E. (2003). The economic performance of regions.Harvard Business School. Institute for Strategy and Competitiveness.

Solow, R.M. (1956). A contribution to the theory of economic growth. *The Quarterly Journal of Economics*, 70(1): 65–94. MIT Press [Internet]. MIT Press. Available from: *http://www.econ.nuy.edu/user/debroj/Courses/Readings/Solow.pdf*

Tsertseil, J. and Ordov, K. (2016). Cluster's innovation development through the territory of the regions. *In:* Bedcirogullari, Z., Minas, M.Y. and Thambusarny, R.X. (*eds.*), Conference: 3rd International Conference of Political Science, International Relations and Sociology. *Book Series*: *European Proceedings of Social and Behavioral Sciences*, 10: 50–62.

Tsertseil, J. and Ordov, K. (2016). The development of the regions on the cluster's territory: Evidence of central and Volga-region federal districts on the territory of Russian Federation. GSTF 2016: Proceedings of the 6th Annual International Conference on Qualitative and Quantitative Economics Research, pp. 9–15.

Tsertseil, J.S. (2014). The prospects of development of clusters on the territory of the regions. *CS Canada International Business and Management,* 10(2): 1–5. Epub 2015 April 30.

Van de Ven, A.H. (1995). Explaining development and change in organizations. *Academy of Management Review,* 20(3): 510–540. Available from: *web.mit.edu*

3

Modelling of Relation Between Electricity Supply Hours (Reliability) and Non-Farm-Enterprise Income in India

ALI GHAHREMANLOU[1]*

ABSTRACT

The power outages are still occurring in India frequently despite of different schemes which were introduced to enhance the quality of electricity supply. This problem has been known to exist everywhere consisting of Non-Farm-Enterprises but this awareness is qualitative instead of quantitative among the policy making institutions. This paper aimed at quantifying the relation between electricity supply hours and Non-Farm-Enterprises income in India. This relation is studied at three different levels; State, District and Village level through a cross sectional data obtained from India Human Development Survey of 2011–2012. For quantification, a Linear Mixed-Effects Model has been used and to deal with the endogeneity a Two Stage Least Square Instrumental Variable has been employed. Eventually, it can be seen that a significant dependency of Non-Farm-Enterprises income on electricity supply hours exists at each level and the other demographic as well as infrastructure variables are having a meaningful and significant coefficients.

***Key words*:** Power outages, Access to electricity, Electricity reliability, Econometric modelling, Linear mixed-effects model.

[1]Master of Arts, Department of Economics, Savitribai Phule Pune University, Pune, India

**Corresponding author*: E-mail: ali.ghahremanlo7272@gmail.com

INTRODUCTION

Electricity has been proved far more important among the other sources of energy. Access to electricity can not only bring lightning which can enhance the literacy, especially among women but it can also create a spare time for doing an extra job. However, lack of access to adequate, affordable, reliable, safe and environmentally benign energy is a severe constraint on development (DFID, 2002).

In this paper, focus is on the access to the electricity and its supply hours per day as well as its impact on the total income of Non-Farm-Enterprises. In theory or in qualitative terms, everyone knows that access to electricity and a better reliability can create better atmosphere among the Non-Farm-Enterprises to adopt more and efficient technologies that in turn will increase their income. However, this has been proved in quantitative terms very rarely especially in India.

This way, we quantify the relation between electricity supply hours and total income of Non-Farm-Enterprises in this paper. To do this, initially a descriptive analysis will be done and then the type and source of data will be outlined. Thereafter, the methodology which is consisting of a strong econometric tool called as Linear Mixed-Effects Model is used to have the relation quantified and then a Two-Stage Least Square Instrumental Variable is used to test for endogeneity. Then, the results of this paper are compared with a study of 2004–05 IHDS data (Rao, 2013) and finally the conclusion is made.

Objectives

In this project, the objectives are as below

1. To show the relation between electricity supply hours and Non-Farm-Enterprises income.
2. To quantify the said relation,
   - 2.1. First at the state level by controlling the variation at this level.
   - 2.2. Second at the district level by controlling the variation at this level.
   - 2.3. Third at the village level by controlling the variation at this level.
3. To control the endogeneity problem
4. To see the improvement in the results since 2004–05.

REVIEW OF LITERATURE

Different studies have been carried out on electricity and its different advantages around the globe. Some of the studies have been around the electrification and its impact on households' income, expenditure and education. In Bangladesh a study was done on these areas where a cross sectional data of 20000 households were collected in 2005 and estimated that the gain in total income due to electrification can be as much as 30 percent and as low as 9 percent (Khandker, 2009). Likewise, a study was done in Rwanda where they check the impact of electrification on income but mainly on lightning (Bensch, 2001). Almost another same study of demographic characteristics and the reason to opt for electricity supply are extensively illustrated in a World Bank report (An IEG Impact Evaluation, 2008). Another study has tried to make a monitoring system through which they can show the causality between electricity and development outcomes (Alvarez, 2009).

There has been some works on small scale and large scale enterprises. A study of electricity access in Bolivia, Tanzania and Vietnam show the financial dimensions and job opportunities along with better quality goods through a rise in small scale enterprises on the basis of supplying electricity (Kooijman-van Dijk, 2010). According to this study, enterprises are a secondary job for many households who just try to diversify their income earnings in order to reduce the vulnerability of rural living. Similarly, a study has been done on Non-Farm-Enterprises in rural Indonesia. In this study, they look at the quality of infrastructure; road and electricity and propose an idea regarding how they generate employment and increase income and then they check the gains from provision of these facilities (Gibson, 2010).

There are studies related to productive uses of electricity in the rural areas where they look at the electricity or more broadly energy productive use on increasing the Gross Domestic Product (Cabraal, 2005). Besides, there is a study which talks about the power outages and its impact. This study shows that when there is a frequent power interruption then this affects negatively the household electricity connection and its consumption for which the expected advantages of rural electrification is decreased (Khandker, 2012). Lastly, a research study shows that how power outages affect the Non-Farm-Enterprises income at a micro level and the impact of a rise in electricity supply hours on total income benefit which would be around 0.1 percent of India's GDP (Rao, 2013).

Descriptive and Exploratory Data Analysis

The electricity supply interruption occurs quite frequently at both household and industrial level. This problem takes place especially during the peak demand times like afternoons when people usage of electricity for utilisation of their electric appliances and their cooling system at home rises. Nevertheless, many of households have found the electric supply very unreliable for which they have different back-up systems like batteries and inverters.

This unreliability of electricity supply differs from state to state and it is even more at the rural level than that of urban level. According to International Energy Agency, the unreliability at the rural level is because of the loss involved in electricity distribution by the local distribution companies which is mainly due to the poor metering and inefficient billing and collection which has led to a poor performance, inadequate investment and finally regular power outages. This loss is also said to be due to the subsidies given to residential consumers and agricultural sector which is not in turn compensated by tariffs paid by commercial and industrial consumers for which financial problems have discouraged the local distribution companies to provide a better and reliable electricity supply.

This unreliability has increased the costs of production in many enterprises and industries as well. According to Federation of Indian Chambers of Commerce & Industry[1], 21 percent of industries face at least 4 hours of power outages per day for which as mentioned earlier they rely on many other facilities to mitigate the side effects of these power outages and these facilities in turn lead to a cost elevation of less than 2 percent. Besides, the same cost impact can be on Non-Farm-Enterprises[2], which will be naturally more as their revenue can be lower as compared to industries.

Households with Non-Farm-Enterprises

Table 1[3] is based on 42152 households of IHDS data 2011–12. Initially, it should be noted that the number of households with Non-Farm-Enterprises and with electricity access is more than those with Non-Farm-Enterprises and without access which indicates the importance

[1]http://ficci.in/sector-surveys.asp?secid=30 or http://www.briefindia.com

[2]According to Economic Census of India; 2005, Non-Farm-Enterprise is an entrepreneurial unit, which is engaged in production and/or distribution of goods and/or services other than crop production and plantation and may have or not hired worker on a fairly regular basis.

[3]In this table, the total number of households is mentioned as 39954 which is lower than 42152 by 2198 which is due to removal of North-Eastern and Union Territories. Besides, the sum of with and without electricity access becomes 39810 instead of 39954 which is due to 144 missing values.

of electricity access in these enterprises. Besides, the presence of households with Non-Farm-Enterprises is more in urban area than rural areas which can be due to better institutional factors. In addition, the households with Non-Farm-Enterprises have almost 55 percent more annual income than those with no Non-Farm-Enterprises. Moreover, their monthly expenditure is more by 1.12 percent.

Table 1: Characteristics of households with and without NFE (Non Farm-Enterprise)

	No NFE	*With NFE*	*All Household*
No. Households	31564 (79.0%)	8390 (21.0%)	39954 (100%)
With Elec. access	27078 (77.7%)	7762 (22.3%)	34840
Without Elec. access	4371 (87.9%)	599 (12.1%)	4970
Location			
Rural	22073 (84.5%)	4061 (15.5%)	26134
Urban	9491 (68.7%)	4329 (31.3%)	13820
Household characteristics	***Mean***	***Mean***	
Income (Tot. Annual. Rs)	112288	174425	
HH. Exp. Capita. Monthly (Rs)	26940	27243	
ASSETS[a]	14.62	18.32	
EDU. HH (years)	2.33	3.19	
N Adult (21+)	2.8	3.3	
N Teen (15–20)	0.60	0.65	
N Child (0–14)	1.34	1.48	
Elec. HRS[b]	15.18	15.81	

[a] This is a set of assets (durable consumer goods) coded from 0 to 30, including books, vehicle, clothes and etc.; [b] Households were asked to recall the hours of electricity supplied in the last month.

Similarly, those households with electricity access have bigger family and own more durable goods. Lastly, households with Non-Farm-Enterprises and with electricity access have about 1.6 hours of better electricity supply. This better electricity supply can be also observed from the Fig. 1 where more Non-Farm-Enterprises are in areas with more electricity supply.

However, few states show that as much as electricity supply hours increase, their income instead of increasing is decreasing. This is because when the infrastructure availability rises, it leads to a tougher urban competition (Straub, 2008). For this, few Non-Farm-Enterprises might not desire to enter into this competition and therefore, their income benefit falls in comparison to other states while the electricity supply hours are increasing.

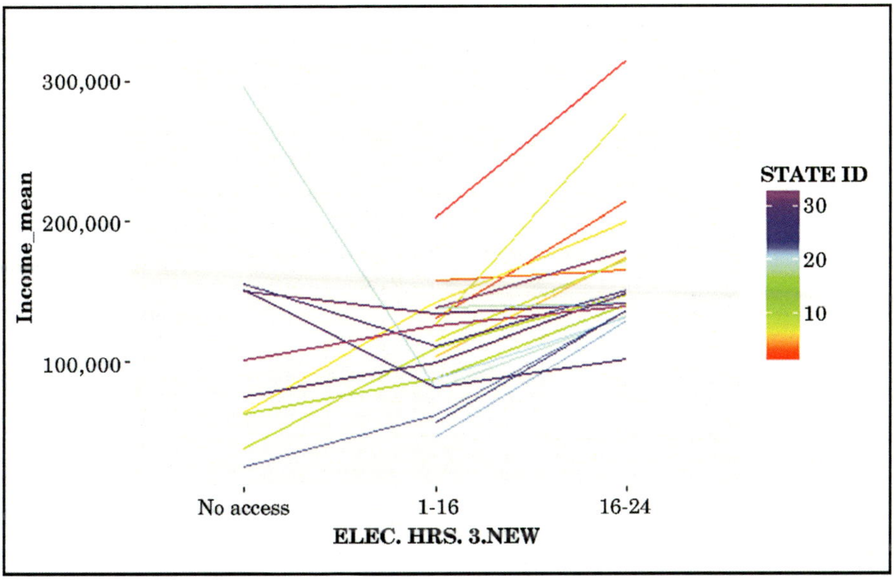

Fig. 1: States' Gain from further infrastructure availability

Similarly, the Fig. 2 shows the states that have a diminishing gain with infrastructure availability which are Jharkhand, Maharashtra, Andhra Pradesh and Goa. In Jharkhand, the number of household with no access are only 4 out of 731 so on the basis of their Non-Farm-Enterprises types they might have a quite high income for which that specific bar of no access in Jharkhand is very high. Similarly, in Maharashtra the number of households with no access is 9 out of 3123; in Andhra Pradesh 2 households with no access out of 2130; in Goa 3 households with no access out of 186 households.

Relation between income, assets[4] and electricity supply hours per day

In this section, the main scope of the paper is outlined which is the relation between total income of Non-Farm-Enterprises and the electricity supply hours per day. This part not only suggests that improving the supply hours will increase the Non-Farm-Enterprises income but it shows that a better electrified rural areas will enhance

[4]Assets are ownership of 1=House 2=Books 3= Household class 4=Bicycle 5=Sewing Machine 6=Generator Set 7=Mixer 8=Motor Cycle 9=Black & White Television 10=Colour Television 11=Cooler 12=Clock/watch 13=Electric Fan 14=Chair or table 15=Cot 16=Telephone 17=Mobile Phone 18=Refrigerator 19=Pressure cooker 20=Cable/Dish T.V 21=Car 22=Air Conditioner 23=Washing Machine 24=Computer 25=Laptop 26=Credit Card 27=Microwave oven 28=clothes 29=shoes or chappals.

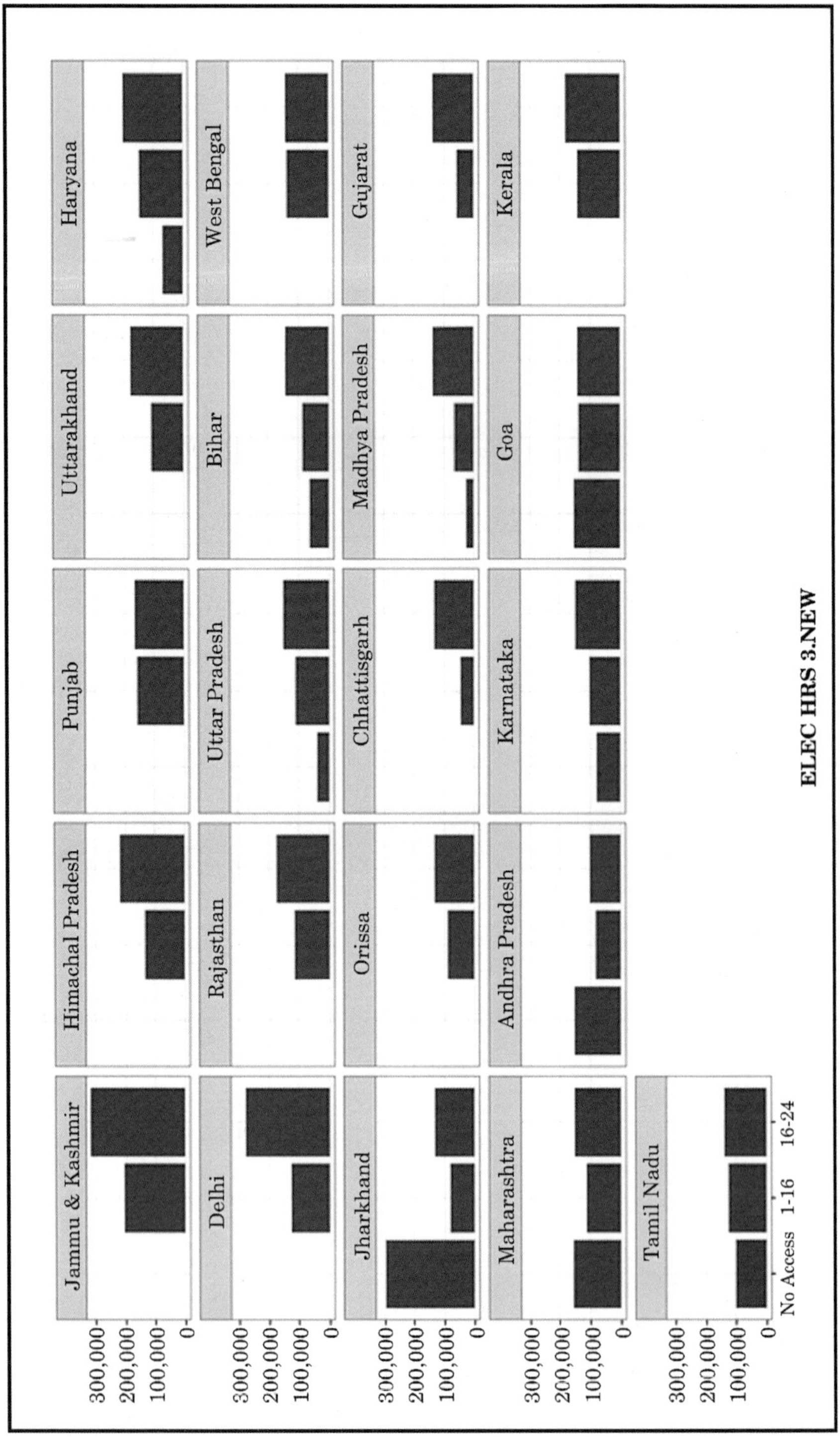

Fig. 2: States' Gain from infrastructure availability

the rural development which is a driving factor in growth of developing countries. Already, in Fig. 1 it is showed that as much as a Non-Farm-Enterprise goes to higher tranches of electricity, a higher income is gained by them. Likewise, households with Non-Farm-Enterprises and a higher electricity supply will have more income as compared to those with no Non-Farm-Enterprises which is shown in Fig. 3 with a continuous electricity supply hours and no tranches of supply hours.

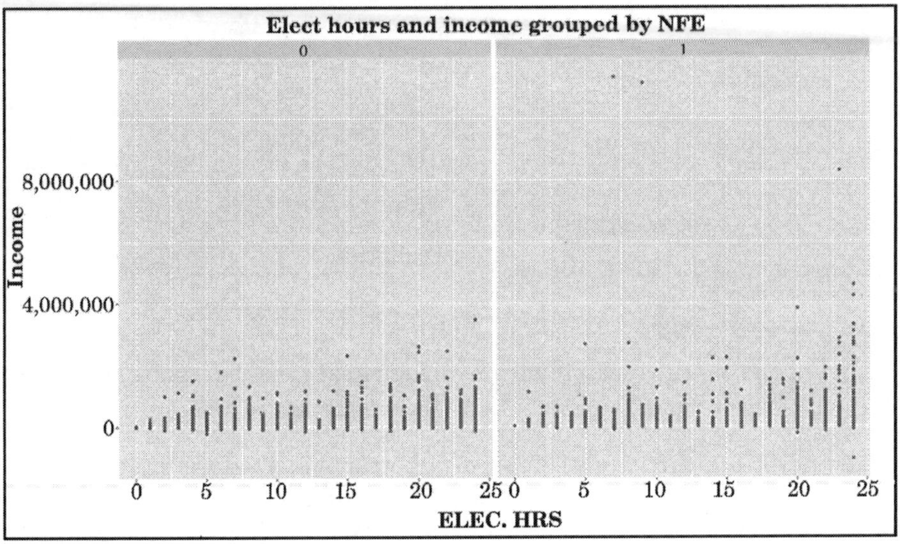

Fig. 3

From development policy making point of view, it is noteworthy to indicate as well that rural development can be enhanced if electrification is elevated in these areas along with betterment of institutional factors like political factors and household's demand for electricity and economic factors like better credit facilities to boost the demand for electricity in such a way that more Non-Farm-Enterprises will be attracted to these areas as well.

This way from the Fig. 4, it can be realized that when a rural household is with electricity and no Non-Farm-Enterprises then their income is less but when this household is with Non-Farm-Enterprises then their total Non-Farm-Enterprises income is scattered more towards a higher income specially with better electricity supply. The same case can be seen in the urban area where better institutional and economic factors exist and with electricity and with Non-Farm-Enterprises, the households are having more income at higher electricity supply hours as against the urban case with no Non-Farm-Enterprises. Therefore,

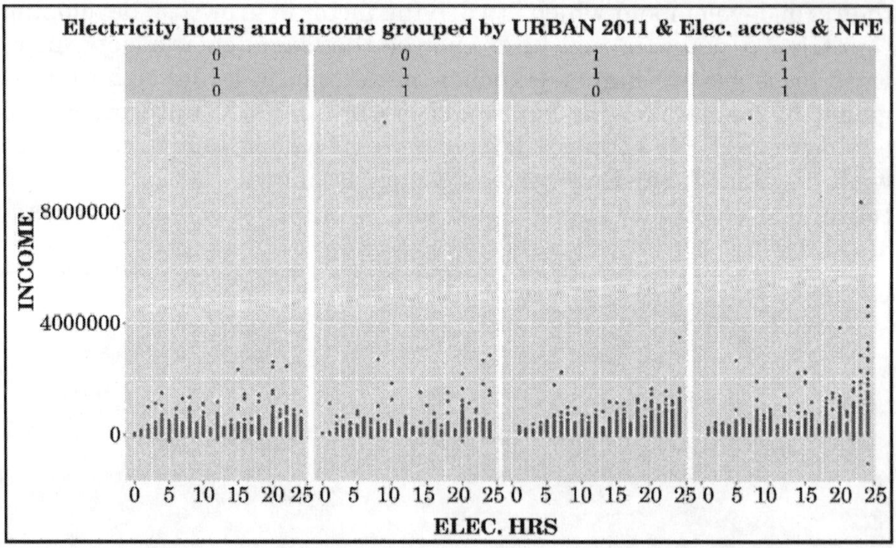

Fig. 4

with improving the electrification at the rural area it can be expected to have the same income condition as like as urban area.

In addition, the causal effect of a better electricity supply on Non-Farm-Enterprises income is of both direct and indirect. The direct effect is when electricity is utilised as an input in the production process which can be particularly observed in manufacturing sector of Non-Farm-Enterprises. The indirect effect, however, is observed mainly as lightning of working places and cooling of the premises which can lead to a higher productivity and efficiency notably during summer season. Besides, in the rural areas, electricity access can reduce the time spent on chores and collecting woods as a source of energy. However, if there are frequent power interruptions then not only this will increase the costs (as already illustrated by purchasing batteries as a back-up system) but also it will discourage the households to demand for electricity access and in turn it will discourage Non-Farm-Enterprises to select those areas since it would not be profitable for them. Moreover, it is good to see also from the following Fig. 5 where we have four tranches of electricity hours and as much as we go to higher electricity tranches like the last one which is 18 to 24 hours, it can be seen that the number of assets (as well as the median asset) is rising. In the last tranche, it can be observed that the asset number 20 and above are more possessed by the households or it can be said that those assets are having a higher frequency in the last tranche (The horizontal lines show the frequency of the assets).

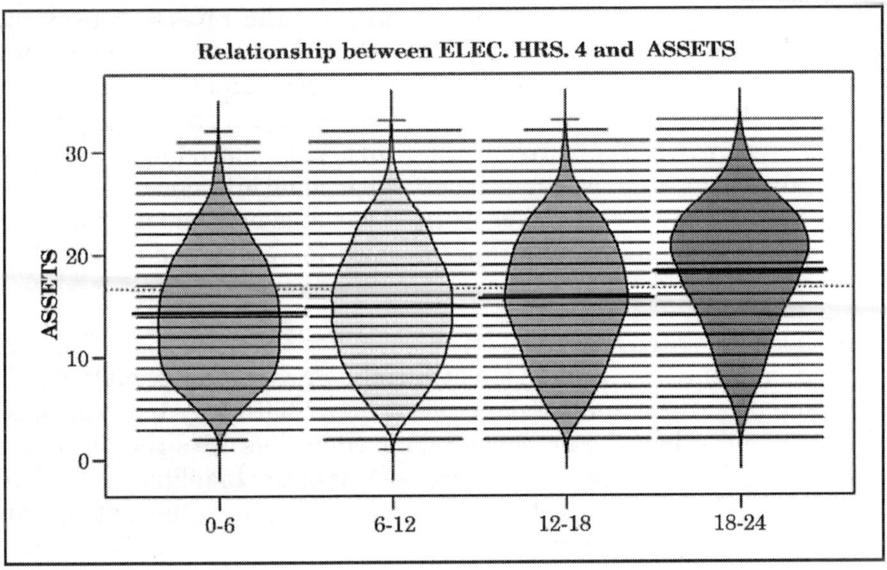

Fig. 5

Data

This paper is working on Indian Human Development Index which is a national survey of 42152 households in India. This survey is assembled in three parts; Individual, Household and Eligible women. For this paper, Household dataset has only been used.

For the analytical part, 21 states have been taken into consideration out of 35 states. The omitted states are the North-Eastern and Union-Territories due to lack of sufficient data. This way, 39954 households are remaining which have been used for Exploratory Data Analysis. However, for the modelling part, a random sample of 8388 households have been selected which is almost 21 percent of the 39954 households.

METHODOLOGY[5]

To quantify the relationship between income and electricity access and its supply, a linear mixed-effects model (multilevel mixed-effects model) is used where both fixed-effects and random-effects exist. Then, an

[5]In this section, the whole idea of what methodology to be used has been adopted from a study of 2004–05 IHDS data (Rao N.D, 2013). However, in this paper instead of a multivariate regression model with fixed effect, a linear mixed effect model has been used where random effects also exist. In IV regression model also, the instrument is different from what that has been used in the study cited here.

Instrument Variable (IV) is used to check for the reverse causation. This mixed method is used because of working on a cross-sectional data which is famous for endogeneity problem which can be due to reverse causation. Endogeneity is when our variables are correlated with the error terms for which our results can turn to be biased. On the same line, reverse causation is when on one side income influences electricity access (and supply level) and/or omitted variable bias and on the other side electricity access and supply proxies for other conditions that influence income[6].

It should be noted that fixed effect variables are those that affect the population mean and random effect variables are those associated with sampling procedure and random effects contribute only to covariance structure of the data[7]. Furthermore, mixed models are either based on Maximum Likelihood (ML) or Restricted Maximum Likelihood (REML). This paper does its modelling based on ML since the data is an unbalanced design/structure. One disadvantage of REML is that likelihood-ratio (LR) tests based on REML are inappropriate for comparing models with different fixed-effects specifications and ML is appropriate for such LR tests and has the advantage of being easy to explain and being the method of choice for other estimators[8].

Instrumental Variable is used to check for reverse causation with the presence of endogeneity. This method allows us a consistent estimation of the regression coefficients. Instrument Variables simply isolate that part of our variables which are not correlated to the error terms and provide us with the isolated part for β s[9]. This way, consistent estimators α, β and γ can be constructed without any biasedness[10].

Mixed-Effects Model

In this model, the dependent variable is a log of income since income is always skewed and the other variables are demographic characteristics,

[6]Rao N.D., Does (better) electricity supply increase household enterprise income in India? Energy Policy (2013), http://dx.doi.org/10.1016/j.enpol.2013.02.025.

[7]Linear Mixed-Effects Modeling in SPSS: An Introduction to the MIXED Procedure, Technical report; IBM, http://www.spss.ch/upload/1126184451_Linear%20Mixed%20Effects%20Modeling%20in%20SPSS.pdf

[8]Stata Multilevel Mixed-Effects, Reference Manual Release 13; A Stata Press Publication StataCorp LP College Station, Texas, https://www.stata.com/manuals13/me.pdf.

[9]Econometric Analysis; William H. Greene.

[10]Industry groups are under the main headings of: Agriculture, Mining, Forestry, Manufacturing, Construction, Restaurants, Transport, Services, Wholesale, Retail, Hotels, Education, Health, Other, and Unknown.

infrastructure, electricity access, industrial location and fixed effect of locations.

$$\log(Yi,j,k) = \beta 1Xi,j,k + \beta 2Ii,j,k + \beta 3ElAcci,j,k + \beta 4ElAcci,j,k * ElHrsi,j,k + \beta 5Indi + \beta 6Loj + ui,j,k$$

Here, $X_{i,j,k}$ is a vector of demographic variables; $I_{i,j,k}$ is a vector of infrastructure variables; $ElAcc_{i,j,k}$ is a dummy for electricity access and $ElHrs_{i,j,k}$ is the supply of electricity in hours/day and it is of 4 trenches of size 6 hours. This division is to obtain more information regarding the supply reliability and its impact on income. Indii[11] is the industry effect and is included to control the endogeneity in the model since the income dependence of people is based on which industry they are working in as industries differ in profit from one another. Thus, this variable has to be a fixed effect to reduce the biasedness. Besides, the profitability of these industries is also based on the variation in location for which location Lo_j is included to adjust to the variation in location with respect to other variables. Other unobserved/omitted variables which are correlated to this location variation which can have an impact on the profitability of industries and finally on the income of people are like market conditions or availability of credit. However, this industry fixed effect is at State level since the variation is extreme at this level but at District and Village level, this is not so. But, the main thing is that the uptake of electricity by people is based on their income and this as pointed out can change by different enterprises which again alter from one another due to location variation. Therefore, a reverse causation can be witnessed from these three region levels as the village is a subset of district and district is a subset of the state.

The coefficients β_k are interpreted as the percentage change in net income from Non-Farm-Enterprises for a unit change in the respective variables. β_3 is a coefficient of electricity dummy so it represents the percentage change in income due to having access to electricity (1) as compared to those who do not have access to electricity (0). In our sample, those with access are 7263 households and without access are 1088 households. β_4 is the supply of electricity in hours/days of those who have access to electricity. β_1 and β_2 show impact of change in some selective variables on income which will be outlined in the covariates section.

[11]Julia L. Bienias. *et al.*, Diagnostics For Random Coefficient Mixed Models With Unweighted And Weighted Data

Covariates

The regressors which have been selected are a combination of variables that have an impact on the income of the household and on their choice of whether taking electricity or not. The first set of variables is to show the demographic characteristics of the households. They are as, the education level of the head of household (EDU.HH) through which we can realize that as much as the head is more literate then he/she is more likely to demand for electricity access and then number of rooms (Rooms) of each household which is a proxy for the size of the house and another one which is the number of working-age members of each household. Here, the number of rooms is a better proxy for the house size than that of the size of land because as much as more rooms are there, then your demand for electricity will be more which can compel you to demand more electricity. Thereafter, we have variables related to infrastructure like in-house access to piped water (Water) which indicates that the household does not need to go outside to collect water.

Then we have electricity access (Elec. Access) and its supply in terms of hours per day (Elec. HRS). We have Urban/Rural conditions (Urban, 2011) which is a proxy for many conditions like the market size or the availability of financial institutions which differ from urban to rural area. Since our main focus is on the income of Non-Farm-Enterprises then the market conditions are important. As the market size is larger, there can be a greater demand which can increase the prices and yield a greater profit. To have an eye on the variation in the prices, the market price of the rice (Rice) is taken as a primary proxy for overall price levels. This commodity is chosen because it is one of the basic household food items which can show us the difference between the incomes of NFEs based on being in urban or rural areas. These set of variables are enough for the analysis and in case more variable are added then there might come the problem of multico linearity but as of now this is not a problem because almost all the regressors have pair correlation of less than 30 percent.

Part 1: Controlling state level variation

In this part, the industry group (NFE.Types) is taken as fixed effect and the random effects are associated with the State variation. However, the main analysis is between the electricity supply hours/days and income. For this, we adjust the variation of supply hours to the change in state which will give us more unbiased results.

Table 2: Estimates of fixed effects[a]

Parameter	Estimate	Std. error	Df	T	Sig.	95% Confidence interval	
						Lower bound	Upper bound
Intercept	9.390196	.048627	4763.630	193.106	.000	9.294864	9.485527
Rooms	.082258	.008401	4690.615	9.791	.000	.065787	.098728
EDU.IIII	.035238	.003152	4765.800	11.181	.000	.029060	.041417
Water	.129405	.027666	4482.070	4.677	.000	.075166	.183644
Rice P	.018913	.001471	4524.177	12.854	.000	.016028	.021798
Elec. Access	.104523	.054735	4472.335	1.910	.056	–.002784	.211831
Urban 2011	.230206	.027865	4675.672	8.262	.000	.175578	.284833
NFE.Types	.000190	.000379	4752.652	.501	.616	–.000553	.000934
N Adult	.218616	.009251	4761.397	23.633	.000	.200480	.236751
N Child	.017125	.008679	4764.708	1.973	.049	.000111	.034140
N Teen	.110132	.013569	4764.162	8.117	.000	.083531	.136734
Interaction	.057227	.017108	109.351	3.345	.001	.023320	.091134

[a] Dependent variable: Ln_Income.

It can be observed from Table 2 that all the parameters are significant at 10 percent level of significance except NFE. Types which are due to large missing values therefore, it is not significant.

It can be seen as well from Table 3 that per hour of electricity supply lead to a rise in income which is equal to 0.057 percent as shown by the interaction coefficient. Here, due to Interaction variable which is of electricity access and supply hours/day only those who have access (1) are considered since, due to the multiplication of the electricity dummy to supply hours/day the zeros (no access) are omitted. The random effect of Interaction which is adjusted to state change is significant which means that it should be included in the model. Besides, in mixed models the normality of residuals at the end are very important and as it can be seen from the normality curve, Fig. 6, that residuals are normally distributed.

Table 3: Estimates of covariance parameters[a]

Parameter	Estimate	Std. error	Wald Z	Sig.	95% confidence interval	
					Lower bound	Upper bound
Residual	.613954	.012607	48.701	.000	.589737	.639167
Interaction subject = Variance stateid]	.001943	.000750	2.590	.010	.000911	.004141

[a] Dependent variable: Ln_Income.

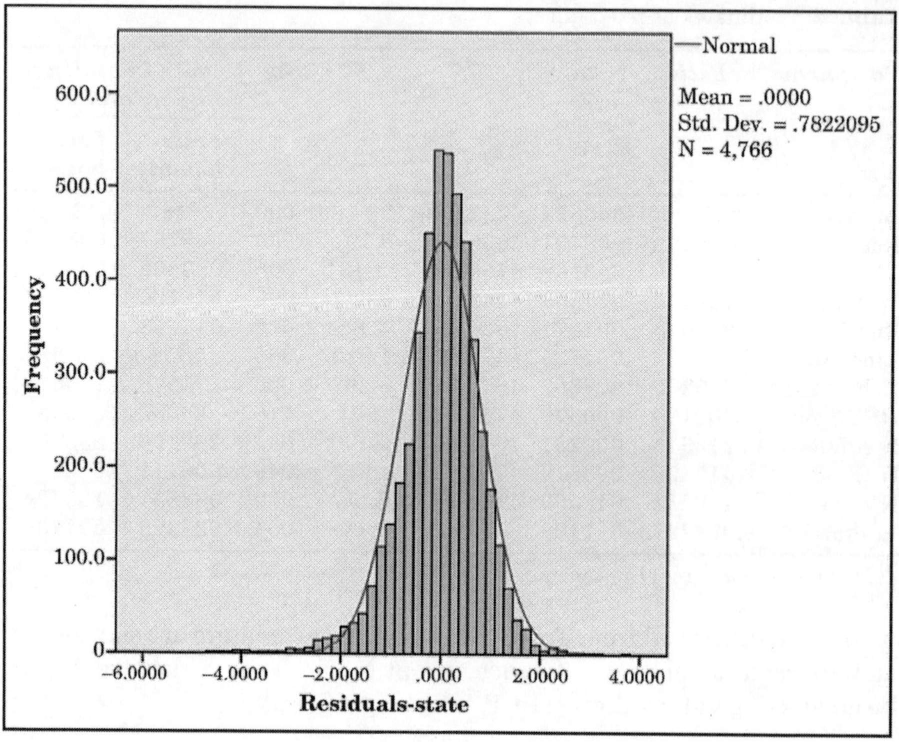

Fig. 6: Normality test of residuals through state level data

Regarding the heteroscedasticity in these models, it should be noted when the residuals are plotted against the predicted values then we have a pattern that suggests there are some outliers.

But, it can be seen from Fig. 7 that the spread of residuals to the right which is towards a higher predicted values and this has been said not to be strong enough to raise much of an alarm[12]. Therefore, it can be concluded that there is no heteroscedasticity. In the other two parts, the same result is achieved for which we do not repeat them anymore.

Part 2: Controlling district level variation

In this part, NFE.Types is not fixed anymore and the relation of Interaction with income is checked while the Interaction is adjusted to changes in the district as a subset of each state.

[12]Please refer to Rao, N.D., Does (better) electricity supply increase household enterprise income in India? Energy Policy (2013), http://dx.doi.org/10.1016/j.enpol.2013.02.025.

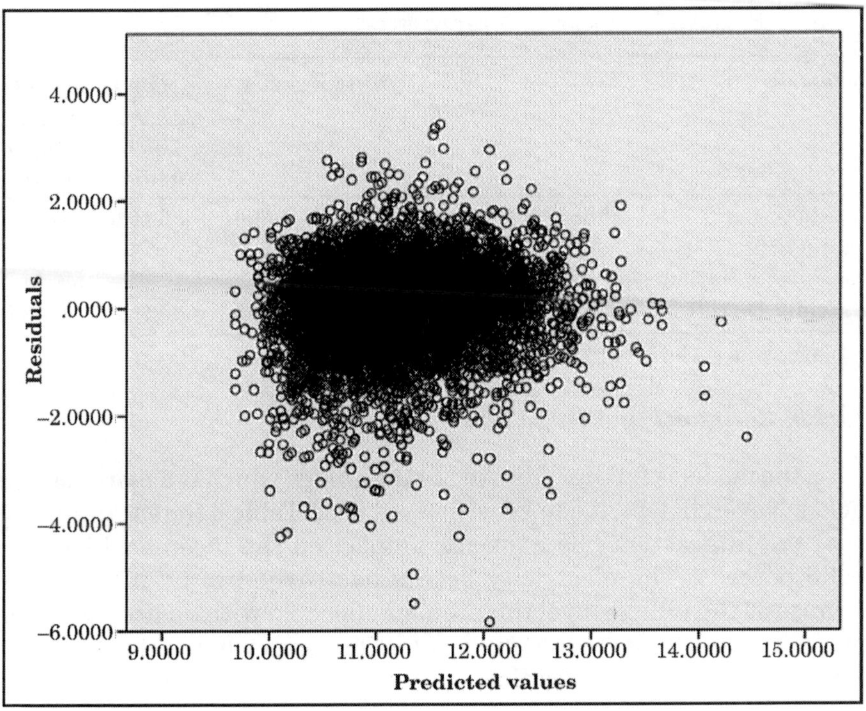

Fig. 7: Test for homoscedasticity condition through scatter plot

Table 4: Estimates of fixed effects[a]

Parameter	*Estimate*	*Std. error*	*Df*	*T*	*Sig.*	*95% confidence interval*	
						Lower bound	*Upper bound*
Intercept	9.410577	.047427	4732.256	198.421	.000	9.317598	9.503557
Rooms	.086178	.008325	4655.526	10.352	.000	.069857	.102499
Edu.HH	.033391	.002967	4762.420	11.253	.000	.027574	.039209
Water	.123731	.027758	4110.600	4.457	.000	.069309	.178153
Rice.P	.018240	.001453	4538.018	12.556	.000	.015392	.021088
Elec. Access	.096941	.053821	4400.561	1.801	.072	–.008576	.202458
Urban 2011	.224991	.029149	2676.565	7.719	.000	.167834	.282148
N Adult	.217230	.009170	4734.823	23.688	.000	.199252	.235208
N Child	.015498	.008575	4760.076	1.807	.071	–.001314	.032309
N Teen	.107195	.013427	4761.605	7.984	.000	.080873	.133517
Interaction	.056304	.014456	1408.080	3.895	.000	.027946	.084661

[a] Dependent variable: Ln_Income.

It can be evaluated that the Interaction from Table 4 has almost the same effect on income by 0.056. The random effect, Table 5, in this model is also significant so it should be included in the model.

Table 5: Estimates of covariance parameters[a]

Parameter	*Estimate*	*Std. error*	*Wald Z*	*Sig.*	*95% confidence interval*	
					Lower bound	*Upper bound*
Residual	.588395	.012453	47.249	.000	.564486	.613315
Interaction [subject = Variance Stateid * Distid]	.004466	.000810	5.512	.000	.003130	.006373

[a] Dependent variable: Ln_Income.

Part 3: Controlling village level variation

Here, the model is further adjusted to the village which is a more complex model. Nevertheless, it can be witnessed from Table 6 that at the village level the Interaction has a greater impact on the income which is by 0.066 percent. The electricity access has turned to be insignificant because at the village level the number of people with no access is more but we are checking for the impact of Interaction which is of those with access only and this makes electricity access insignificant.

Table 6: Estimates of fixed effects[a]

Parameter	*Estimate*	*Std. error*	*Df*	*T*	*Sig.*	*95% confidence interval*	
						Lower bound	*Upper bound*
Intercept	9.384705	.046642	4353.891	201.206	.000	9.293262	9.476147
Rooms	.087817	.008207	4694.375	10.701	.000	.071728	.103906
Edu.HH	.034414	.002988	4695.521	11.516	.000	.028556	.040273
Water	.140308	.027307	4102.855	5.138	.000	.086771	.193846
Rice.P	.019505	.001432	4702.959	13.622	.000	.016698	.022312
Elec. Access	.070722	.051548	4580.100	1.372	.170	–.030336	.171781
Urban 2011	.231569	.028945	2371.544	8.000	.000	.174809	.288329
N Adult	.215141	.009224	4724.680	23.325	.000	.197058	.233224
N Child	.016176	.008560	4714.410	1.890	.059	–.000606	.032958
N Teen	.111476	.013385	4714.206	8.328	.000	.085236	.137717
Interaction	.066285	.013152	3714.640	5.040	.000	.040499	.092071

[a]Dependent variable: Ln_Income.

The covariance parameters from Table 7 also suggest that random effects are still significant even at village level for which it should remain in the model.

Table 7: Estimates of covariance parameters[a]

Parameter	*Estimate*	*Std. error*	*Wald Z*	*Sig.*	*95% confidence interval*	
					Lower bound	*Upper bound*
Residual	.559541	.013618	41.089	.000	.533477	.586878
Interaction [subject = Stateid Distid * Vnid] Variance	.007369	.001062	6.937	.000	.005555	.009775

[a]Dependent variable: Ln_Income.

Instrumental Variable

Here, we check for an instrument through which we can get consistent coefficients for our analysis. It should be noted that whatever instrument chosen, it should be correlated with the endogenous variable (Electricity access) and it should not be correlated to our error terms. This can be written as below:

$$\text{Instrument relevance} : cov\ (ELEC.ACCESS,\ VP) \neq 0$$

$$\text{Instrument exogeneity} : cov\ (VP,\ \varepsilon) = 0$$

We chose the total number of individuals who have access to electricity in a village (VP). The rationality in choosing this instrument is that the peer pressure of it will motivate a household to take electricity. This occurs this way that, a household while observing his neighbours with daily electricity and its impact on their life like income, education and the most important one that is the lightning at night, will inspire the other household to get an electricity access which is the relevance part of the IV assumption.

This correlation is also checked which is 34 percent. Besides, this VP does not influence the income directly because the income of a household is mainly based on their expenditure structure and the number of working family members. Therefore, this VP will not be correlated to the error terms (ε) as well.

$$EAi, j, k = \alpha 1Xi, j, k + \alpha 2Ii, j, k + \alpha 3VPi, j, k + vi, j, k \quad \text{First Stage}$$

$$\log\ (Yi, j, k) = \beta 1Xi, j, k + \beta 2Ii, j, k + \beta 3EAi, j, k + \beta 4Indi + \beta 5Loj + ui, j, k$$

Second Stage

This is a two-stage-least square IV regression model wherein the first stage, Table 8, the relation between VP and electricity access (EA) is checked. Moreover, in the second stage, Table 9, the is the representative of electricity access with its instrument embodied. In addition, the supply hours has been omitted because no instrument variable could be found out for it. For this, our dependent variable will

Table 8: Instrumental variable regression, first stage

First-stage regressions

Number of obs	= 8171	F (9, 8161) =	218.01
Prob > F	= 0.0000	R-squared =	0.1938
Adj R-squared	= 0.1929	Root MSE =	0.3032

Elec. Access	***Coef.***	***Std. err.***	***t***	***P>|t|***	***[95% Conf.***	***Interval]***
Edu.HH	.0043032	.0009331	4.61	0.000	.0024741	.0061324
Rooms	.0200325	.0021836	9.17	0.000	.0157521	.0243128
N Adult	.0204429	.0026148	7.82	0.000	.0153173	.0255685
N Teen	.0032987	.0039241	0.84	0.401	–.0043936	.010991
N Child	–.0149066	.0024642	–6.05	0.000	–.0197371	–.0100761
Water	.0867909	.0078604	11.04	0.000	.0713825	.1021993
Urban 2011	.0427464	.0079785	5.36	0.000	.0271065	.0583863
Rice.P	.0031966	.0003977	8.04	0.000	.002417	.0039762
Vill_indi_with_ele	.0159652	.0006054	26.37	0.000	.0147784	.0171519
_Cons	.5709535	.011659	48.97	0.000	.5480989	.593808

Table 9: Instrumental variable regression, second stage

Instrumental variables (2SLS) regression

Source	***SS***	***df***	***MS***		
				Number of obs =	8171
Model	2991.55149	9	332.39461	F (9, 8161)	= 450.36
Residual	5949.03601	8161	.728959197	Prob > F	= 0.0000
Total	8940.5875	8170	1.09431916	R-squared	= 0.3346
				Adj R-squared	= 0.3339
				Root MSE	= .85379

ln_income	***Coef.***	***Std. err.***	***t***	***P>|t|***	***[95% Conf.***	***Interval]***
Elec.Access	.4942975	.1067799	4.63	0.000	.2849816	.7036134
Edu.HH	.0299143	.0026684	11.21	0.000	.0246836	.0351449
Rooms	.0983604	.0064952	15.14	0.000	.0856281	.1110927
N Adult	.1966363	.007754	25.36	0.000	.1814365	.211836
N Teen	.1062074	.0110533	9.61	0.000	.0845402	.1278746
N Child	.0150921	.007201	2.10	0.036	.0009763	.0292079
Water	.1876006	.024565	7.64	0.000	.139447	.2357543
Urban 2011	.2873375	.023764	12.09	0.000	.2407539	.333921
Rice.P	.0198401	.0011958	16.59	0.000	.0174961	.0221841
_Cons	9.191909	.073238	125.51	0.000	9.048344	9.335474

Instrumented: Elec.Access

Instruments: Edu.HH; Rooms; N Adult; N Teen; N Child; Water; Urban 2011; Rice.P; Vill_indi_with_ele

be interpreted in the second stage with respect to the changes in the average supply of electricity hours in the access variable. The output of this 2 SLS model is as below:

In the first stage, the instrument variable which is Vill_indi_with_ele (VP) has the highest t-statistics value (= 26.37, ignoring the t value of constant) which means that it has a high accuracy in estimating our dependent variable (Electricity access) and the p-value of the t-statistics is 0.000 which indicates that our VP has a significant impact on the electricity access. Similarly, the R^2 is equal to 0.20 that means the instrument has a good amount of explanatory power since its difference with adjusted R^2 is minimal.

The main part of this 2sls IV regression model is the second stage which will be used for further analysis. This result of 2sls IV regression shows a similar income effect as compared to the linear mixed-effects model. Besides, the endogeneity test shows that the electricity access is exogenous since the p-value (= 0.0751) of Chi2 (1) (= 3.16772) is not significant at 0.05 percent level of significance for which we fail to reject the null hypothesis (H_0). This means that there is no endogeneity or no observed reverse causation in the original model.

This way the IV cannot provide us with consistent coefficients though all the indicators illustrated above are showing VP to be a good instrument but literature as well shows IV is not always efficient so better to stick to the original model in analysing the coefficients. The Hausman F-test also suggests the same result as it has the same null hypothesis and almost the same p-value which will be rejected at 0.05 percent.

Tests of endogeneity

Ho: Variables are exogenous

Durbin (Score)	chi^2 (1)	= 3.16772 (p= 0.0751)
Wu-Hausman	F (1, 8160)	= 3.16469 (p=0.0753)

Comparison of the electricity reliability with 2004–05 study[12]

To begin with, it is worthwhile to point out that the dependency of Non-Farm-Enterprises income on electricity reliability based on 2004–05 IHDS data study was 0.006 at the state level but now based on 2011–12 IHDS data the Non-Farm-Enterprises income dependency has risen to 0.057227 (almost 0.06) as it can be seen from Table 10. This means that based on the average growth rate formula,

$$\text{Average Growth Rate} = \left(\frac{\text{Present}}{\text{Past}}\right)^{\frac{1}{n}} - 1$$

where n is the number of years then we can say that if 2005 is the past ending point and 2012 is the present ending point then n=8 and the present value is 0.057227 and past value is 0.006. Therefore, based on the formula, the average growth rate of this dependency on electricity reliability over a span of 8 years has improved by 0.3256*100 = 32.56 percent at the state level.

Table 10: Summary of final hierarchical modelling

Log (Total NFE income)	***(Part 1)FE***	***(Part 2)FE***	***(Part 3)FE***	***IV***
Industry group fixed effects	***Yes***	***No***	***No***	***Yes***
Location fixed effects	***State***	***District***	***Village***	***State***
Household characteristics				
Edu.HH	.035238***	.033391***	.034414***	.0299143***
	(.003152)	(.002967)	(.002988)	(.0026684)
Rooms	.082258***	.086178***	.087817***	.0983604***
	(.008401)	(.008325)	(.008207)	(.0064952)
N Adult	.218616***	.217230***	.215141***	.1966363***
	(.009251)	(.009170)	(.009224)	(.007754)
N Teen	.110132***	.107195***	.111476***	.1062074***
	(.013569)	(.013427)	(.013385)	(.0110533)
N Child	.017125**	.015498*	.016176*	.0150921**
	(.008679)	(.008575)	(.008560)	(.007201)
Infrastructure conditions				
Elec.Access (0/1)	.104523*	.096941*	.070722	.4942975***
	(.054735)	(.053821)	(.051548)	(.1067799)
Interaction[a]	.057227***	.056304***	.066285***	
(Electricity supply h/day)	(.017108)	(.014456)	(.013152)	
Water (0/1)	.129405***	.123731***	.140308***	.1876006***
	(.027666)	(.027758)	(.027307)	(.024565)
Urban 2011 (0/1)	.230206***	.224991***	.231569***	.2873375***
(Market industry conditions)	(.027865)	(.029149)	(.028945)	(.023764)
RICE.P	.018913***	.018240***	.019505***	.0198401***
(Market price of rice)	(.001471)	(.001453)	(.001432)	(.0011958)
Constant	9.390196***	9.410577***	9.384705***	9.191909***
	(.048627)	(.047427)	(.046642)	(.073238)

IV: Endogeneity Test (H0: Exogenous); Chi^2 (1) = 3.16772; p-value = 0.0751
The parentheses include standard error. *$p < 0.1$, **$p < 0.05$, ***$p < 0.01$
[a]Here the supply hours is of 4 tranches of 6 hours each for better accuracy.

The Non-Farm-Enterprises income dependency has increased by an average of 29.77 percent at the district level. This clearly indicates a better institutional and economic factor at the state level. However, the article for 2004–05 does not have the information of electricity supply hours at the village level but based on our results, it can be seen that, the dependency

Of Non-Farm-Enterprises income on electricity reliability at the village level is more than the state and district levels which show that the recent schemes (*e.g.*, Rajiv Gandhi Grameen Vidyutikaran Yojana) have been improving the efficiency of the electricity supply hours over this period of time as one of the factors. And since this value is more, it can be claimed as well that the total income of Non-Farm-Enterprises at the village level will increase further since it is highly significant also, at higher electricity supply hours if the same scenario continuous over time. Besides, another reason for this rise in dependency can be due to emergence of new Non-Farm-Enterprises which are more profitable and electrified.

CONCLUSIONS

Through the modelling of the data and analysis of the results in this paper, the following points can be concluded that over this span of time the dependency of Non-Farm-Enterprises income on electricity supply has increased which indicates that if the power reliability is enhanced then the Non-Farm-Enterprises income can rise further as already mentioned with respect to the earlier period. This dependency should be taken into consideration while policy making since the exact amount of change can be measured as the impact of an increment of one hour better electricity reliability which can be seen from the results at each level separately. Likewise, the size of households have expanded at all the locations; the education of the head of households have almost remained same at the state and district level but interestingly, it has risen at the village level which is a positive point from economic development point of view. Besides, the importance of number of adults, teens and children can be observed from the significant values of them in comparison to 2004–05 study. However, it should be noted that the number of children has remained less significant but the other two have become extremely significant. This goes with the theory as well that the number of adults does contribute more in total income of Non-Farm-Enterprises than number of children. Regarding the infrastructure conditions; water supply and market/industry conditions, it can be said that, over this span of time, they have reduced slightly at all the state, district and village levels but they have remained highly significant to the total income of Non-Farm-Enterprises. Moreover, the market price of rice shows a moderate fall at all the three levels but this has also remained highly significant in contribution to total income of Non-Farm-Enterprises.

END NOTE

I am grateful to those who helped me in developing this paper. This paper is done with three software namely; SPSS, STATA and R and the commands and syntaxes can be provided upon request.

REFERENCES

Alvarez, D. (2009). Optimizing long-term monitoring and evaluation metrics for public sector projects–large-scale energy infrastructures and their impact on the millennium development goals. Columbia University School of International and Public Affairs.

An IEG Impact Evaluation (2008). The welfare impact of rural electrification: A reassessment of the costs and benefits. Worldbank.org. Available from: *http://www.worldbank.org/ieg*

Bensch, G., Kluve, J. and Peters, J. (2011). Impacts of rural electrification in Rwanda. *Journal of Development Effectiveness*, 3(4): 567–588.

Cabraal, R., Barnes, D. and Agarwal, S. (2005). Productive uses of energy for rural development. *Annual Review of Environment and Resources,* 30(1): 117–144.

Energy for the Poor Underpinning the Millennium Development Goals [Internet] (2002). 1st ed. Department for International Development. Available from: *https://www.ecn.nl/fileadmin/ecn/units/bs/JEPP/energyforthepoor.pdf*

Gibson Jolivia, S. (2010). The effect of infrastructure access and quality on non-farm enterprises in rural Indonesia. *World Development,* 38(5): 717–726.

Khandker, S., Barnes, D. and Samad, H. (2009). Welfare impacts of rural electrification a case study from Bangladesh. The World Bank development research group sustainable rural and urban development team. Policy research working paper 4859.

Khandker, S., Samad, H., Barnes, D. and Ali, R. (2012). Who benefits most from rural electrification? Evidence in India. The World Bank development research group agriculture and rural development team. Policy research working paper 6095.

Kooijman-van Dijk, A. and Clancy, J. (2010). Impacts of electricity access to rural enterprises in Bolivia, Tanzania and Vietnam. *Energy for Sustainable Development*, 14(1): 14–21.

Rao, N. (2013). Does (better) electricity supply increase household enterprise income in India? *Energy Policy*, 57: 532–541. Available from: *http://dx.doi.org/10.1016/j.enpol.2013.02.025*

Straub, S. (2008). Infrastructure and growth in developing countries: Recent advances and research challenges. The World Bank development research department research support team. Policy research working paper 4460.

4

Theoretical Basis of External Transport Pricing

NEJIA ZAOUALI[1*]

ABSTRACT

Transportation is essential to our economic, political and cultural. They resemble the citizens of each other and they facilitate trade and international exchanges. The evolution of transport has always been linked to competitiveness economic but also to the creation of direct and indirect jobs. Given the gravity and the stress of transport problems many governments have taken in recent years, measures to improve the efficiency of transport by encouraging the managing congestion, decreased number of accidents and victims of transport and the reduction the impact of transport on the environment. The objective of this paper is to launch a discussion on how transport policy, pricing instruments can contribute to solving the most important transport problems. To analyze the general problem of externalities and which policy instruments are, in principle, available to address them.

***Key words*:** Transport costs, Pricing externality, Internalization, Economic instruments

INTRODUCTION

Faced with the strong growth in transportation need, transport infrastructures are increasingly overloaded or badly maintained and often negative externalities (congestion, air pollution, noise and

[1]Faculty of Economic Sciences and Management of Mahdia, University of Monastir, Tunisia

**Corresponding author*: E-mail: nejiaonline@yahoo.fr

accidents) are not supported by the users. A prerequisite for a pricing policy aimed at internalizing external costs is the monetary evaluation of the negative effects associated with transport.

Transportation is a vector of economic growth and an indispensable means of human activity. Indeed, it allows everyone to move to enjoy the variety of jobs that arise, it facilitates the movement of goods, etc. Beyond these positive effects on economic development, transportation, however, generates very significant nuisances that degrade living conditions. Mention is mainly congestion, air pollution, noise, accidents, damage to buildings, etc.

The concerns about the negative effects have increased from the moment we realized quils are not supported by transport users. As pointed out by the Green Paper in 1995, solutions must be found regarding the payment mechanisms for the use of transport infrastructure. A prerequisite for a pricing policy is to distinguish between travel costs. So we can classify the generalized cost of transportation into three main categories: private costs, external costs and public costs.

Table 1: Classification of the costs of transport (Commission of the European Communities,1995)

Cost categories	***Social costs***	
	Internal/Private costs	***External costs***
Transport expenditure	• Fuel and vehicle costs: tickets/fares	• Costs paid by others (*e.g.*, free Provision of parking spaces)
Infrastructure costs	• User charges, vehicle taxes and fuel excises	• Uncovered infrastructure costs
Accident costs	• Costs covered by insurance own disbenefits	• Uncovered accident costs (*e.g.*, pain and suffering Imposed on others)
Environmental costs	• Own disbenefits	• Uncovered environmental costs (*e.g.*, noise disturbance to others
Congestion costs	• Own–time costs	• Delays/time costs imposed on others

Indeed, all transport activity generates a series of costs. The separation of these costs is carried out according to the person who pays (Commission of the European Communities, 1995). We distinguish in particular between: the so-called private costs, that is to say, those incurred by the users themselves. The so-called external costs, that is to say, those caused to other users or to society as a whole and not be borne by transport users. Finally, the so-called public cost that is to say those who are supported by the State, local and regional authorities.

Although it has been used since the 20s, in the transport field the concept of externality is still the subject of much debate. An externality is when the welfare of an individual varies due to the activity of other individuals. Externalities are a consequence dune activity that does not give rise to monetary consideration. The social cost of transport includes not only the private costs borne directly by the user but also the external costs (environmental costs, congestion costs and accident costs).

THE ESTIMATION PROCEDURE OF EXTERNAL COSTS

In recent years, there has been a great diversity on the evaluation methodology of transport externalities. The European Commission convened a High Level Group on pricing objective in May 1999. Transport infrastructure is to establish a common procedure for estimation of transport externalities. To achieve a more efficient use of transport infrastructure and to ensure greater transparency and consistency in the pricing of the transport system, the European Commission convened a group of transportation specialist to examine in more detail how to define and 'Cost estimate.

- ***First step*:** The definition of costs

  There is talk of a marginal external cost lorsqu.une additional transport unit (vehicle, train, barge, boat, plane) uses the infrastructure.
- ***Second step*:** The definition of cost categories

  Once the nature of costs is dé.nie, it is important to determine their categorization depending on the time of travel (peak hour, off-peak hour), the type of vehicle (motorcycle, car, bus, trucks, aircraft, etc.), the type of engine (diesel or electric), etc. The categorization of costs is essential because it allows the charge with the greatest possible precision to those who are responsible.
- ***Third stage*:** Evaluation of the causes and impacts

  The causes are determined using a technical expertise and medical.
- ***Step four*:** Cost allocation

  In a pure pricing system, prices vary depending on the variation in costs. Indeed, for each category must charge the cost to the corresponding user.
- ***Fifth step*:** Calculating the monetary value

The calculation of the monetary value is based on the choice of estimation method namely money market transactions, investigations of the willingness to pay and willingness to accept, etc.

Table 2: External costs components and level of externality

Cost component	***Private and social costs***	***External part in general***	***Differences between transport modes***
Costs of scarce infrastructure (Congestion and scarcity costs)	All costs for traffic users and society (Time, reliability, operation, missed economic activities) caused by high traffic densities.	Extra costs imposed on all other users and society exceeding own additional costs	For non-scheduled transport (Road sector), the external cost component is the difference between marginal cost and average cost based on a congestion cost function. For scheduled transport services (Rail, air), the external cost component is the difference between the willingness to pay for scarce access slots and the existing access slot charge.
Accident costs	All direct and indirect costs of an accident (Material costs, medical costs, production losses, suffering and grief caused by fatalities).	Part of social costs which is not considered in own and collective risk anticipation and not covered by (Third party insurance).	There is a debate on the level of collective risk anticipation in individual transport, are the costs of a self-induced accident a matter of (Proper) individual risk anticipation or a collective matter? Besides, there are different levels of liability between private insurance schemes (Private road transport) and insurance schemes for transport operators (Rail, air, waterborne)
Environmental costs	All damages of environmental nuisances (Health costs, material damages, biosphere damages, long term risks).	Part of social costs which is not considered (Paid for).	Depending on legislation, the level of environmental taxation or liability to realize avoidance measures differs between modes.

Source: (Handbook on estimation of external costs in the transport sector, February, 2008)

THE PRINCIPLE OF INTERNALIZATION OF EXTERNAL COSTS

A policy of internalizing external costs is to get the user of a mode of transport to bear the overall cost of their trip to know the private costs borne directly but also external costs. The aim of such a policy is to ensure both economic efficiency and equity. There are basically four different elements in a transport strategy:

- ***Regulatory instruments*:** The regulatory approach sets standards, restrictions, administrative procedures, etc.
- ***Cooperation agreements*:** The cooperative agreements get all the people engaged in a specific issue of voluntary negotiation.
- ***Information instruments*:** Information instruments about transport can serve as a basis for more rational transport decisions of transport users.
- ***Economic instruments*:** The price mechanism serves as a policy enforcement. By changing the price of private transport, the decisions of the users can be guided into more favourable directions.

From an economic point of view pricing is the best policy instrument to internalize external costs, since it has a direct impact on all dimensions of travel behavior (*e.g.*, choice of route or mode of transportation). In addition, compared to the regulatory pricing generates income. However to ensure a better allocation of transport economists support the idea that the price paid by the transport user must be calculated on the basis of marginal social cost. This corresponds to the extra costs incurred by a new user on the network.

According to economic theory, the existence of externalities creates a divergence between private costs, that is to say, those incurred by the person performing the transport activity, and social costs. It follows thus that the balance achieved in the transport market does not correspond to the optimum situation. Two approaches have been discussed in the literature in order to internalize these externalities. The regulatory approach corresponds to institutional measures to act on individuals through institutional measures namely the emission standards, the facilities planning territories, etc. The tariff approach corresponds to institutional measures through incentives in the form of price signals to know the axle taxes, fuel taxes, vignette, tolls, etc. Today economists support the idea that pricing has the best cost-effective than regulation, since it affects all dimensions of travel behavior and compared to the regulatory pricing generates income.

Marginal External Costs Pricing

It should be sufficient to ensure an organization efficient transport systems, to impose a pricing marginal cost (TCM). Any deficit resulting from the difference between the infrastructure and operating costs and revenues from transport could be financed by lump sum taxes. In practice, this method of pricing and financing is inapplicable because of market imperfections and limited opportunities to differentiate the cost function of space, time, and various types of users.

The transport entails negative externalities: congestion, chemical pollution or acoustic, accidents, violations infrastructure. Coase says these externalities can be integrated through negotiations. But haggling to Coase is practically out of the question on the transport market, given the large number of parties involved, the high transaction costs, and information events imperfect and/or asymmetric. Pricing is used to take account of these externalities by confronting users with the entire CM (marginal cost) of social move.

In economic literature, the external cost charge back to the work of Pigou (1920), Knight (1924), Walters (1961) and Vickrey (1969). They showed that to maximize social welfare, internalization of external costs charges should be calculated on the basis of marginal social costs (marginal private cost + external marginal costs). Marginal external costs are all costs that an additional user causes to other users or to society as a whole, and which are not included in the fare.

Consider Figure below, which is a classic graph Price - Quantity. The cost per trip is represented on the vertical axis and the volume of traffic, or amount of trips by time unit, on the horizontal axis. For the case of a negative externality, assume the production of for example a

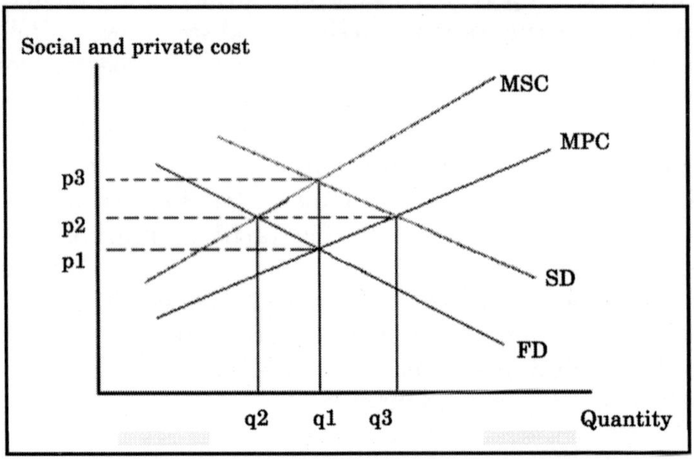

polluting activity, production at quantity q3 with the price p2, reflecting only the marginal private cost. In order to reach optimality the SD should equal MSC. This is done at quantity q1 and price p3. Hence, the result is a decrease in production being imposed by the corresponding increase in price which is the result of internalizing the negative externality by way of a tax for example.

The marginal social cost of short term is optimal if the following conditions are met:

- Competition markets
- No transaction cost
- No optimal taxes or fees
- No information problems
- No redistribution problems

These conditions are not met exactly, and so that, strictly speaking, the marginal cost is never applicable. The reality is instead marked by opposite conditions:

- There are shortcomings approach
- Transaction costs can be very significant
- Applicable taxes are not optimal
- Information is imperfect
- The community still has concerns redistribution

But the theory provides insights and solutions all these concrete situations. Rapidly examine these cases.

Ramsey Pricing

Walters (1974) noted that marginal cost pricing constitutes an appropriate pricing. But when the road is congested or when there are economies of scale, it is necessary that authorities set prices higher than average cost. This discriminatory practice is known as the rule of Ramsey, which states that a natural monopoly, like all businesses, is to be profitable, one way or another, pricing at a tariff above the cost marginal. Here, the Ramsey rule states that the price should be much higher marginal cost that the customer has a more elastic demand.

CONCLUSIONS

Here was proposed a very general overview of the externalities of transport. Although, its policies reduce some forms of pollution, improve significant road safety, they do not seem able to remedy situations malfunctioning markets. This result in distortions in the daily decisions moving, too many people use the wrong mode transportation in the wrong place at the wrong time. Most policies developed have direct influence on these decisions. It is possible to effects focus more on the modulation of rates according to the tariff zone of borrowed means of transport, the distance covered or the period of the week or the time of day. In effect, to get users to pay the real cost of their travel policy must complement regulatory policy and other policies.

The problem of transport externalities has already been the subject of several studies especially Bonnafous (1992), Quinet (1994), National Account Passenger transportation (1998), Vivier (1999), Lame (2001), Ricci (cf. de Palma Quinet, 2004). These authors analyze the external costs to using a global approach. They give an overall assessment of external costs enabling a balance sheet (account passenger), compared to national level (as % of GDP) etc. A deepening of that work could be by using a marginal approach that allows evaluate costs caused by traffic additional unit. It is based on the monetization of externalities by mode, for period of travel or types of effects. This subsequently allows to study the effect of certain tariff policies on the behavior of users in the choice of transport mode.

REFERENCES

Alberini, A. *et al.* (1999). "Mortality risk valuation for environmental policy, Resources for the future", discussion paper, pp. 99–47.

Arnott, R., De Palma, A. and Lindsey, R. (1993). "The welfare effects of congestion tolls with heterogeneous commuters", Boston College Working Papers in Economics 231, Boston College Department of Economics.

Arnott, R., De Palma, A. and Lindsey, R. (1993). A structural model of peak-period congestion: A traffic bottleneck with elastic demand. *American Economic Review*, 83(1): 161–79.

Boiteux, M. (2001). Transport, pour un meilleur choix d'investissement, la documentation française Paris.

Boniver, V. and Thiry, B. (1994). "Les costs marginaux externes du transport public de personnes en milieu urbain-estimations chiffrées pour la Belgique". *Cahiers Economiques de Bruxelles*, 142.

Bonnafous, A. (1992). Transports et environnement comment valoriser et maîtriser les effets externes? *Economie et Statistique n*, 258–259: 121–128.

Commission of the European Communities. Towards fair and efficient pricing in transport, Green Paper 1995, Brussels.

Commission of the European Communities (1998). Fair payment for infrastructure use: A phased approach to a common transport infrastructure charging framework for the EU, White paper, Brussels, p. 153.

Handbook on estimation of external costs in the transport sector, Produced within the study Internalisation Measures and Policies for All external Cost of Transport (IMPACT), version 1.1 February 2008.

Knight, F. (1924). Some fallacies in the interpretation of social costs. *Quarterly Journal of Economics,* 38(4): 582–606.

Kunzli, N., Kaizer, R., Medina, S., Studnicka, M., Chanel, O., Herry, M., Horak, F., Puybonnieux-Texier, V., Quenel, P., Schneider, J., Seethaler, R., Vergnaud, J.C. and Sommer, H. (2000). "Public-health impact of outdoor and traffic-related air pollution: A European assessment". *Lancet*, 356: 795–801.

Lambert, J. (2001). "Le bruit des transports en Europe-Exposition de la population, risques pour la santé et coût pour la collectivité". Echo bruit, (96 - Numéro spécial le bruit en Europe), ISSN 0755-4397, pp. 6–11.

Lamure, C. (1990). "Environmental considerations in transport investments". *In:* Transport Policy and Environment, European Conference of Ministers of Transport (ECMT), Paris, OCDE, pp. 108–146.

Nash, C., Sansom, T. and Still, B. (2001). Modifying transport prices to internalize externalities: Evidence from European case study. *Regional Science and Urban Economics*, 31: 413–431.

Pigou, A.C. (2001). *The Economics of Welfare*, London: Macmillan.

Proost, S., Delhaye, E., Nijs, W. and Van Regemorter, D. (2009). Will a radical transport pricing reform jeopardize the ambitious EU climate change objectives? *Energy Policy*, 37(10): 3863–3871.

Quinet, E. (1997). Full social cost of transportation in Europe. *In*: Greene, Jones and Delucchi (*eds.*), the full social costs and benefits of transportation, Springer-Verlag.

Quinet, E. (2004). A meta-analysis of Western European external costs estimates. *Transportation Research Part D: Transport and Environment*, 9(6): 465–476.

Ricci, A. (2004). "Evaluation des costs externes et définition des politiques". *In*: de Palma, A. and Quinet, E. (*eds.*), La tarification des transports: Enjeux et défis, *Economica*, pp. 179–196.

Vickrey, W.S. (1969). Congestion theory and transport investment. *American Economic Review*, 59: 251–260.

Vivier, J. (1999). Comparaison des costs externes de transport public et de l'automobile en milieu urbain: Cas de la région Ile de France", UITP, Mai.

5

Is Development Relevant/Required?

M. Kunhaman[1]*

ABSTRACT

In the massive and burgeoning literature on development studies there has been no unanimity of views on the concept, source and measure of development. What is development, what type of development and whose development or development for whom; all these are still unsettled questions. Development, as it was conceived and perceived since the Second World War has been state-led and project centric. People's thinking was appropriated; they had been simply considered as the objects rather than subjects of development. Subjectivity and people's agency role had been ignored. But the same period witnessed thinking about not only alternative development but also alternative to development. Some scholars even speak about the post development era. Development should be individualized. Its genesis should be considered as freedom of the individual. Liberalism and classical individualism are back at the centre stage. The state should be a laissez-faire state. Choice of economic activity should be left to individuals. Individuals should not just part take of the growth of the system; Instead, the growth of the system should be the sum total of individual benefits and contributions. There should be shifts from rulers to leaders; from employers to entrepreneurs; and from skill to innovation. The state can play an enabling rather than a leading role.

Key words: Development, Liheralism, Economic activity

---

[1]Tata Institute of Social Sciences, Tuljapur Campus, Tuljapur P.O. Osmanabad District, Maharashtra.

Paper presented at the National Seminar on "Sustainable Development: Searching a Policy Frame for Kerala" organized by the C. Achutha Menon Foundation in Trivandrum, Kerala, 4–6, March 2016.

**Corresponding author*: E-mail: mkunhaman@rediffmail.com.

INTRODUCTION

This paper, premised on the dialectical conflicts over primitive accumulation and resistance thereto, raises the question development, as it is practiced today or in alternative forms, is necessary at all. Is the relevant question development, or alternative development or alternative to development? It is, in a sense, a subaltern critique of development, particularly the deplorable tendency to consider every question as a development question and to counter the resistance of the development dropouts to state-sponsored and state-supported dispossession and deprivation as anti-development. It also takes the position that the once-unquestioned razz-ma-tazz about, and the abracadabra of development itself, must be replaced with the spotlight on individuals alongside ensuring a rural-urban osmosis. There has been no unanimity regarding the concept, source and measure of development. Development of what type of development, whose development, and by whom? All these are important, but still contentious questions.

When we consider development, the state comes in. Policy, programs and projects are the focal themes: policy priorities are important. Development is state-led and project-centric. State means power. Power is used by the strong against the weak. State is an instrument of oppression. It has legitimacy of and monopoly over instruments of violence. Whose knowledge and ideas shape policies? Ruling ideas are ruling class ideas. Ruling class controls wealth, knowledge and power. Power has a tendency for concentration and centralization. The Post Second World War period heralded the development era.

In the newly independent countries, the process became state-led, and top down almost universally. People's thinking is externalized/ appropriated. People are treated as mere objects: object of development and object of domination. Scholars, thinking for the people; experts, preparing plans for the people; bureaucracy, implementing plans for the people; political parties, struggling for the people. A formidable development establishment comprising politicians, bureaucrats, Contractors, NGOs has emerged and become entrenched. Development is, in fact, for this establishment. It resists the emergence of an alternative to development. And the process is top-down, whether it is centralized or decentralized development.

Socio-spatial specificities are ignored

The same period also witnessed the emergence of two other schools: one that argued for alternative to development and the other that talked about the post- development era.

The accelerated process of globalization based on "space-time compression" witnessed the attrition of the state to a "minimalist" position.

Development is dead; obituary of development is omnipresent. The two pillars of global economic expansion are technology and market.

Liberalism and Classical individualism are universally acclaimed and demanded: a vindication of Adam Smith.

Of course, there is special concern for the poor. But why? It's condescending and demoralizing; it saps the self-worth of the poor. It is trendy to talk to the poor, talk about the poor, and talk for the poor but it is dangerous to talk with the poor. The poor are not asking for development. They are asking for resources, education, employment and social security. People are not against profit; they are against primitive accumulation. The tribal's are not asking for airports or multi star hotels or multi-specialty hospitals in their hamlets/settlements. They are just asking for land, water, and forest which historically and constitutionally belong to them. It is a paradox under the development regime that people don't get what they ask for; they get what they don't ask for. Developmentis used as an instrument to intimidate, suppress and silence the poor. If people are anti-development, that does not mean that they are a threat to internal security. Why is it that the poor are entitled only to the BPL card, or the Dalits and Adivasi are entitled only to community certificates?

Inequality is not the creation of the neo-liberal economic policy. The emergence of Inequality of wealth and income should be traced to pre-capitalist, feudal mode of production (Joseph Stieglitz and Thomas Piketty). Neo-liberal economic policy only accentuated them. People seem to be not overly bothered about inequality. They demand resources, a living family income and social security.

Those who conspired to defeat Ambedkar in the first general election after Independence are now showing sympathy to dalit students' unions and not to Ambedkar students' associations on various University campuses in the country. These political leaders may be well-advised to remember Ambedkar's famous observation that those who forget history cannot create history.

Political leaders (career politicians) lament that youngsters are not joining their political parties. This is a legitimate survival concern for these leaders. But the youngsters, *i.e.*, the aspirational class, demand quality education, gainful employment, and career prospects.

These leaders exhort the students of poor/marginalized sections to get education in mother tongue even as they send their own children to English medium schools and ivy league universities abroad. A few of these top leaders speak at meetings in their home states in English while some lesser beings translate their speeches for the ordinary mortals. The poor children need not study English; they are for slogan shouting, poster-pasting and getting beaten up by police. The academia and the media, the two sites of knowledge production, collation and dissemination are controlled by the upper castes. In the media, Dalit/ Adivasi presence is nil, while in the academia, they have a pale/ insignificant presence. In the Universities, there are "Empirical Sudhras" and "Theoretical Brahmin" (Sarukkai, 2012). At academic seminars, dalit/adivasi scholars get invited to speak on dalit/adivasi issues, not on general issues.

Post-colonial development perspectives in India: A kaleidoscopic overview.

Indian Independence meant the transfer of power from Western rulers to Westernalised Indian rulers, without any change of attitude.

India launched planning in a feudal social framework. Policies and priorities were set by the powerful.

Two development approaches were followed: one for the rich and one for the poor. The rich were free while the poor were made dependent on the state. The outcomes were natural and unsurprising: victors and victims. Development and deprivation.

A critical look is taken here at the various development perspectives emerging/prevailing towards the end of the colonial period and at the beginning of the post-colonial period. It is instructive to bear in mind that important issues relating to policies and programs pertaining to planning, development, land reforms, democracy and numerous other subjects to be pursued since Independence had been engaging the minds of leaders (political, social and corporate) and scholars. Regarding development, four major perspectives deserve mentioning. (a) The Nehruvian perspective, set out in his book, The Discovery of India published in 1940, aiming at catching up with the developed countries;

(b) Ambedkar's perspectives, specifically on land and water; (c) Gandhian perspective based on decentralized production and participative democracy; and (d) The Communist Party perspective based on the agrarian questions and class relations. It may be mentioned that these perspectives cannot be synthesized in a non-encaustic manner; at best, what can be attempted is to is develop a Christmas tree approach to development aiming, though not always completely successfully, to satisfy everybody of the four, it was, expectedly, Nehru's perspective that ultimately prevailed, pulling the plug on others and conferring on him the honorific of being the architect of Indian planning and development primarily because he was powerful and he was in power. This was quite natural as everywhere and always, it is the knowledge and thinking of the powerful that shape policies. After all, to be accepted, ideas should move with power. Also, in our system, what is said is less important than who says it.

A NEW / DIFFERENT TYPE OF POLITICS

The enthusiasm of the middle class, tepid to electoral politics for a long time since Independence, in discussing issues in the social media and participating in elections is a new phenomenon resulting from deep disenchantment with maledictions such as corruption, cronyism, nepotism, crime against women, and dynastic politics. A new politics, leaderless and party less, has emerged and ramped up the clamor for clean and corruption-free governance, a trend that helped, in no small measure, the emergence of a new breed of political leaders. It may be observed, parenthetically, that serious policy debates have shifted from obstreperous legislatures to social media platforms. A welcome trend, indeed.

Individualism and classical liberalism are heralding a new economic paradigm based on individual enterprise, competitive efficiency, new, (though not-cutting-edge) technology, and burgeoning market opportunities. Family enterprises of yore are being juxtaposed with new ones being established by first generation start-up enterprises. Mention may be made first of women. Highly qualified, skilled and competent women are moving into leadership positions in industrial and business enterprises in the organized sector in increasing numbers. Women entrepreneurship has been flowering also at middle and lower enterprises. Women have been showing unprecedented grit in breaking loose of the caste-class-patriarchy- cultural axis which had blocked their mobility for centuries. Microfinance-driven women's Self Help Groups (SHGs) are empowering women to face the challenges being thrown up by a rapidly changing social order. Also pertinent to mention is the emergence of a class of dalit entrepreneurs (Devesh Kapur, 2014) breaking shackles and arousing entrepreneurial spirit. Though the appropriateness of the term "dalit-capitalism", is debatable, the Pune-centered DICCI declaring nonchalantly to the world that dalits would be job givers rather than job seekers affirms that provided propitious and enabling circumstances, daring and risk-taking persons form the most marginalized, oppressed sections can thrive and prosper in a competitive/entrepreneurial capitalist economy (Lakshmi lyer, 2013). Land Reforms in India bypassed the dalits. They could not become land-owning farmers, particularly so in Kerala Under the neo-liberal economic policy, many of them has become capitalists. Micro finance, women's SHGS, above all, the Pardhan Mantri Jan-Dhan Yojna stand testimony to the fact that development is freedom (Sen, 1999), and the antidote to the gender and caste oppressions and discriminations of various sorts. India is fast-modernizing economy and society. But it would appear that the country has a capitalist basic structure with a feudal super structure, for primordial values and practices like caste and gender discriminations are still prevalent. However, what is syncretically pertinent is not merely to take note of the opening opportunities but to draw inspirations from the civilizational dimensions

Many of the developed countries/societies of today, so became not on the basis of plans or specific programs for specific socio-economic groups. There might not have been even so much as a talk about development. They inspired and promoted individualism and classical liberalism. And given the fact that individuals were free to enjoy the fruits of their efforts and enterprise after meeting the public obligations like tax payments, they had the incentives to produce more and benefit more. Whereas in India, the well-of sections were given the freedom to use individualism some and liberalism, combined with private property, the poor were made dependent on the state for their very survival, not to speak of development. For them, it has been the caste certificate-determined, state–directed welfare and development programmes coming in dribbles. Naturally, their social space defined and determined their spaces in the economy. In post colonial India, polity became inclusive while the economy remained exclusivist especially for the dalits who have been programmed to go on all fours for handouts, making them quiescent and incapacitating them in benefiting from market opportunities.

There is no reason to suppose that the persons forming and controlling the state have supreme wisdom and divine vision to pursue development, making people mere objects and denying them any subject role. This neurophiliac trend continued through the post-reform phase also even as the philosophy postulated a minimalist state and a maximalist market. The fact of the matter is that the poor do not have the freedom and opportunity to pursue the economic activities of their choice. Experience hitherto is testimony to the fact that development cannot be derived from the transitive verb, for the state has failed in bringing it about through its statured programmes and projects. The creaky development establishment comprising a hypocritical political class, a lethargic and status quoist bureaucracy, a self-seeking class of contractors and pesky NGOs miserably failed in heralding development. The pre-reform development in India is a cock and bull story told by a cockeyed and slimy planner who has inevitably and irreverently been put on the back-foot owing to the unsavory realization that the promises given turned out to be just pie in the sky and the dystopia that resulted instead created all-round cynicism. The state is an incubus, playing fast and loose. Development is an instrument of intimidation an enervation. The argument is necessarily for an alternative to development, not alternative development. As state-directed development has been a failure, it must be given thumbs down; the alternative *viz.*, a free market competitive economy deserves a thumbs up. Such a perspective does not envisage the disappearance of the state, but rather, it's redefining and repositioning. It has a serious role to play, *viz.*, nationalizing resources and distributing them equally among the people. Its other function are: defense, law and order, provision of infrastructure, maintaining an impartial legal system and provision of social security system. This line of advocacy is based on the conviction that, of the paradigms that prevailed in history, the best has been the perfectly competitive a la Smith (not monopolistic or patrimonial) capitalism. Creating and maintaining such a society should be the indispensable and immediate necessity.

The deprived and marginalized like the poor dalits and adivasis are not asking for development; rather, they are fighting for resources. One can see this more pointedly in the case of the advises who have been waging a resource politics contrary to the power politics of the mainstream. Diagnosis of these two types of politics, *i.e.,* resource politics and power politics forms the basis and underpinnings of the paradigm outlined above. Inheritance is an important factor in development. While the rich inherit wealth, knowledge, self confidence and optimism, the deprived and the socially excluded inherit deprivation, poverty, oppression, fear, inferiority complex and diffidence resulting in visceral negativism. This rich-poor divide is seemingly unbridgeable. The depressed need, basically to shed their inferiority complex and build confidence; they must be mentally brought on an equal footing with the others so as to bring down hierarchical rigidities and institutionalised inequities. The question needs to be asked when, in the case of upper castes, capitalism succeeds, why should it fail in the case of dalits and adivasis, who are increasingly becoming literate, politically conscious, spunky and aspirationally mobile? Why should their only entitlement be the caste certificate? Why should the sole entitlement of the poor, desperate to catch at any straw, be the BPL card? The approach adopted here-to-fore has disproportionately benefitted the rich and deprecatingly short-changed the poor. The rich and the poor should be covered under the same policy and philosophy so as to synergistically release their kinetic energy for creative economic activity, rather than pushing the poor into a tail spin. What is sauce for the goose is sauce for the gander. Development must be given a neat burial and a solemn obituary. Nobody, least of all the mendacious state and the mendicant NGOs should worry about the development of the others. The demise of the and rogynous developer ipso facto means the beginning of human liberation and is in conformity with the zeitgeist. Scholars have started talking about the "post-development era [which] is to be free of the illusions, ideological perversions, hypocrisy and falsehoods that prevailed in the development world" (Rahnema, 1997: p. 391). The development tide has begun to turn. It should be driven home in unambiguous terms that those who are preparing the epitaph of capitalism are wrong. Equally wrong are those who envision a crisis-free capitalism.

Entrepreneurial capitalism (Schumpeter, 2005), promotes efficiency. Hence, unleashing entrepreneurial energy and creativity is the need of the hour, irrespective of whether one likes capitalism or not. State is a poor entrepreneur. There is a strong case for delinking economics from politics. The bourgeoning lumpen political class with its deadpan leadership should be relegated to a corner. Today's world needs, not rulers, but leaders. Rulers have power; leaders have imagination. Rulers are for today (and, today only); leaders look beyond today. Concurrently, equity is a desired and sought-after value inescapable also for sustainability. Hence, the challenge, the world over, is to combine competitive efficiency with equity. India also should plump for the same. Eternal vigilance is called for to prevent concentration of wealth and power. Equally important is to maintain the symbiosis between economy and environment.

SOME RANDOM OBSERVATIONS

Systemically, poverty seems to be bottoming out, not due to the structural characteristics of the growth process; rather, it has been the result of welfare programs and pro-poor state and social interventions.

Inclusive growth is an illusion. The poor are sought to be included as manual laborers and not as independent producers. In a country that is on the upswing, any meaningful and sustainable inclusion is possible only through the provision of resources, *viz.*, land, water, skill/education and finance through a drastic redistributive reform rather than corvee. The humongous program, *viz.*, MGNREGA is a sham. No political party has a program for equality of wealth and income. Enunciation of such a program may disable political parties in the existing competitive, democratic, parliamentary politics.

Equality of Opportunities has not Ensured Equality of Outcome

Unlike Soviet Russia or China, India did not launch planning after a revolution followed by establishment of socialism. Hence, the planner was not left with a tabula rasa. This made it inescapable that no plan, in the real sense of the term, was made for the 1951–56 period; rather, the programs and projects (a whole raft of them) already under execution and which had their provenance in the pre-planning era, were listed and given the name, the First Five Year Plan. Resources were mainly under private ownership, necessitating a mixed planning: an imperative planning for the fledgling public sector and an indicative planning for a strong private sector. Resource mobilization for the public sector which could be based almost exclusively on progressive taxation has ever been a formidable task with the government facing the double whammy of perpetual budget/fiscal deficit and exponentially increasing public expenditure commitments. Administrative controls were a poor substitute for resource controls. And intrusive/invasive state developed an unavailing, obstructionist and oppressive attitude towards citizens, killing their freedom, initiative and enterprise.

Besides, in a multiclass, multi-caste society with parliamentary democracy, it is impossible to adopt a singular and concrete objective acceptable to all. In a socialist society, where resources are owned and controlled by the state, central planning is the mechanism for managing the resources in such a way that the benefits of planning accrue to everyone equally. In a multi party, competitive democracy, on the other hand, no such unanimity on the objective of development is possible. Any programme or project acceptable/beneficial to any particular socio-economic group would necessarily alienate and antagonize others, eroding the political support base of the rulling party and the opposition parties taking advantage thereof (Kohli, 2004). Hence, the use of such abstract and recondite objectives as "growth and justice", "growth with justice", "welfare of all", "inclusive growth", "equitable growth" etc. After all, parliamentary democracy- a costly electoral system wherein a few privileged get elected and become entitled to squander public money with gay abandon-thrives on falsity, ambiguity and hypocrisy. Every government tries to pursue a line of least resistance.

Nehru could see India, but could not see Indians. Particularly, he could not understand the inequalities of various sorts-incomes, wealth, education, status and power: nor did he have the grit and gumption to tackle them. Ambedkar, on the other hand, could clearly see India and Indians. Had Ambedkar been the first Prime Minister of India, given his right diagnosis of the basic maladies of Indian society, India's development story would not have been so staid and insipid; the egregious inequalities would not have assumed such infernal proportions.

It can be said, in retrospect, that there were two freedom struggles in India: one led by Gandhi for India's freedom and the other by Ambedkar for Indians' freedom. Ambedkar clearly discerned the patterns of inequality *i.e.*, graded inequality. Terms such as liberty and equality were rightly included in the Preamble to the Constitution as guiding, parametric principles. It bears reiteration that the core problem emphasized by Ambedkar, *viz.*, inequality is the basic and most formidable problem that is being faced by India, a problem for which there seems to be no solution within the extant framework of parliamentary democracy.

A word about Gandhi, the paterfamilias of the Indian National Congress. He, was anything but a social analyst; not a modernist but a revanchist; his assertion about ancestor's calling is particularly repulsive and abominable. He lacked the vision for building a modern economy and society.

The neo-liberal economic policy has opened the economy, offering infinite opportunities in various fields. Like the globalized world economy, the fate of the Indian economy hinges on innovation, technology, market and management. People's mobility of various sorts, especially aspirational has been in the ascendant.

India is an ancient civilization. It never imposed its core values, ideas and world views on others; rather, these were accepted by others of their volition. It never conquered and colonized other regions of the world. It could attain development on its own and that prosperity attracted conquerors from outside. Subsequently, the resources were plundered. None-the-less, the civilizational values/core remains intact. This civilization and historical fact must be the inspirational wellspring for the aspirationally mobile who is the indefatigable strength, real and potential, of the country today.

REFERENCES

Amartya Sen, J.D. (1999). *India: Economic Development and Social Opportunity.* Clarendon Press.

Amin, S. (2008). Anuradha Ghandy Memorial Lecture. Mumbai.

Balakrishnan, P. *Economic Growth in India: History and Prospect.*

Chatterjee, P. (2006). The politics of the governed reflections on popular politics in most of the world.Columbia University Press.

Chomsky, N. Class warfare. Pluto Press.

Devesh Kapur, D.S. (2014). Defying the odds: The rise of dalit entrepreneurs.Vintage Books.

Fromm, E. (1982). Greatness and limitations of Freud's thought.

Hinrichsen, D. (1987). Our common future: A reader's guide.Oxford University Press.

Immanuel Wallerstein, R.C. (2013). Does capitalism have a future? New York: Oxford University Press.

Jaffrelot, C. (2003). India's silent revolution: The rise of the lower castes in North India. C. Hurst and Co. Publishers.

Jaffrelot, C. (2005). Dr. Ambedkar and Untouchability: Fighting the Indian Caste System. Columbia University Press.

Kalyan, S. (2007). Rethinking capitalist development. Routledge.

Kannabiran, K.G. (2004). *The Wages of Impunity: Power, Justice and Human Rights.* Orient Blackswan.

Kohli, A. (2004). State-directed development political power and industrialization in the global periphery. Princeton University, New Jersey.

Lakshmi Iyer, T.K. (2013). *Caste and Entrepreneurship in India,* Vol: XLVIII.

Munshi, I. (2012). The adivasi question: Issues of land, forest and livelihood. Orient Blackswan.

Pai, S. (2012). Developmental State and the Dalit Question in Madhya Pradesh: Congress Response. Routledge India.

Piketty, T. (2014). Capital in the Twenty-First Century.Harvard University Press.

Popper, K. (2005). *The Logic of Scientific Discovery.* Routledge.

Rahnema, M. (1997). The Post-Development Reader. Zed Books.

Sarukkai, G.G. (2012). The cracked mirror: An indian debate on experience and theory. Oxford.

Schumpeter, J.A. (2005). Business cycles: A theoretical, historical and statistical analysis of the capitalist process.Martino Pub.

Sen, A. (1999). Development as Freedom.Oxford University Press.

Sengupta, A. (2007). Report on conditions of work and promotion of livelihoods in the unorganised sector. Goverment of India.

Stiglitz, J.E. (2012).The price of inequality: How today's divided society endangers our future. W.W. Norton and Company.

Subrahmanyam, K. (2015). Poverty and social structure. The Hindu.

Thorat Sukhadeo and Katherine, S. (2012). Krieger School of Arts and Sciences (2012). Blocked by caste economic discrimination in Modern India. Oxford India.

6

Designing the Strategy of "Change": Meaning of Accounting in Budget Policy Case Study in Jembrana Regency of Bali

SYARIFUDDIN[1] AND RATNA AYU DAMAYANTI[1]

ABSTRACT

Whether we realize or not, managing the strategy of change in local government is not strategically simple. Even until now there is no consensus on the meaning behind the statement "managing strategically" in the context of local government administration. According to some experts, even if a strategic approach can be implemented in the sense of "not stated explicitly" or "implicitly without a formal document strategy", "changing" is still not an easy job. The objective of this article is to describe how local government manage strategies of change in the environment of local government that is massively complex and not simple. This is because the kind of problems that are addressed by local government are difficult and complex problems, it could even be said that it is not possible to diagnose the symptoms caused by problems. The method used is plot analysis. The study found that for actors (accounting man), accounting has the power to change the disclosure patterns of an organization so that the affairs of the internal world can be seen by the public. That is, if accounting is used carefully and with caution, accounting can play a role in strategically changing the managerial awareness, which has variety of internal problems. Different forms of political pressure can be put into the organization and will produce strategic agreements including accounting policies.

Key words: Budgeting, Strategic planning, Economic planning, Bali, Local government.

[1]Faculty of Economic and Business University of Hasanuddin, Indonesia
**Corresponding author*: E-mail: syarif1963@yahoo.com

INTRODUCTION

Local governance is a very complex organization, as well as being in a turbulent environment. Therefore, manager in the organization is expected to predict demand, identify and react to social, demographic and economic complexity and environmental problems (Thompson and Scholes, 1993). Thus, responding to the expectations of a changing society, responding to the expectations of citizens, and allocating scarce resources effectively and efficiently is something very important in policy formulation (Rittel and Webber, 1973; Hassal and Worral, 1997).

As we know, change in leadership will be accompanied by changes in political values and ideology in government organizations. These changes are often accompanied by changes in the concept of thoughts in the public sector, which relates to social, economy and public services issues, and the limits of government lifeworld. But it should be noted that change does not come by itself, but achieved/made consciously. That is, an individual or organization gradually changes, either on their own will or from an external drive. So, the change must be planned, and the planning can achieve its objectives if it is managed strategically.

However, whether we realize or not managing the strategy of changes in local government is not easy. Even until now there is no consensus on the meaning behind the statement "managing strategically" in the context of local government administration (Worrall *et al.*, 1998). According to Worrall *et al.* (1998), even if a strategic approach can be implemented in the sense of "not stated explicitly" or "implicitly without a formal document strategy", "changing" is still not an easy job. As stated by Whittington and Stacey (1994: 14), managing the strategy of change in the world of local government that is massively complex is not simple. According to Rittel and Webber (1973: 23), this is because the kind of problems that are addressed by local government are "difficult" problems, it could even be said that it is not possible to decipher the symptoms only from the problems.

Flood and Jackson (1991) suggested that in a situation in which the government body constantly changes, it takes an intervention (strategy) to direct the purpose of change. According to them one of the way is to avoid an overlap in the structure of problem. Thus, local governments need to develop a "lateral" capability to ensure a level of consistency between the organization's strategy and host strategy/basic strategy (education, housing, environment, anti-poverty, information systems, finance, and others) that they have. If not, then "chaos" and "obscurity" will be the everyday life of the organization (Hassal and Worral, 1997).

Therefore, a leader need a simple way, both in structure and imagination in order to avoid chaos (Flood and Jackson, 1991).

In the issue of changes and policies, positivist believed that a policy issues is an objective condition in which their existence can be created easily in a specific condition (Parsons, 1997: 77). According to him, this naive view of the nature of policy issues, fails to recognize the same facts. For example, government statistics show that crime, pollution, and poverty always changes, is often understood differently (subjectively) by the policy actors. Therefore, the same information that is relevant to a policy can generate different definitions and explanations. This is mainly because the stakeholders have different understandings about human nature, social changes, as well as the policy object itself.

Thus, the policy can be seen as the reflection of meaning of stakeholders' on the subject of policy (*e.g.*, accounting). Meanwhile, change itself is a sign and the form of change [policy] as a marker. Therefore, in driving change towards an accounting policy as in Jembrana, I think it is important to know how stakeholders interpret accounting as a sign, and how does the strategy of change needs to be played to achieve the desired objectives. This article will discuss how stakeholders manage change and construct policies, as sign and form of change as markers, based on their understanding of accounting [budget].

In the context of this paper, I chose the case of Jembrana because of its uniqueness. Jembrana is one of the local governments in the province of Bali which have very limited resources because it is not a tourist area like the other local governments in the province of Bali. However with limited resources, the leadership of the organization in the 2000s was able to do a very significant change that is to provide free education and health services for the people. Meanwhile, at the time the policy was something impossible because Indonesia has yet to devise and implement it. In the context of this article, I want to show how the head of the organization was able to perform the strategy of change and strategies to assure that the changes can be accepted by the local legislature.

BUDGET POLICY: ACCOUNTING MAN SUBJECTIVE MEANING OF ACCOUNTING

An important issue in the context of local government strategy is concerning the relationship between accounting man and context (space and time). Therefore, budget policy as a strategy in response to changes seems to be very influenced by how actors understand accounting [budget].

Recently, in literatures, accounting has been conceptualized as information (Prakash and Rappaport, 1977), language (Belkaoui, 1978; Boland, 1989; Laovie, 1987), political (Burchell *et al.*, 1980), magic (Gambling, 1977), myth (Boland, 1982), ideology (Tinker *et al.*, 1982), and exploitation (Tinker, 1985; Morgan, 1988). Meanwhile, evidence of Syarifuddin's Research (2013) found accounting policies [budget] as an "opportunity" (change), "hope" and "promise" in the metaphorical sense. Stakeholders' interpretation on budget in the study, is seen as one of the drivers for stakeholders in directing and managing change.

The views expressed above, can be traced through the following evidence. For example, the finance staff of Jembrana local government understands budget policy as something real and is the result of social construction, Ketut (informant), a finance staff, for example, stated that: "The budget policy of Jembrana local government to free education for the community is something real, can be felt not only by us directly in charge of the related sector expenditure, but also for the people who benefit from it". The same thing was expressed by another informant, a student parent's of SDN Jembrana, "Jembrana government policy to free education is indeed very helpful and pro-poor, like me. I see the budget policy as a hope given by the ruler to the people".

Two of the above evidence, clearly views budget policy as hope and promise that is as the way they feel. For Lefebvre (1998: 40) this view refers to accounting that has been materialized. In this case, accounting becomes a material or object that can be defined empirically. Thus, it is fitting what was stated McPhail (1997: 5) that accounting is something real, and socially produced. According to him, accounting in this case budget is something that is felt (real as a promise), because budget is something tangible, can be accurately measured and described. In this case, accounting policy is defined as a production process of a material form of social interaction, so that it can be presented as a medium, and the result of social activity. That is, "hope" that is perceived from budget policies is material, however, does not mean that it is physical in nature. Instead, accounting is the result of social practice, and depends on social practice for its existence. That is, the above interpretation of stakeholders on budget policies, are indication of a process, in which "hope" on the budget policy is measured and labeled empirically.

The proof above reminds me of an imaginary dialogue that I experienced the week before in the finance department room when I first visited. It was still early in the morning, Jembrana Regency employees had not yet arrived, today. I intentionally come early, I meant to observe the office setting without employees. I find an office building laden with Balinese architecture that tells me stories about what it has seen all this time. The first room I visited was the local secretary of finance [accounting] of Jembrana Regency. The rooms suddenly greet me and tell a story about what it has been through. "I'm glad you could visit here, there is so much I can tell, but this is just between the two of us" called this room that I heard through the ears of my heart, a greeting full of strong feelings of friendship and closeness. Suddenly this room believes that I could be the outlet to out poure its heart: "tell me, and I will keep all your story neatly, except to people who are also the same with me, who want to hear and care about your stories".

An empty room, with rows of tables and chairs that seems a bit dense in comparison with the space that is not that big. It then continued its story,

> Here, officials used to always try to work as hard as possible to meet the obsession of the leaders. Previously, they did not fully understand what the final shape of their work really was. They were merely a backdrop dancer of the famous "kecak[1]" dance.

The room paused,

> Their voice was only cak... cak... cak... up and down, slowly and then harder, depending on the accompanying music. They do not understand the direction of the dance and why they should dance.... cak... cak... cak... it was the only instruction for them to do... while raising their hands.

"Did they complained", I asked, curious:

> Yes, some of them were even frustrated.... Newcomers (regent) forced them to do what they do not understand.

"Why do they not protest", I began to insist:

> Some of them wanted to do so... but this is a government cubicle, you have very little space to say no... (sighs) therefore, although not understanding, most of them was convinced that this dance was important and attractive... they want to be part of this drama and watch whether the director can give an interesting show.

[1]Kecak is a traditional Bali dance to worship the gods.

"Do they still dance without feeling today", I tried to further uncover the atmosphere of the past it had felt:

> Not anymore... this time, they are well aware of their dance... this time, their body and soul sing along... and this room, now feels more so spacious... they feel that there is a huge opportunity for them to not just shout cak... cak... cak..., but that cak... cak... cak... is also as a surge of happiness... triumph... opportunities... and independence.

"You must certainly feel very happy", I asked, teasing him:

> I believe in one thing, that we are moving in an uninterrupted continuum line,... and form a circle, these people will go and replaced by the other, another generation, who have seen this show... may be they can dance as good as this... or even better... but for those who are really new would start again from zero... dancing without feel... cak... cak... cak...

The room was quiet for a moment, as if it was drowning in an emotional state, and then it continued. Sure enough its voice was a little heavy,

> I actually want them to stay here, filling my room, because I am their physical space, but this space gets bigger while the spaces in their hearts also gets bigger, they also create another space they call budget.

"How do they appreciate the budget that you so called the other space in this room?" I asked curious:

> The budget is a space of hope and a promise that must be met, which is limited but large enough for them to incorporate their ideas, their interests,... but as the other space, everyone tries to occupy a larger space, leaving less for others... .

The room then continued,

> They improvise, negotiate, imagine and contemplate in the budget space... I guess everyone has territorial boundaries in that space, and they know it... but some of them are trying to enter the others territory... we call it intervention.

"Is the budget space big enough for them to pour all their interests and political ideas?", This time I asked, while staring at the ceiling that looks new, has a new layer of paint, yes the paint could still be smelt. And he recalled that:

> Actually, the budget is very spacious for those who understand it, but too narrow for those who are bound by regulations, such as the walls of this room... actually this room should not be framed if only its contents does not create a frame for themselves.

My imaginary dialogue with the finance department room in charge of the budget policy, could be concluded that the budget and all forms of policy at the top, shows the budget policy as an "opportunity" (change), "hope" and "promise". That is, budget policy is not only regarded as a series of numbers alone, but also another social form that can be felt by human beings as the benefeciary.

Sudantra (informant), turned out not only considers budget as a "promise" (discourse space) but as head of finance department he felt dedicated and responsible for that promise. "When I woke up, I instantly remember about the budget and allocations that I had to face today. At the office my job is to check back and observe the obstacles that I will face in the budget. Before I sleep, I think, how to manage the budget, so that all the priority programs can be done?". This shows that Sudantra (informant) has regarded the budget as a part of his life, he was the inhabitant of that policy. He is inside and determines the happiness, anxiety, color, and rainbow of the budget policy.

Slightly different from the previous view, Regent Gede Winasa (informant), looks at the budget policy as a concept to achieve its political goals. This interpretation is far from the materiality of accounting. Winasa argued: "budget is not the goal. It is a means to an end... I have ideals, an ideology... have a moral basis, and I need budget to achieve my idea".

Very pragmatic, as I thought beforehand, Blumer, the sociologist, was right! The above statement shows how human attitude is full of interpretation and understanding. That is a view that is aligned and become what is called by functionalist as the social structure. Blumer (1969: 17) prefer to call this phenomenon as a collective action, or socially organizing different actions from different participants. For Blumer, this view is more than just a single performance described in the explanation of "impression management" (Blumer, 1969: 18).

While in my opinion, the evidence above suggests that budget policy is a conceptuality that is understood and interpreted as a means to achieve the goal of an embraced political ideology. "Opportunity" is understood as a source of epistemological power, representation of power and ideology, control and supervision, which manifests itself as a system of verbal signs.

The view of Winasa regarding accounting that attention is shifting from language to discourse and metaphore. The movement was a shift from using language to see accounting to views which see language or discourse as an "opportunity", or more specifically as a surface.

STRATEGIES TO MANAGE CHANGES: IDENTIFYING STAKEHOLDER VIEWS

> An important issue in the context of local government strategy is concerning the relationship between accounting man and context

Recognizing "confusing" changes is something that is very useful especially when you want to reflect on how budget policy is effected by various environmental changes that are complex and plural. This awareness has pushed practitioners and researchers in the field of accounting to continue developing new concepts in observing changes. Hopwood (1989) for example illustrates that:

> Accounting is not an autonomous phenomenon, other social, political and economic factor is now seen as being able to provide bases for accounting change.

This fact is evident from the emergence of the use of analysis and policy studies on various matters relating to accounting changes. These analysis of changes use various new knowledge, especially in interpreting the economic, political and social aspect which is the basis of changes in budget policy. As described by Kade Nirwana (informant), an employee of Jembrana Regency Education Department, that:

> Power shift from the old to the new Regent (Pak Gede Winasa) obviously brings a very fundamental change. Almost all aspects of governance including public policy changed drastically. I think every *new leader carries out a renewal* to realize their political dream.

Thus, it can be said that this kind of school of thought has played an important role in influencing the course of transformation. As disclosed by Sudantra:

> To allow the creation of conceptual visibility, budget policies need to accommodate and explain the important role of social, politics and organizational problems.

This means that actors *(accounting man)* should be able to show how budget policy is influenced by perceptions, and use budget policy as an everyday language through various dialogs. Through this way, it is expected that these policies can seep into various priorities and concerns, as well as new possibilities to be expressed in the form of policy.

Thus, focusing budget policy as a reflection of the changing patterns of visibility/transparency, will provide empirical examples of how these changes occur, managed strategically and formed a new change (policy). It can be achieved by appreciating how strategy could be implicated in the process of organizational change that is reflected in the form of policies (control of change strategy).

The discussion of strategy in this article was developed to discuss key issues in the budget process, resource allocation, service priorities and thematic priorities. According to (Worrall *et al.*, 1998) in any context, it is not possible to design the "best" strategy, but it is important to design a coherent and consistent strategy in dealing with the serious issues regarding public policy. Coherence in this context includes the preparation of policy formulation and consideration of alternative strategies available. Coherence may also include improving the clarity of the position of different stakeholders, and improving communication among stakeholders in the strategy preparation phase.

Such coherence in changes and strategy ideas is what lead to the people of Jembrana when talking about free education and health care, can not stop talking about Regent Winasa. In fact the development of the region is equated with the presence of Winasa. Although, when it comes to the strategy of shaping the policy, they are somewhat confused. As with most of the terms used in the public domain, strategy is often raised and used but not well understood[2]. On one occasion after leading an echelon II meeting in Jembrana Regency, Gede Winasa the Regent chattered that, "strategically managing local government is not easy, it even seems that there is not much consensus on the meaning of "strategic management "in the context of local government". He continued:

> While many local governments have corporate strategy (latest estimates indicate about 60 percent). I see that this does not mean strategic approaches are executed in all these organizations. For me, strategy is a pattern of behavior, strategy is position, strategy is intention, strategy is perspective.

[2]Although many practitioners use this term, but 'strategic management' is interpreted differently in different organizational settings.

Mintzberg (1994) takes a more pragmatic view about strategy and differentiate between intended strategy (what you want to be done the first time), unrealized strategy (what cannot be done), deliberate strategy (what do you want to do or accomplish), emergent strategy (what you want to do during implementation), and realization strategy (what is the end result).

What emerges from the interpretation of Mintzberg on strategy is the result of a process, and the process itself. This is also based on thc idea of consistency and dependency of time-strategy cannot be ephemeral, especially in the context of local government with the complex issues discussed by them. In line with this view, Vijoen (1994, 32) saw strategy as:

> The process of identifying, choosing and implementing activities that will enhance the long-term performance of an organization by setting direction and by creating an ongoing compatibility between the internal skills and resources of the organization and the changing external environment in which it operates.

Similar with that, Thompson (1994: 112) sees strategy as:

> The direction and scope of an organization over the long-term: ideally, which matches its resources to its changing environment, and in particular its markets, customers or clients so as to meet stakeholder expectations.

Clark (1994) has developed a biological metaphor to identify the key competencies required for an organization to act .strategically, which can be used to assess the organization capability. The views he proposes is that:

> An ability to gather data about the organization's external environment, about the firm's internal operation, performance and competencies and about the organization's dynamic interrelationship with its environment (Clark, 1994: 12–56).

While from the cognitive aspects, he put forward the following strategy:

> The analytical capability to derive meaning from data (*i.e.*, derive information and intelligence from data), to assess the implications of this information for the organization and to learn by continually questioning key assumptions and values (Clark, 1994:12–56).

From the statement above, it can be said that an organization starts to learn when assumption is given precedence, assessed and continually questions that assumptions and values. Therefore Clark (1994: 12–56) proposed the motoric aspects of strategy as: "the ability to implement action to achieve aims and objectives and to modify the relationship of the organization to its environment".

Therefore, there is a view that the evolutionary process of strategies often begins with the belief that acting defensively (muddling through) is not an effective way to manage an organization as complex as local government (Lindblom, 1958). Under this view, policy development only differs marginally from the existing policy, because budget policy is restricted by rules that impede the development of synergies in several functional or pragmatic area. Sudantra expressed similarly that:

> In local government, existing rules often caused the inability of "strategy" to respond to radical political agenda. This becomes a major problem. These constraints are likely to increase dissatisfaction and the search for a more methodological and rational way in running the organization.

The above statement explains that strategy is a political process in a given period. This means, strategy is seen as a process to identify and resolve policy decisions, searching for leadership, as well as considering the available resources. According to Collinge and Noble (1993: 78) a strategy cannot be seen as 'something' composed of words and paper that can be produced within a few weeks, but a series of thorough decision, which is recorded and published as a strategy document. According to Sudantra:

> Pros and cons shows that free education in its relationship with priority based budget was preferred but at that time was regarded as difficult to implement. Therefore, the presence of strategic processes developed through a rational process, inductive priority was needed. Hence, at that time we started with a strategic plan to get priority in the budget.

The above statement is in line with the alternative view obtained from organization theory. This theory suggests that organizations develop through the resolution of internal and external forces that are complex, and an overall change in direction appears spontaneously through this process. Strategic decision makers in this case seek to oppose, or give supportive comments regarding the unavoidable event (*e.g.*, Mintzberg, 1994; Thompson and McHugh, 1995).

As for Waldrop (1992), the above phenomenon is a picture of a deliberate intention to change, designed by those who have power and resources. Unlike the emergent change, where the organization found its way by accident, this change is designed in relation with a deliberate process, and a rational management.

The above description shows that an understanding of accounting provides the basis for a radical change in the physical process using as a reason, the criteria of various considerations, which is implicated directly in the physical process itself, such as in the economic and financial sectors. In many ways the understanding of accounting as an opportunity, hope and promise provides a variety of strategies that provide a way that both affects and induces changes in budget policy.

An understanding of accounting gives a very strong meaning to compare between social politic conditions and economic conditions. Accounting gives knowledge facility of how the economic trends are made. And in that way, accounting helps decision makers to determine objectives to be achieved and weight that would be given to economic and financial affairs.

The other side of the subjective view of accounting policy, is to view budget policy as a representation of space for people caught in the field of budget policy vision, because they live in the budget policy space, a space generated specifically to be read. Sudantra explains:

> Budget policy can be read or produce something to read. However, budget policy is not intended to only be read by people outside them. Budget policy should also be able to be read and understood by those who are in it.

This indicates that accounting policies have the power to change the disclosure patterns of an organization, so that the affairs of the external world can penetrate and influence the internal affairs of the organization. That is, if used carefully and thoroughly, awareness of accounting can play a role in strategically changing the managerial awareness. This awareness is far away from problems that only revolved around internal affairs that are

> Focusing budget policy as a reflection of the changing patterns of visibility/transparency, will provide empirical examples of how these changes occur, managed strategically and formed a new change (policy). It can be achieved by appreciating how strategy could be implicated in the process of organizational change that is reflected in the form of policies

interdependent, but leads to a view of the external position of the organization or to the main segment of the organization.

For Sudantra, budget policy complements the environment with a sign, so that the results of budget policy can be read by people in the budget policy space. However, based on transparency could still be able to hide the strategic intent of the policy. Because there is a difference between the two sides of the dialectical space representations, which is between the "inside" and the "outside" while understanding the accounting policies produced.

SUMMARY

Aware that interpretation can direct a change (policy), I was then fascinated to think of more detailed ways regarding of how accounting is effected by a greater process of change. In this regard, I developed some conventional manner regarding the relationships between accounting and change.

The above evidence clearly shows that to the actors (accounting man), accounting has the power to change the disclosure patterns of an organization, so the internal affairs of the world can be seen by the public. That is, if used carefully and thoroughly, awareness of accounting can play a role in strategically changing the managerial awareness, far away from various problems revolving around internal interdependency, but leads to a view of the external position of the organization or to the main segment of the organization. Various forms of political pressure can be put into the organization and will produce strategic agreements including accounting policies.

In the context of this article, it is demonstrated that through various organizational configurations and budget policy changes [accounting], government organizations in the policy-making process will be more oriented toward the public interest. This is because the public acts as the "watch dog".

Thus, it can be said that disclosure patterns are changing. Therefore, policies including accounting policy are also undergoing an adjustment, which is pro-actively shaping and changing concepts of government of what is important and what is not important. An understanding of accounting, in this case budget, has the potential in changing managerial awareness of the public in making a change with regard to its policies.

It should be noted, that in study of budgeting in Jembrana Bali Syarifuddin (2013) found that budget policy is a dialectic space that enhances the mobility of moral and ethical commitment to society. His study also found that budget policy, goes through strategy control, not only individually control.

And finally I understood that both in appreciating and activating a wide range of change, it takes more than just a technical view of accounting alone. To understand what is happening, the needs for accounting need to be appreciated in the context of strategic organizations. Accounting, in this case budget, cannot be seen only as something that reflects a wide range of organization state, but also as a phenomenon that can play a role in changing the organization.

REFERENCES

Belkaoui, A. (1978). Linguistic relativity in accounting. Accounting Organizations and Society, pp. 97–104.

Blumer, H. (1969). Symbolic interactionism: Perspective and method. Prentice Hall Inc. New Jersey.

Boland, R.J. (1982). Myth and technology in the American accounting profession. *Journal of Management Studies,* pp. 107–127.

Boland, R.J. (1989). Accounting and the interpretative act. Accounting Organizations and Society, pp. 125–146.

Burchell, S., Clubb, C., Hopwood, A., Hughes, S. and Nahapiet, J. (1980). The roles of accounting in organizations and society. Accounting Organizations and Society, pp. 5–28.

Clark, C. (1994). Who's who in strategic management: Dynamics of strategy. Surrey European Management School. University of Surrey.

Collinge, C.J. and Noble, J. (1993). Budget making through priorities. Local Government Chronicle.

Flood, R.L. and Jackson, M.C. (1991). Creative problem solving: Total systems intervention. Wiley, Chichester.

Gambling, T.M. (1977). Accounting and morale. Accounting organizations and society, pp. 141–151.

Hassall, J. and Worrall, L. (1997). Developing a fuzzy approach to the measurement of organizational effectiveness: A local government perspective. Second International Conference on the Dynamics of Strategy. SEMS. University of Surrey, pp. 200–13.

Hopwood, A. (1989). Behavior accounting in retrospect and prospect. *Behavior Research in Accounting*, Vol. 1.

Laovie, D. (1987). The accounting of interpretations and the interpretation of Accounts: The communicative function of the language of business. Accounting Organizations and Society, pp. 579–604.

Lefebvre, H. (1998). The production of space. Trans. Donald Nicholson-Smith. Cambridge. Blackwell.

McPhail, K.J. (1997). The threat of ethical accountants: An application of *Foucault's* concept of ethics to accounting education and some thoughts on ethically educating for the other. Wards Working Paper Series, 97/8. University of Glasgow.

Mintzberg, H. (1994). The rise and fall of strategic planning. Prentice Hall. Hemmel. Hampstead.

Morgan, G. (1988). Accounting as reality construction: Towards a new epistemology for accounting practice. *Accounting, Organizations and Society*, 13(5): 477–485.

Parsons, W. (1997). Public policy: An introduction to the theory and practice of policy analysis. Edward Elgar Publishing Limited. UK.

Prakash, P. and Rappaport, A. (1977). Information inductance and its significance in accounting. Accounting Organizations and Society, pp. 29–38.

Rittel and Webber (1973). Wicked problems. *Policy Sciences*, 5(1): 77–87.

Syarifuddin (2013). [Re] Construction of accountability: A study of accounting from local prespective. *Ekuitas Journal Economics and Finance*, 17(2).

Thompson, J.L. (1994). Strategic management: Awareness and change. Chapman and Hall. London.

Thompson, P. and Mc. Hugh, D. (1995). Work organizations: A critical introduction. Mac. Millan. Basingstoke.

Tinker, A.M., Merino, B.D. and Neimark, M.D. (1982). The normative origins of positive accounting theories: Ideology and accounting thought. Accounting Organizations and Society, pp. 167–200.

Viljoen, J. (1994). Strategic management: Planning and implementing successful corporate strategies. Longman. Melbourne.

Waldrop, M.M. (1992). Complexity. Penguin. London.

Whittington, R. and Stacey, R. (1994). Strategic management and organizational dynamics. *Journal of Management Studies*, 31(3): 453–55.

Worall, L, Chris, C. and Tony, B. (1998). Managing strategies in local Government. *International Journal of Public Sector Management*, 11(6): 472–493.

7

Introduction to Causal Inference Methods in Social Science Research

QIHUI CHEN[1]*

ABSTRACT

Increasingly more research projects in social sciences seek to understand the causal effect operated from a socio-economic variable of interest to another, such as the effect of class size on test scores, the effect of fertility on female labor supply, and the effect of population control policies on sex-ratios, etc. Choosing the most suitable tool to conduct casual analysis is the key to success of these projects. This chapter is, therefore, devoted to an in-depth introduction of a set of empirical methods that have been widely adopted in the fields of demography, economics, education, and sociology in the recent decades. Specifically, the methods discussed in this chapter include randomized controlled trials, instrumental variables, regression discontinuity design, difference-in-differences and propensity score matching. These methods are formally formulated in each section, followed by discussions on case studies that adopted these methods.

Key words: Causal inference, Randomized controlled trials, Regression discontinuity design, Instrument variables, Difference-in-differences, Propensity score matching

INTRODUCTION

Social scientists are often interested in questions such as: Will hiring more police officers reduce crime? Can class size reduction improve

[1]Department of Applied Economics and Center for Food and Health Economic Research, College of Economics and Management, China Agricultural University, Beijing, China.

**Corresponding author*: E-mail: chen1006@umn.edu

students' academic performance? Does fertility affect female labor supply? Did population control policies lead to imbalanced sex ratios in Asia? Each of these questions asks about the causal effect of a socio-economic variable on another. Not only are these causal effects of academic interest, but they are also of great policy relevance.

However, causal relationships are usually difficult to identify. For example, if we observed that children who wear eyeglasses outperformed those who do not wear eyeglasses on exams, can we conclude that wearing eyeglasses raises children's test scores? Not without further information. It could be that eyeglass-wearing students scored higher because they worked harder (which may be the reason why they have to wear eyeglasses in the first place). Eyeglass-wearing students may also have better-educated parents,[1] who are willing and able to help these children with schoolwork. Without ruling out these possibilities, we cannot be sure if wearing eyeglasses really causes higher test scores. In general, to identify the causal effect operated from an explanatory variable (*e.g.*, wearing eyeglasses) to an outcome variable (*e.g.*, test scores), one needs to rule out the influences of all confounding factors (*e.g.*, diligence, ability, family background, etc.), usually with the help of statistical methods.

This chapter introduces a set of causal inference methods that have become popular in the fields of demography, education, economics and political science. More specifically, it covers randomized controlled trials, instrumental variables, regression discontinuity design, difference-in-differences, and propensity score matching methods. While mathematical notations are used for ease of illustration, the focus of this chapter is placed on relevant concepts, rather than on technical details. For more technical treatments, interested readers are referred to Angrist and Pischke (2009), Blundell and Dias (2009), Morgan and Winship (2007), Imbens and Wooldridge (2009), Khandker *et al.* (2011), Ravallion (2008), Todd (2008) and Wooldridge (2010).

1. The Problem Defined

1.1. *Potential outcomes, counterfactual and causal effect*

Many of the causal relationships of interest in social sciences fit into the potential outcome framework.[2] As a working example, consider a job

[1]For example, Glewwe *et al.* (2016) found that mothers' years of education has a significantly positive impact on the probability of wearing eyeglasses among primary school students in rural China.

[2]For important works developing this framework, see Rubin (1974) and Holland (1986).

training program. To define the causal effect of the program on the outcome of interest, Y, say, wage, it is important to recognize that, at any time, any individual either participates in the program (*i.e.*, "treated") or does not participate (*i.e.*, "untreated"). Thus, for any individual i, there are two potential outcomes associated with his/her program participation (treatment) status, P: Y_{1i} is the outcome in the state that person i is treated ($P = 1$); Y_{0i} is the outcome in the state that person i is not treated ($P = 0$). Formally,

$$Y_i = \begin{cases} Y_{1i}, \text{ if } P_i = 1; \\ Y_{0i}, \text{ if } P_i = 0. \end{cases} \tag{1}$$

The *causal* impact of the program on individual i, Δ_i, is defined as the difference between his/her potential outcomes in the two states at the same time:

$$\Delta_i \equiv Y_{1i} - Y_{0i}, \tag{2}$$

that is, the *change* in one's potential outcome due to program participation.

While Δ_i is theoretically well-defined, empirically it is not very operational, because we never see both potential outcomes at the same time for any individual. Such a "missing data" problem gives rise to a concept called the "counterfactual" outcome, which, for a treated person, say person j, is the outcome we would have observed in the absence of the program for this person (*i.e.*, the untreated outcome, Y_{0j} of a treated person j). Given this concept, the causal effect of the program, Δ_i, is the difference between the observed and the counterfactual outcomes for a treated individual i. The task of causal inference is, therefore, to find a plausible estimate of the counterfactual outcome for this treated person.

1.2. *Causal parameters of interest*

Unless under very strong assumptions, it is difficult (if not entirely impossible) to estimate the counterfactual for a given individual. But we are usually not interested in the causal effect of the program on any particular individual. Rather, we are often interested in some "average" effects defined over certain subgroups. The most commonly discussed causal parameters of interest are the Average Treatment Effect (ATE) and the Average Treatment Effect on the Treated (ATT):

$$\Delta^{ATE} \equiv E(\Delta_i) = E(Y_{1i} - Y_{0i})$$

$$= E(Y_{1i}) - E(Y_{0i}); \quad (3)$$

$$\Delta^{ATT} \equiv E(\Delta_i \mid P_i = 1) = E(Y_{1i} - Y_{0i} \mid P_i = 1)$$
$$= E(Y_{1i} \mid P_i = 1) - E(Y_{0i} \mid P_i = 1), \quad (4)$$

where "E()" and "E(|)" are, respectively, the "expectation" and "conditional expectation" operators.[3]

Before discussing how to empirically estimate these causal parameters, it is useful to understand the meaning of them. ATE is the average impact of the program on the entire *population* of eligible individuals (or a representative evaluation sample drawn from it). For example, suppose that of a total of 1,000 individuals eligible for our job training program, 600 participated and 400 did not. Then, ATE is the impact of the program averaged over all those 1,000 eligible individuals. It also measures the expected effect of extending the program to a similar population. In contrast, ATT is the average impact on the 600 participants. Since ATT is defined over the treated sample, it also measures the average benefit *generated* by the program.

Note that ATE and ATT can be quite different in size. An important case is where only those who expect to receive positive benefits participated in the program while those who expect little gain (or even a loss) did not:

$$\text{"}P_i = 1 \text{ if } Y_{1i} > Y_{0i} \text{ and } P_i = 0 \text{ otherwise".} \quad (5)$$

Such a decision rule implies that ATT > ATE.

1.3. *Selection bias*

The missing data problem noted above implies that we are unable to directly calculate ATE or ATT. It is tempting to use the observed outcomes to estimate these parameters, but this will usually lead to biased estimates. To see this, consider a "naïve" estimator, δ^N,[4] which compares the average observed outcome between the treated and the untreated:

$$\delta^N = E(Y_i \mid P_i = 1) - E(Y_i \mid P_i = 0)$$
$$= E(Y_{1i} \mid P_i = 1) - E(Y_{0i} \mid P_i = 0) \quad \text{(by Eq. 1)}$$

[3]Similarly, we can define the *average treatment effect on the untreated* (ATU) as $E[\Delta \mid P = 0]$.

[4]We use Δ to denote a parameter of interest and use δ to denote an *estimator*.

$$= \mathrm{E}(Y_{1i}\,|\,P_i = 1) - \mathrm{E}(Y_{0i}\,|\,P_i = 1) + \mathrm{E}(Y_{0i}\,|\,P_i = 1) - \mathrm{E}(Y_{0i}\,|\,P_i = 0)$$

$$= \Delta^{\mathrm{ATT}} + [\mathrm{E}(Y_{0i}\,|\,P_i = 1) - \mathrm{E}(Y_{0i}\,|\,P_i = 0)]. \qquad (6)$$

Eq. (6) suggests that while δ^N provides some information on ATT, it also contains something extra, *i.e.*, the term $\mathrm{E}(Y_{0i}\,|\,P_i = 1) - \mathrm{E}(Y_{0i}\,|\,P_i = 0)$, the so-called "selection bias". Clearly, if this term is nonzero, δ^N will provide a biased estimate of ATT.

Table 1: Potential and observed outcomes of a hypothetic job-training program

	Untreated (P = 0)	***Treated (P = 1)***
Average monthly wage (Y_0)	**\$760**	\$680
Average monthly wage (Y_1)	\$740	**\$720**
Δ	–\$20	\$40
Observations	400	600

Note: Boldfaced figures are observable outcomes.

Table 1 illustrates the influence of selection bias for our job-training example. If the counterfactual outcome for the treated, Y_0, were *observed*, we can easily calculate that ATT is \$40 (=720–680).[5] In contrast, based on the observed outcomes, the δ^N estimator yields an estimate of –\$40 (=720–760), implying a selection bias of size –\$80. But since the selection bias here is unobservable (due to the unobservability of the counterfactual term, $\mathrm{E}(Y_{0i}\,|\,P_i = 1)$, in it), we are unable to recover ATT from δ^N. Fortunately, although we are unable to directly estimate selection bias, we may be able to eliminate it and thus obtain some sensible estimates of the causal parameters, *e.g.*, ATT in Eq. (6). In fact, "to estimate the counterfactual for the treated" and "to eliminate selection bias" are the two sides of the same coin of causal inference. Different methods eliminate selection bias in different ways.

2. Randomized Controlled Trials

2.1. *Randomization eliminates selection bias*

Randomized controlled trials (RCTs) use random treatment assignment to eliminate selection bias. RCTs randomly assign individuals from the population of interest (or a representative evaluation sample from it) into two groups: treatment and control.[6] Those assigned to treatment

[5]In this example, ATE = (740×0.4+720×0.6) – (760×0.4+680×0.6) = \$16 < ATT, which is consistent with the behavior described by the decision rule Eq. (5).

[6]Randomized controlled trials are sometimes called "randomized evaluations" or "social experiments".

are treated while those assigned to control are not. If the group assignment is indeed random, any systematic difference in the mean observed outcomes between the treatment and control groups should only be due to the difference in their treatment status.

In other words, randomization eliminates selection bias. In a sufficiently large evaluation sample, randomization ensures that all population characteristics flow evenly into treatment and control. Fig. 1 provides an illustration. Suppose that of the 1,000 individuals in a given evaluation sample, 45% are females, 20% have a college degree, 80% are rural residents, etc. When these 1,000 individuals are randomly assigned to treatment and control, each group will consist of (approximately) 45% females, 20% college-degree holders, 80% rural residents, etc. Not only these observable characteristics, but also unobservable ones, such as "being introverted", will be statistically balanced across groups because of randomization. Most importantly, the distributions of the potential outcomes, Y_1 and Y_0, will be similar between treatment and control, with only differences due to sampling errors. It follows that $E(Y_{0i} | P_i = 1) = E(Y_{0i} | P_i = 0)$, which eliminates the selection bias in Eq. (6).

Study sample (N=1,000)	**Treatment (N=500)**	**Control (N=500)**
45% are female	45% are female	45% are female
20% with a college degree	20% with a college degree	20% with a college degree
80% reside in rural areas	80% reside in rural areas	80% reside in rural areas
35% love pizzas	35% love pizza	35% love pizza
70% are introverted	70% are introverted	70% are introverted
...	...	...
$E(Y_0)$	$E(Y_0)$	$E(Y_0)$
$E(Y_1)$	$E(Y_1)$	$E(Y_1)$

Fig. 1: Randomized treatment assignment

Table 2 provides a real-world example, using data from a famous conditional cash transfer program in Mexico, PROGRESA, which provided monetary benefits to eligible households in 506 poor villages, aiming to improve their children's human capital outcomes. Of these 506 villages, 320 were assigned to treatment and 186 to control. Table 2 indicates that, as a result of random treatment assignment, the means of a large set of village characteristics are similar between treatment and control.

Table 2: Selected characteristics of PROGRESA localities

Characteristics	*All*	*Control (186 villages)*	*Treatment (320 villages)*
A. *Education facilities*			
Preschool	0.82	0.83	0.82
Primary school	0.97	0.95	0.98
Tele-secondary	0.17	0.25	0.13
Secondary school	0.01	0.01	0.01
High school	0.01	0.02	0.00
B. *Heath facilities*			
Health ministry clinic	0.10	0.13	0.08
Medical aids	0.60	0.62	0.58
Dispensary	0.07	0.09	0.06
Midwives	0.32	0.25	0.36
Witchdoctors	0.12	0.12	0.13
Mobile health centers	0.75	0.76	0.74
Pregnancy supervision	0.28	0.26	0.29
Delivery supervision	0.25	0.24	0.25
Baby checkups available	0.32	0.26	0.35
Immunizations available	0.79	0.77	0.81
Diarrhea prevention	0.50	0.42	0.55
Family planning	0.44	0.39	0.47
Hospitalization	0.05	0.03	0.06

Note: Adapted from Skoufias (2005, pp. 72–73).

2.2. *Causal parameters*

By eliminating selection bias, random treatment assignment helps provide unbiased estimates of both ATT and ATE. Start with ATT:

$$\Delta^{\text{ATT}} \equiv \text{E}(Y_{1i} - Y_{0i} \mid P_i = 1) = \text{E}(Y_{1i} \mid P_i = 1) - \text{E}(Y_{0i} \mid P_i = 1)$$
$$= \text{E}(Y_{1i} \mid P_i = 1) - \text{E}(Y_{0i} \mid P_i = 0). \qquad (7)$$

Note that randomization allows us to replace $\text{E}(Y_{0i} \mid P_i = 1)$ with $\text{E}(Y_{0i} \mid P_i = 0)$ in the last equality, which ensures that both terms on the right-hand side are observable.

Randomization also allows us to estimate ATE using observed outcomes:

$$\Delta^{\text{ATE}} \equiv \text{E}(Y_{1i} - Y_{0i}) = \text{E}(Y_{1i}) - \text{E}(Y_{0i})$$
$$= \text{E}(Y_{1i} \mid P_i = 1) - \text{E}(Y_{0i} \mid P_i = 0). \qquad (8)$$

Note that we replaced $\text{E}(Y_{1i})$ with $\text{E}(Y_{1i} \mid P = 1)$ and $\text{E}(Y_{0i})$ with $\text{E}(Y_{0i} \mid P = 0)$ in the last equality, because randomization ensures that population characteristics, $E(Y_{1i})$ and $E(Y_{0i})$, are "preserved" in the two randomly assigned groups.

Simply put, with the help of randomization, the δ^N estimator based on observed outcomes (Eq. 6) is able to provide unbiased estimates of both ATE and ATT. In practice, one can estimate ATE and ATT by either computing the relevant means in Eq. (7)–(8) or running a simple regression. To construct the regression model, note that individual *i*'s observed outcome, Y_i, can be written as

$$\begin{aligned} Y_i = P_i Y_{1i} + (1 - P_i)Y_{0i} &= Y_{0i} + P_i (Y_{1i} - Y_{0i}) \\ &= Y_{0i} + P_i \Delta_i. \end{aligned} \tag{9}$$

Taking expectations of both sides, conditional on *P*, yields

$$\begin{aligned} E(Y_i \mid P_i) &= E(Y_{0i} \mid P_i) + P_i E(Y_{1i} - Y_{0i} \mid P_i) \\ &= E(Y_{0i}) + P_i E(Y_{1i} - Y_{0i}) \qquad (= \beta_0 + P_i \Delta^{ATE}) \\ &= E(Y_{0i}) + P_i E(Y_{1i} - Y_{0i} \mid P_i = 1) \ (= \beta_0 + P_i \Delta^{ATT}). \end{aligned} \tag{10}$$

This implies that both ATE and ATT can be estimated by the following regression model, using observed information on all individuals in the sample:

$$Y_i = \beta_0 + \beta_1 P_i + \varepsilon_i, \tag{11}$$

where the constant term $\beta_0 = E(Y_{0i})$ and the error term $\varepsilon_i = Y_{0i} - E(Y_{0i})$, which implies that $E(\varepsilon_i) = E(\varepsilon_i \mid P_i) = 0$. This in turn implies that the ordinary least-squares (OLS) estimate of β_1 is an unbiased estimate of both ATE and ATT.

One can also include pre-determined characteristics, $\mathbf{Z}$, such as socio-demographic characteristics, as covariates in the regression:

$$Y_i = \beta_0 + \beta_1 P_i + \mathbf{Z}\beta_2 + \varepsilon_i. \tag{12}$$

The inclusion of additional covariates can help (a) increase the precision of the estimate and (b) assess the robustness of estimation results–if randomization is done correctly, the inclusion of additional covariates should not lead to a substantial change in the estimate of β_1.[7] However, one should avoid including variables that may be affected by the program: such variables, the so-called "bad controls", may lead

[7]Another routinely performed check is to run regressions of each of the **Z** variables on the program participation dummy, *P*, to see whether these variables are balanced between treatment and control.

to bias. See Angrist and Pischke (2009, pp. 64–68) for more discussions on bad controls.

The basic setup in Eq. (11) can be extended in at least three important ways. First, the treatment-status variable P can be defined more broadly. The "program" behind it does not have to be an officially implemented physical program. For example, P could denote one's educational attainment (*e.g.*, whether attended college) or health status (*e.g.*, whether having poor vision), whether one "lives in an area with heavy precipitation", etc. As long as the value of P is randomly determined, β_1 will measure some average casual effect of the "program".

Second, while P is specified above as a binary variable, it can be replaced with a continuous variable, P^{cont}. As long as the *value* of P^{cont} is randomly determined, β_1 will measure the causal effect of changing the value of P^{cont} by one unit. For example, a strand of research in education exploits random roommate assignment in certain colleges to identify the causal effect of roommates' academic ability on students' academic outcomes (*e.g.*, Sacerdote, 2001, Zimmerman, 2003; Carrell *et al.*, 2009; Chen *et al.*, 2014). In these studies, P^{cont} is specified as the (average) pre-college test score of one's college roommate[s].

Finally, there may be multiple treatments. In that case, P can be replaced with a set of binary variables, P_1, P_2, ... P_K, each denoting one's treatment status with respect to the kth treatment (k =1,..., K). The coefficient on P_k, then, captures the causal effect of the kth treatment, relative to the control group.

2.3. *Randomized controlled trials at work*

As a powerful tool for obtaining credible causal estimates, RCTs have become increasingly more popular in development projects, especially education and health interventions. The Mexican PROGRESA program is among the most famous. Exploiting its experimental design, a series of studies have been conducted to examine its impact on Mexican children's education (Schultz, 2004) and health outcomes (Gertler, 2004). A number of other famous RCTs come from Africa. For example, Glewwe *et al.* (2004) and Moulin *et al.* (2009) examined, respectively, the impacts of flip charts and textbooks on test scores in Kenyan primary schools. Miguel and Kremer (2004) examined the effects of deworming on Kenyan children's education and health outcomes in Kenya. The following case study discusses a pioneering RCT conducted in the United States.

Case study 1: Can smaller classes raise test scores?

A question that has been under heated debate in education is: does class size matter for students' academic performance? The Tennessee STAR experiment, conducted in 1985–86 in the United States, was designed to answer this question. The experiment was implemented for a cohort of kindergarteners, involving about 11,600 children. Children in each participating school were randomly assigned to one of three groups: (a) small classes with 13–17 children, (b) regular classes with 22–25 children and a part-time teacher's aide, or (c) regular classes with a full-time teacher's aide. Groups (a) and (c) were the treatment groups and group (b) was the control group.

Exploiting this experimental design, Krueger (1999) estimated the impacts of smaller classes and full-time teachers' aide on children's scores on the Stanford Achievement Test. Because randomization eliminates selection bias, the treatment-control difference in mean test scores captures the average causal effect of class size and that of a full-time aide, relative to regular classes with a part-time aide. Krueger found a statistically significant small-class effect of about 5 percentile points but found no significant regular-class + aide effect. Adding additional covariates, such as gender and teacher characteristics, does not substantially change the estimate of the small-class effect, but does increase the precision of it.

2.4. *Practical issues*

While RCTs have many desirable properties, these properties are derived based on the assumption that the experiment is done correctly, which means at least three conditions hold: a large enough evaluation sample, full compliance and no sample attrition. Since Section 3 will discuss the problem of non-compliance in detail, we briefly discuss the other two problems here. More detailed discussions can be found in Duflo *et al.* (2008).

Nonrandom sample attrition can lead to estimation bias. For example, if treated individuals who received little benefit from the program dropped out of the evaluation sample, then estimation using data on those who remained will overestimate the impact of the program. It is thus important to keep track with all individuals involved in the study.

Two issues concern the size of the evaluation sample. First, a large sample is needed to ensure that population characteristics flow evenly into treatment and control. This property may not hold in small samples. For example, if we randomly drew only *two* persons from the population of interest, then simply by chance, these two persons may have very different characteristics (*e.g.*, one being poor and the other being rich). No matter how we assign these two persons to treatment and control, these characteristics will always be imbalanced between the two groups. A large sample, however, would allow these characteristics to be balanced in an *average* sense.

The second issue is: how big a sample is needed to detect potential treatment effects? In general, a larger sample reduces the variance of an estimate, making it easier to detect potential treatment effects. However, the functional relationship between sample size and the minimum detectable effect size is usually nonlinear, and it also depends on other factors, such as the desired statistical power, the level of randomization (*e.g.*, individual level versus school level), the number of treatments and costs entailed, etc. These factors should be taken into account in sample size determination. Interested readers are refer to Duflo *et al.* (2008) and Gertler *et al.* (2011) for more details.

Finally, RCTs are usually costly to implement. For example, the Tennessee STAR experiment cost $12 million. Besides the explicit costs of implementation, there could also be ethical costs. Take health interventions, for example. If we discovered that some individuals in the control group suffer from acute diseases, then these individuals ought to be treated for ethical reasons. But then the control group is contaminated with treated observations, which undermines the experimental design.

3. RCTs with Non-compliers: Instrumental Variable Method

3.1. Non-compliers in randomized controlled trials

In the discussions of RCTs above, we assumed that all individuals involved in the program complied with the group assignment. But this assumption may fail in reality. Some individuals assigned to treatment may refuse to participate (*e.g.*, for religious reasons); some individuals assigned to control might find their own way (*e.g.*, by bribing the staff) to participate. Such non-compliance behaviors cause estimation problems.

For ease of illustration, Table 3 provides a hypothetical example of an RCT with non-compliers. Suppose that $n\%$ (*e.g.*, 10%) of the individuals in the evaluation sample are "never-takers", who will never participate regardless of their group assignment. Another *a%* (*e.g.*, 20%) are "always-takers", who will always participate, even if they are assigned to control. The rest *c%* (*e.g.*, 70%) are "compliers". They will participate if assigned to treatment, and will not participate if assigned to control.

Table 3: Different groups in a randomized controlled trial with non-compliers

	(1)	*(2)*	*(3)*
	Treatment $T = 1$	***Control*** $T = 0$	***Observed difference in Y*** $\delta = (1) - (2)$
(1) Always-taker (*a%*)	(a) $P = 1$: $Y = Y_1$	(b) $P = 1$: $Y = Y_1$	0
(2) Compliers (*c%*)	(c) $P = 1$: $Y = Y_1$	(d) $P = 0$: $Y = Y_0$	$\Delta = Y_1 - Y_0$
(3) Never-taker (*n%*)	(e) $P = 0$: $Y = Y_0$	(f) $P = 0$: $Y = Y_0$	0

Note that the treatment status of non-compliers (*i.e.*, never-takers and always-takers), *P*, may not always equal their treatment assignment, *T*. This creates problems. To see this, consider the naïve estimator d^N (Eq. 6), which provides unbiased estimates of ATE and ATT in RCTs with full compliance. Now, this estimator compares the mean observed *Y* of groups (a)-(c) with that of groups (d)-(f) in Table 3. The problem is that while groups (c) and (d) are comparable, the combined group of (a) and (b), both being "always-taker" groups, and the combined group (e) and (f), both being "never-taker" groups, may not be comparable.

Formally,

$$\begin{aligned}
\delta^N &= E(Y|P=1) - E(Y|P=0) \\
&= [\text{Prob}(P=1, T=1) \times E(Y|P=1, T=1) \\
&\qquad + \text{Prob}(P=1, T=0) \times E(Y|P=1, T=0)] \\
&\qquad - [\text{Prob}(P=0, T=1) \times E(Y|P=0, T=1) \\
&\qquad + \text{Prob}(P=0, T=0) \times E(Y|P=0, T=0)] \\
&= [(a\% + c\%) \times E(Y|P=1, T=1) \\
&\qquad + a\% \times E(Y|P=1, T=0)] - [n\% \times E(Y|P=0, T=1) \\
&\qquad + (n\% + c\%) \times E(Y|P=0, T=0)] \\
&= c\% \times [E(Y|P=1, T=1) - E(Y|P=0, T=0)] \\
&\qquad + a\% \times [E(Y|P=1, T=1) + E(Y|P=1, T=0)]
\end{aligned}$$

$$
\begin{aligned}
&\quad - n\% \times [\mathrm{E}(Y \mid P = 0, T = 1) + \mathrm{E}(Y \mid P = 0, T = 0)], \\
&= c\% \times [\mathrm{E}(Y_1 \mid P = 1, T = 1) - \mathrm{E}(Y_0 \mid P = 0, T = 0)] \\
&\quad + a\% \times [\mathrm{E}(Y_1 \mid P = 1, T = 1) + \mathrm{E}(Y_1 \mid P = 1, T = 0)] \\
&\quad - n\% \times [\mathrm{E}(Y_0 \mid P = 0, T = 1) + \mathrm{E}(Y_0 \mid P = 0, T = 0)], \\
&= c\% \times \mathrm{E}(Y_1 - Y_0 \mid \text{compliers}) + a\% \times \mathrm{E}(Y_1 \mid \text{always-takers}) \\
&\quad - n\% \times \mathrm{E}(Y_0 \mid \text{never-takers}) \\
&= c\% \times \mathrm{E}(\Delta \mid \text{compliers}) + a\% \times \mathrm{E}(Y_1 \mid \text{always-takers}) \\
&\quad - n\% \times \mathrm{E}(Y_0 \mid \text{never-takers}), \qquad (13)
\end{aligned}
$$

where "Prob(x)" denotes "the probability of x occurring". While the derivation of Eq. (13) seems complicated, the result is simple and informative. The first term on the right-hand side of the last equality in Eq. (13), $c\% \times \mathrm{E}(\Delta \mid \text{compliers})$, captures something causal: it is the average treatment effect on the compliers, deflated by their proportion in the sample. However, the last two terms, $a\% \times \mathrm{E}(Y_1 \mid \text{always-takers}) - n\% \times \mathrm{E}(Y_0 \mid \text{never-takers})$, reflect some sort of *selection bias*: the difference in the (deflated) mean observed outcome between always-takers and never-takers. In general, this difference does not capture anything causal, because (as suggested by their names) always-takers and never-takers may have little in common.

3.2. *Intention-to-treat effect*

Let us turn to other estimators. Note first that even with non-compliers, the treatment assignment is still random. Thus, the contrast between the mean of observed Y for the treatment group ($T = 1$) and that for the control group ($T = 0$) captures something causal, although it is unlikely to be ATT or ATE:

$$\Delta^{\mathrm{ITT}} = \mathrm{E}(Y \mid T = 1) - \mathrm{E}(Y \mid T = 0). \qquad (14)$$

The parameter Δ^{ITT} captures the *intention-to-treat* effect (ITT), *i.e.*, the effect of offering the program, allowing individuals to make their own decisions on whether or not to participate.[8]

Another interpretation of ITT is provided by Table 3. Note that random treatment assignment ensures that the fractions of compliers, always- and never-takers are all statistically identical between the

[8]It is easy to see that in RCTs with full compliance, ITT = ATE = ATT.

treatment and control groups. Thus the means of the observed Y for always-takers in the two groups, both being $E(Y_1 \mid \text{always-takers})$, cancel each other out (Row 1). Similarly, the means of the observed Y for never-takers in the two groups, both being $E(Y_0 \mid \text{never-takers})$, are also canceled out (Row 3). The only thing captured by ITT, then, is the average effect on the compliers (Column 3).

This can be shown using a little math:

$$\Delta^{ITT} = \text{Prob(compliers)} \times E(Y_1 - Y_0 \mid \text{compliers}).^{[9]} \quad (15)$$

Since Prob(compliers) <1, ITT is a deflated estimate of the average treatment effect on the compliers. Yet if we have an unbiased estimate of Prob(compliers), we can recover the average treatment effect on the compliers, *i.e.*, the local average treatment effect (LATE) due to Imbens and Angrist (1994), from ITT.

3.3. *Local average treatment effect*

How, then, do we estimate the probability of being a complier (*i.e.*, the proportion of compliers) in the evaluation sample? With the presence of non-compliers, compliers cannot be identified directly. In particular, compliers cannot be distinguished from always-takers in the treatment group, because they are both treated ($P = 1, T = 1$). But if we are able to figure out the proportion of always-takers in the treatment group, we can subtract it from the proportion of treated individuals (*i.e.*, compliers and always-takers) in that group to obtain the proportion of compliers:

$$\text{Prob (compliers}, T = 1) = \text{Prob} (P = 1, T = 1) - \text{Prob (always-takers}, T = 1). \quad (16)$$

---

[9] $\Delta^{ITT} = E(Y \mid T = 1) - E(Y \mid T = 0)$
$= [\text{Prob} (P = 1, T = 1) \times E(Y \mid P = 1, T = 1) + \text{Prob} (P = 0, T = 1) \times E(Y \mid P = 0, T = 1)] - [\text{Prob} (P = 1, T = 0) \times E(Y \mid P = 1, T = 0) + \text{Prob} (P = 0, T = 0) \times E(Y \mid P = 0, T = 0)]$.
$= [(a\% + c\%) \times E(Y \mid P = 1, T = 1) + n\% \times E(Y \mid P = 0, T = 1)] - [a\% \times E(Y \mid P = 1, T = 0) + (c\% + n\%) \times E(Y \mid P = 0, T = 0)]$
$= c\% \times [E(Y \mid P = 1, T = 1) - E(Y \mid P = 0, T = 0)] + a\% \times [E(Y \mid P = 1, T = 1) - E(Y \mid P = 1, T = 0)] + n\% \times [E(Y \mid P = 0, T = 1) - E(Y \mid P = 0, T = 0)]$
$= c\% \times [E(Y_1 \mid P = 1, T = 1) - E(Y_0 \mid P = 0, T = 0)] + a\% \times [E(Y_1 \mid P = 1, T = 1) - E(Y_1 \mid P = 1, T = 0)] + n\% \times [E(Y_0 \mid P = 0, T = 1) - E(Y_0 \mid P = 0, T = 0)]$,
where the last two terms are both zero. It follows that $\Delta^{ITT} = c\% \times [E(Y_1 \mid P = 1, T = 1) - E(Y_0 \mid P = 0, T = 0)] = E(Y_1 \mid \text{compliers}) - E(Y_0 \mid \text{compliers}) = E(Y_1 - Y_0 \mid \text{compliers})$, which is the average treatment effect defined on the compliers, multiplied by the proportion of compliers in the sample.

Although we do not know directly who the always-takers are in the treatment group, we do know that, by randomization, the proportion of always-takers in the treatment group equals that in the control group. And we know that those with $P=1$ and $T=0$ are the always-takers in the control group. Thus, we can use the proportion of always-takers in the control group to replace Prob(always-takers, $T=1$) in Eq. (16). And since Prob(compliers, $T=1$) = Prob(compliers) by randomization, we have:

$$\begin{aligned} \text{Prob(compliers)} &= \text{Prob}(P=1, T=1) - \text{Prob}(P=1, T=0) \\ &= \mathrm{E}(P \mid T=1) - \mathrm{E}(P \mid T=0). \end{aligned} \tag{17}$$

Then we can recover LATE, using Prob(compliers) as the inflating factor:

$$\Delta^{\text{LATE}} = \frac{\Delta^{\text{ITT}}}{\text{Prob(compliers)}} = \frac{\mathrm{E}(Y \mid T=1) - \mathrm{E}(Y \mid T=0)}{\mathrm{E}(P \mid T=1) - \mathrm{E}(P \mid T=0)}. \tag{18}$$

To estimate LATE,[10] it is useful to recognize that both the numerator and the denominator of LATE are captured by certain parameters in some regression equations of interest. The numerator, ITT, is captured by the parameter γ_1 in the following regression of the observed Y on treatment assignment, T:

$$Y = \gamma_0 + \gamma_1 T + u. \tag{19}$$

The denominator of LATE, the proportion of compliers in the evaluation sample, is captured by the parameter λ_1 in the following regression:

$$P = \lambda_0 + \lambda_1 T + v. \tag{20}$$

An unbiased estimate of LATE can then be constructed as $\hat{\Delta}^{\text{LATE}} = \hat{\gamma}_1 / \hat{\lambda}_1$, where "^" denotes the estimate of a given parameter. Note that for $\hat{\Delta}^{\text{LATE}}$ to be well-defined, $\hat{\lambda}_1$ should not be zero in statistical

[10]For Eq. (18) to really identify the local average treatment effect, another assumption, the so-called "monotonicity" (or "no defiers") assumption, must hold. This assumption says that $P_{1i} - P_{0i} \geq 0$ or $P_{1i} - P_{0i} \leq 0$ for all i, where P_{1i} is the value of P_i when $T_i = 1$ and P_{0i} is the value of P_i when $T_i = 0$. Intuitively, this assumption means that when the treatment assignment, T, switches on (=1) and off (=0), it should push the value of P for all individuals in the same direction. If, for example, T pushes some individuals from $P=0$ to $P=1$ while others from $P=1$ to $P=0$, when switching from $T=0$ to $T=1$, then we are unable to define *compliers* in a consistent way.

terms; in other words, it should be significantly different from zero in the regression estimating Eq. (20).

Imbens and Angrist (1994) showed that LATE can be estimated using a two-stage least-squares (2SLS) regression, with

$$Y = \eta_0 + \eta_1 P + w \tag{21}$$

being the second-stage equation and Eq. (20) being the first-stage equation. Using T is as an instrumental variable (IV) for P,[11] the 2SLS estimate of the parameter η_1 in Eq. (21) is the LATE estimate. The scope of application of the IV method is wider than the case of RCTs with non-compliers discussed here. More technical details on 2SLS regressions can be found in texts by Greene (2002) and Wooldridge (2010). For more details on how the LATE formula (Eq. 18) relates to the 2SLS estimator, see Imbens and Angrist (1994), Angrist and Imbens (1996) and Angrist and Pischke (2009).

3.4. *Instrumental variables at work*

While some RCT programs, such as the Tennessee STAR project and the Mexican PROGRESA program, have (nearly) full compliance, allowing one to estimate both ATE and ATT, other programs encountered non-trivial noncompliance problems. For such programs, one can only estimate the average treatment effect for the compliers (LATE) using the IV method, as a second-best alternative. The case study below examines an RCT done in China, which involved many non-compliers.

Case study 2: Does wearing eyeglasses raise test scores?

Does wearing eyeglasses improve students' academic performance? To answer this question, Glewwe *et al.* (2016) implemented an RCT in two counties in Gansu province of China in 2004, providing free eyeglasses to 4–6th graders with poor vision in these two counties. The project

[11]In the standard setting, an instrumental variable is an "exogenous" variable that can be used to address the "endogeneity" problem of an explanatory variable in a linear regression model. Consider the simple model $y = \alpha + \beta x + \varepsilon$, where the explanatory variable x is correlated with the error term ε and is thus said to be endogenous. In this model, the OLS estimate of β is biased, due to the correlation between x and ε (Greene, 2002). A valid IV for x, call it z, is a variable such that it is uncorrelated with ε (hence, exogenous) but highly correlated with x. In our context of RCTs with non-compliers, T is determined by randomization, so it is uncorrelated with the error term in Eq. (21), ε. And to the extent that there are a large proportion of compliers, the estimate of λ_1 in Eq. (20) should be statistically significant. These make T a valid IV for P in the standard sense.

encountered a number of problems. First, random treatment assignment was done correctly in only 25 townships (13 treatment and 12 control townships) of the 37 project townships in the two counties. The analysis was then focused on children from these 25 townships.

Second, even within the 25 townships in which randomization was done correctly, there were many non-compliers. In particular, of the 1,528 students with poor vision in the treatment schools who were offered free eyeglasses, about one third (462) declined the offer! Such a non-compliance problem calls for an IV solution. Using the treatment assignment, T, as the IV for one's treatment status (*i.e.*, whether wearing eyeglasses), P, Glewwe *et al.* estimated the average treatment effect of wearing eyeglasses on compliant students (*i.e.*, LATE). Their IV estimates indicate that wearing eyeglasses for one year increased the test scores (the average of Chinese, math and science scores) of (compliant) students with poor vision by 0.16–0.22 standard deviations. Such an impact is equivalent to the impact of 0.3–0.5 additional years of schooling. Glewwe *et al.* also estimated the ITT effect, by running a regression of children's test scores on the treatment dummy, T. As expected from Eq. (18), ITT is smaller than LATE: offering eyeglasses to the treatment group raised the average test scores in that group by 0.11–0.16 standard deviations.

3.5. *Extensions*

In many applications, the treatment assignment variable T does not have to come from an official intervention program. There are some other variables that are approximately randomly determined, such as gender and multiple births, which can be used as IVs to identify the effect of some causal variable of interest. For example, exploiting American parents' preference for having a balanced sex-mix among their children, Angrist and Evans (1998) used an indicator of the first two children being of the same sex, as the IV for the incidence of having a third child, and found that having a third child significantly reduces women's labor supply. Li *et al.* (2008) used the incidence of twin births as an IV for sibship size and found that sibship size has a significantly negative impact on children's years of schooling in China.

4. Regression Discontinuity Design

4.1. *Basic idea*

RCTs are not always feasible. But in some cases, we are able to design a "localized" RCT, using a regression discontinuity (RD) design.[12] For some programs, the eligibility of participation is determined by a continuous index (*Z*) and a clearly specified cut-off (*c*). For example, a college student may be eligible for a scholarship if her GPA is equal to or above 3.8. A household will receive a governmental cash transfer if its annual income is below $10,000. A male may be eligible for a pension if he is aged 65 or older. In these cases, GPA, income and age, play the role of the continuous index, and the specified values, 3.8, $10,000, and 65, play the role of the cut-off. The index triggers the treatment when its value (smoothly) passes the cut-off:

$$P_i = \begin{cases} 1, \text{ if } Z_i \geq c; \\ 0, \text{ if } Z_i < c. \end{cases} \tag{22}$$

The idea of RD designs is that if all factors except one's treatment status, P_i, vary smoothly when the eligibility index passes the cut-off, the difference in the observed outcome between the treated and the untreated at the cut-off (*e.g.*, points *B* and *A* in Fig. 2) should only be due to the difference in individuals' treatment status between the two groups. Viewed from a different angle, within a small interval around the cut-off, whether one's eligibility index falls on the left side or the right side of the cut-off is approximately *randomly* determined,[13] which creates a localized random experiment.

As with the case of RCTs, there might be non-compliance involved. Corresponding to the cases with and without non-compliers, there are two RD designs: fuzzy and sharp.

4.2. *Sharp RD design*

The sharp RD design applies to the case where one's treatment status is completely determined by his/her eligibility index (Eq. 22), which is similar to the case of a local RCT with perfect compliance. To see how the sharp RD design provides sensible causal estimates, recall the "naïve" estimator Δ^N from Eq. (6):

$$\delta^N = E(Y_i \mid P_i = 1) - E(Y_i \mid P_i = 0)$$

[12]This method was rooted in the studies by Thistlewaithe and Campbell (1960) and Campbell (1969) in the field of educational psychology.

[13]Remember how students who scored one or two points below a passing grade always complained about their bad luck?

$$= E(Y_i | Z_i \geq c) - E(Y_i | Z_i < c) \quad \text{(by Eq. 22)}$$

$$= [E(Y_{1i} | Z_i \geq c) - E(Y_{0i} | Z_i \geq c)] + [E(Y_{0i} | Z_i \geq c) - E(Y_{0i} | Z_i < c)], \quad (23)$$

Again, while the first term on the right-hand side, $E(Y_{1i} | Z_i \geq c) - E(Y_{0i} | Z_i \geq c)$ captures something causal (*i.e.*, ATT), the second term, $E(Y_{0i} | Z_i \geq c) - E(Y_{0i} | Z_i < c)$, is the selection bias. Recall that in the case of RCTs, we use randomization to eliminate selection bias. Similarly, in the sharp-RD case here, we exploit the localized random experiment to eliminate selection bias around the cut-off. More specifically, within a small e-radius interval around the cut-off, $(c - e, c + e)$, there should be little difference in the untreated outcome (Y_0) between the treated and the untreated:

$$\lim_{e \to 0} E(Y_{0i} | Z = c + e) = \lim_{e \to 0} E(Y_{0i} | Z = c - e), \quad (24)$$

where $\lim_{e \to 0}(x)$ denotes "the limit of x, as e approaches 0". In words, the treated and the untreated around the cut-off are comparable in the absence of treatment. Thus, we can use the (mean of) observed Y of the untreated near the cut-off (*e.g.*, B in Fig. 2) as the counterfactual for the treated near the cut-off (*e.g.*, A in Fig. 2).

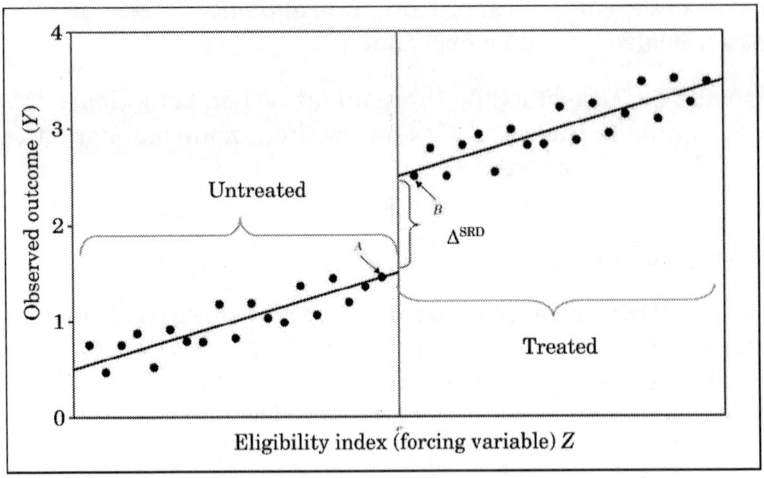

Fig. 2: Treatment assignment by the eligibility index

Taking limits of both sides of Eq. (23) at the cut-off yields:

$$\Delta^{SRD} = \lim_{e \to 0}(\delta^N | c - e < Z_i < c + e)$$

$$= \lim_{e \to 0}\{E(Y_i | Z_i \geq c) - E(Y_i | Z_i < c)\}$$

$$= \lim_{e \to 0}\{[E(Y_{1i} \mid Z_i = c + e) - E(Y_{0i} \mid Z_i = c + e)]$$

$$+ [E(Y_{0i} \mid Z_i = c + e) - E(Y_{0i} \mid Z_i = c - e)]\}$$

$$= \lim_{e \to 0} E[(Y_{1i} - Y_{0i} \mid Z_i = c + e)] + \lim_{e \to 0} [E(Y_{0i} \mid Z_i = c + e)$$

$$- \lim_{e \to 0} E(Y_{0i} \mid Z_i = c - e)]$$

$$= \lim_{e \to 0} [E(Y_{1i} - Y_{0i} \mid Z_i = c + e)] + 0 \qquad \text{(by Eq. 24)}$$

$$= \lim_{e \to 0} [E(\Delta_i \mid Z_i = c + e)]$$

$$= E(\Delta_i \mid Z_i = c), \tag{25}$$

where we assume that $E(Y_{0i} \mid Z_i = z)$ is continuous at c and that $\lim_{e \to 0} [E(\Delta_i \mid Z_i = c + e)]$ exists. Eq. (25) indicates that Δ^{SRD} captures the average effect of the program on individuals *at the cut-off*, by the difference in the limits of the observed Y approached from both sides at the cut-off (*i.e.*, Δ^{SRD} in Fig. 2). Also, the last equality in Eq. (25) suggests that Δ^{SRD} is the "ATT" defined for individuals *at the cut-off*. To the extent that the localized experiment is truly random, so that we can drop the conditioning on P $(= 1(Z_i \geq c))$, Δ^{SRD} also measures ATE (and ITT) for individuals *at the cut-off*.

To empirically estimate Δ^{SRD}, both parametric and non-parameter methods have been devised. The simplest possible parametric model is

$$Y_i = \beta_0 + \beta_1 P_i + f(Z_i) + \varepsilon_i, \tag{26}$$

where $f(Z_i)$ is a flexible function (*e.g.*, a second or third order polynomial) of the eligibility index, Z. This model produces the fitted regression lines depicted in Fig. 2. The estimate of β_1 captures the difference in the intercepts of those two lines (*i.e.*, the difference in the limits of Y approached from different sides) at the cut-off (Δ^{SRD}).

One can further allow $f(Z_i)$ to have different curvatures on different sides of the cut-off, by introducing an interaction between P and $f(Z_i)$ in the model:

$$Y_i = \beta_0 + \beta_1 P_i + f(Z_i) + \lambda\,(P_i f(Z_i)) + \varepsilon_i. \tag{27}$$

For example, a cubic specification of $f(Z_i)$ can be used to capture the curvature of the functions depicted in Fig. 3, which is taken from Lee's (2008) study on the effect of party incumbency (P) on reelection probabilities (Y) of Democratic candidates in the U.S. House of Representatives:

$$Y_i = \beta_0 + \beta_1 P_i + \gamma_{1L} Z_i + \gamma_{2L} Z^2_{\ i} + \gamma_{3L} Z^3_{\ i}$$
$$+ \gamma_{1R}(P_i Z_i) + \gamma_{2R}(P_i Z^2_{\ i}) + \gamma_{3R}(P_i Z^3_{\ i}) + \varepsilon_i, \qquad (28)$$

where Z is the vote share margin in the previous election (*i.e.*, the difference between the Democratic and Republican vote shares), which determines the value of P: $P_i = 1(Z_i \geq 0)$. And $\gamma_{jL}(\gamma_{jR})$, $j = 1, 2, 3$, is the coefficient on the jth-order term of Z on the left (right) side of the cut-off.

Nonparametric models usually use a local linear regression estimator to estimate the limits of the mean observed Y at the cut-off (Hahn *et al.*, 2001). In either type of application, one should determine the bandwidth around the cut-off to be included in the estimation.[14] For more details, interested readers are referred to Imbens and Lemieux (2010).

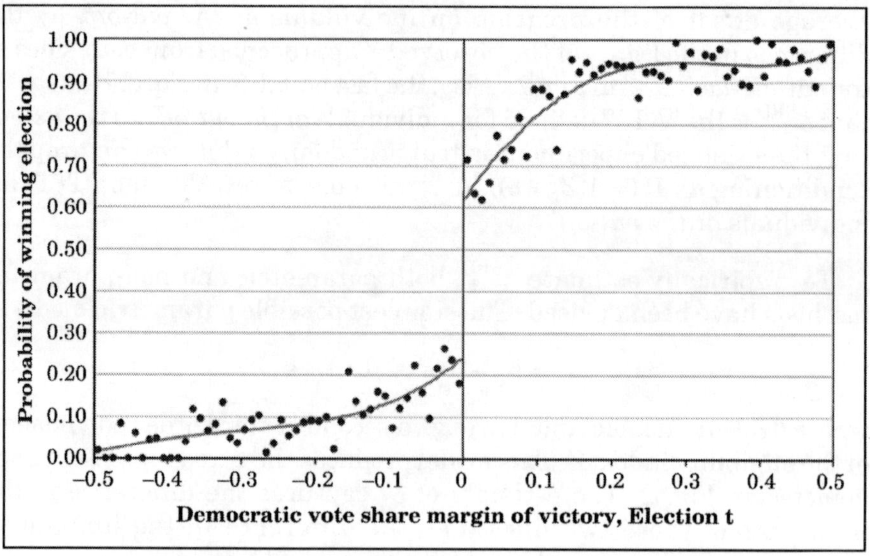

Fig. 3: Probability of winning an election by past vote share

Note: Adapted from Lee (2008). Vote share margin is the difference between the Democratic and Republican vote shares when these are the two largest parties.

[14]In practice, we can first determine a bandwidth by considering the balance in observed characteristics of the population above and below the cutoff, and then repeat the estimation using different bandwidths to assess the sensitivity of the estimates with respect to the chosen bandwidth. See Lee and Lemieux (2010) for how to choose the "optimal" bandwidth.

4.3. *Shape RD design at work*

That a clearly-defined cut-off determines the eligibility for some treatment of interest signifies the possibility of applying the sharp RD design. For example, exploiting the legal cut-off of the eligibility of unionization of American firms, Dinardo and Lee (2004) applied a sharp RD design to estimate the effect of unionization on workers' wage. In some cases, the researcher can even set a cut-off to conduct a policy experiment. Dobkin *et al.* (2010) and Chen and Okediji (2014) provided two recent examples in the field of education. The case study below uses a sharp RD design to estimate the effect of disease diagnosis on one's food consumption behavior in China.

Case study 3: Does information on health status lead to a healthier diet?

As China developed rapidly in the recent decades, the proportion of Chinese residents suffering from hypertension also increased rapidly, from 19.1% in 1991 to 26.8% in 2004, suggesting a positive relationship between income and the incidence of chronic diseases. Such a relationship is puzzling. Normally, one would expect the incidence of chronic diseases to be lower among the rich, because they have easier access to better food, medical care and health information than the poor.

To help explain this puzzle, Zhao *et al.* (2013) hypothesized that people's income may have outgrown their demand for health information during China's rapid growth. Increased income enabled people to consume foods that are tasty but are potentially harmful for their chronic health, and their understanding of these potential harms lagged behind their income growth. To test this hypothesis, a key step is to see whether more health information leads to healthier diets. Yet a simple comparison of diets across people with different amounts of health information may be misleading. For example, it could be that people who care more about their health collect more health information, and it is their preference for better health, rather than health information *per se*, that leads to healthier diets. To identify the causal effect of health information, Zhao *et al.* exploited the medical cut-off for hypertension diagnosis: one is diagnosed with hypertension if his/her "systolic blood pressure ≥140 mmHg". Since people with a 139-mmHg systolic blood pressure and those with a 140-mmHg systolic blood pressure are presumably similar in all aspects except the diagnosis (information), Zhao *et al.* adopted a sharp-RD design for casual inference.

Using data on some 13,000 individuals from nine provinces in China, their (non-parametric) sharp-RD analysis found that "being diagnosed with hypertension" led to a significant drop in fat intake (7.7 g/day, or, equivalently, 10% of daily fat consumption) among the rich, but had little impact on the poor (Fig. 4, where blood pressure reading has been re-centered at 140 mmHg). These findings suggest that when health information is available, the rich are able to switch to a healthier diet, but the poor fail to do so, which lends empirical support to the hypothesis posed by Zhao *et al.*

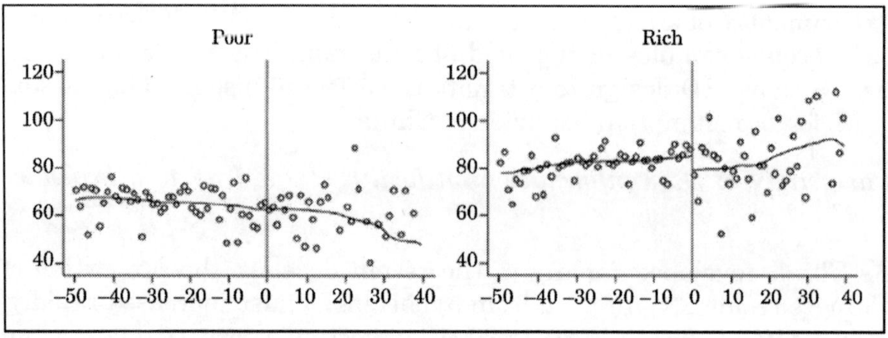

Fig. 4: Daily fat intake by income levels.

Note: Adapted from Zhao *et al.* (2013).

4.4. *Fuzzy RD design*

As with RCTs with non-compliers, there might be non-compliers in localized RCTs: some individuals whose eligibility index is above the cut-off are not treated while some individuals whose eligibility index is below the cut-off are treated. In this case, one's treatment status, P, is determined only *partly* by his/her eligibility index, which makes treatment determination fuzzy. The defining feature of the fuzzy-RD design is that the *probability* of being treated, $\text{Prob}(P_i = 1 \mid Z_i)$, is discontinuous at c:

$$\text{Prob}(P_i = 1 \mid Z_i) = \begin{cases} g_1(Z_i) \text{ if } Z_i \geq c \\ g_0(Z_i) \text{ if } Z_i < c \end{cases}, \text{ and } g_0(Z_i) \neq g_1(Z_i). \quad (29)$$

Recognizing that the sharp-RD parameter is analogues to the ITT parameter in the case of a localized RCT with full compliance, it is easy to see that the fuzzy-RD estimator is analogues to the LATE estimator in the case of a localized RCT with non-compliers. Thus, similar to how we recovered LATE from ITT (Eq. 18), we need to "inflate" the sharp-RD estimator, $\lim_{e \to 0} E(Y_i \mid Z_i = c + e) - \lim_{e \to 0} E(Y_i \mid Z_i = c - e)$, using the proportion of compliers near the cut-off, $\lim_{e\to 0} \mathrm{E}(P_i \mid Z_i = c + e) - \lim_{e\to 0} \mathrm{E}(P_i \mid Z_i = c - e)$, as the inflating factor:

$$\Delta^{\mathrm{FRD}} = \frac{\lim_{e\to 0} \mathrm{E}[Y_i \mid Z_i = c + e] - \lim_{e\to 0} \mathrm{E}[Y_i \mid Z_i = c - e]}{\lim_{e\to 0} \mathrm{E}[P_i \mid Z_i = c + e] - \lim_{e\to 0} \mathrm{E}[P_i \mid Z_i = c - e]}, \tag{30}$$

where the feature that $\mathrm{Prob}(P_i = 1 \mid Z_i = z)$ is discontinuous at $Z = c$ (Eq. 29) guarantees that the denominator of Δ^{FRD} is nonzero. For a formal derivation of the fuzzy-RD parameter, the reader is refer to Hahn *et al.* (2001).

To estimate Δ^{FRD}, one can either obtain the four limits (in means) involved in Eq. (30) using non-parametric methods, or directly estimate Δ^{FRD} using a 2SLS regression framework in which Eq. (26) or (27) serves as the second-stage equation and the "treatment assignment" dummy, $T_i = 1(Z_i \geq \mathrm{c})$, serves as the IV for P_i.

4.5. *Fuzzy RD design at work*

When a clearly-specified cut-off is used to determine treatment eligibility but somebody does not comply with the treatment assignment, the fuzzy-RD design may be used to obtain causal estimates. For example, although almost all countries specify an official age for primary school enrollment, say, "age six by September 1st", there are always some children entering school younger or older than the official enrollment age. To estimate the causal effects of school entry age on students' academic and labor-marker outcomes, a series of studies have exploited the enrollment age cut-off to perform fuzzy RD analyses (*e.g.*, McEwan and Shapiro, 2008; Elder and Lubotsky, 2009; Black *et al.*, 2011; Chen, 2015). As another example, the case study below re-examines the class-size effect discussed in Case Study 1, using a fuzzy RD design.

Case study 4: Can smaller classes raise students' test scores? Revisited.

Angrist and Lavy (1999) employed a fuzzy RD design to answer the same question addressed by the Tennessee STAR experiment. They exploited the fact that class size in Israeli schools is capped at 40 by the "Maimonides Rule". According to this rule, students in a grade with up to 40 students can expect to be in classes as large as 40, but grades with 41 students are split into two classes, grades with 81 students are split into three classes, and so on.

Assuming students are split up into classes of equal size, the predicted class size resulting from a strict application of Maimonides' Rule is

$$M_c = \frac{E}{\text{int}[\frac{E-1}{40}]+1}, \tag{31}$$

where M_c is the predicted class size (in a given grade) assigned to class C, E is enrollment in the grade, and int(x) is the integer part of a real number x. This function, plotted with dashed lines in Fig. 5 for 5th graders in Angrist and Lavy's data, has a sawtooth pattern with sharp drops in M_c at integer multiples of 40 (especially 40, 80, and 120). Maimonides' Rule does not predict class size perfectly, because some schools split grades at enrollments lower than 40, which makes the RD design fuzzy.

Angrist and Lavy used M_c as an instrument variable for class size in a model linking students' Math scores and the size of their class. Here M_c plays the role of T_i, E plays the role of Z_i and class size plays the role of P_i. The resulted 2SLS estimates suggest a strong small-class effect: a 7-student reduction in class size raises Math scores by about 1.75 points, which is not far from the Tennessee RCT estimates.

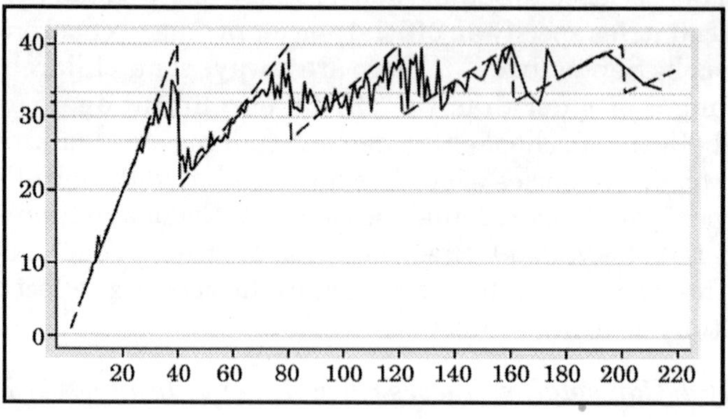

Fig. 5: Maimonides' rule and class size in Israeli schools.

Note: Adapted from Angrist and Lavy (1999).

4.6. *Limitations*

While the idea of RD seems "smart", it has a number of limitations. First, since RD only estimates *local* average effects at the eligibility cut-off, it is unable to provide an average effect for all program participants, or the effects on individuals at other cut-offs. Second, the fact that RD produces *local* causal estimates raises concerns about statistical power. Since only observations around the cutoff are used in estimation, the statistical power for detecting potential effects is reduced. Thus, relatively large evaluation samples are usually required to obtain sufficient statistical power in RD applications. Third, RD estimates may be sensitive to the empirical specification of the relationship between the eligibility index and the outcome variable. In practice, one should try different specifications (linear, quadratic, cubic, etc.) to assess the robustness of the estimates. Fourth, if the specified eligibility cut-off is publicly known, some individuals may be able to manipulate their eligibility index so as to receive the treatment, thereby undermining the localized random experiment. Interested readers are referred to McCrary (2008) for a formal test for such behaviors.

5. Difference-in-Differences

5.1. *Basic idea*

When neither a global nor a localized randomized experiment is feasible, one has to resort to other methods to eliminate selection bias. Under the assumption that the selection bias involved is time-invariant, the difference-in-differences (DD) method exploits repeated observations over time to eliminate selection bias.

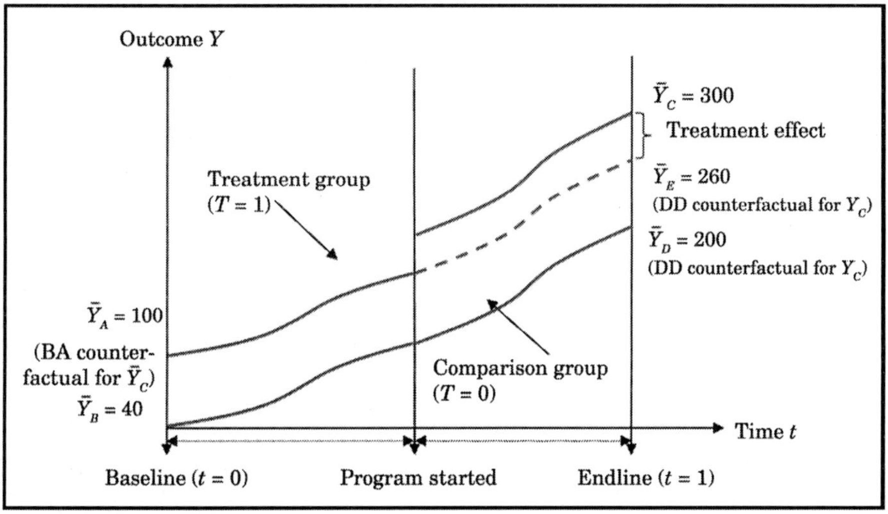

Fig. 6: Before-after, cross-sectional and difference-in-differences estimators

Fig. 6 illustrates the basic idea of the DD method. Suppose that a program (say, our job-training program) started at some point in time t.

Before the program started ($t = 0$, the baseline), nobody was treated. After the program started ($t = 1$, the endline), some are treated (the treatment group, $T = 1$) while others are not (the comparison group, $T = 0$). Suppose we have observations recorded at both the baseline and the endline for all individuals. More specifically, $\bar{Y}_A$ and $\bar{Y}_C$ in Fig. 6 are, respectively, the baseline and endline means of the observed Y for the treatment group, and $\bar{Y}_B$ and $\bar{Y}_D$ are, respectively, the baseline and endline means of the observed Y for the comparison group. Note that, of these four outcomes, $\bar{Y}_C$ is the only treated one. Our task is to estimate the counterfactual for it.

To understand how DD works, consider first the naïve estimator δ^N applied to the endline data, *i.e.*, the cross-section (CS) estimator using the endline outcome for the comparison group, $\bar{Y}_D$, as the counterfactual for $\bar{Y}_C$:

$$\delta^{CS,\ endline} = \bar{Y}_C - \bar{Y}_D = 300 - 200 = \$100. \tag{32}$$

The problem here is that this cross-sectional difference may pick up the underlying systematic difference (in Y) between the two groups that is independent of the program. As indicated in Fig. 6, the two groups are quite different in the mean of Y even at the baseline (*i.e.*, $\bar{Y}_A \neq \bar{Y}_B$), when neither was treated. Indeed, the baseline treatment-comparison difference, $\bar{Y}_A - \bar{Y}_B = E(Y \mid T = 1, t = 0) - E(Y \mid T = 0, t = 0) = E(Y_0 \mid T = 1, t = 0) - E(Y_0 \mid T = 0, t = 0)$, is the selection bias defined at the baseline.

Assuming the selection bias is time-invariant, DD eliminates it by subtracting the baseline treatment-comparison difference (*i.e.*, the baseline selection bias), $\bar{Y}_A - \bar{Y}_B$, from the endline treatment-comparison difference, $\bar{Y}_C - \bar{Y}_D$:

$$\begin{aligned}\delta^{DD} &= \delta^{CS,\ endline} - \delta^{CS,\ baseline}\\ &= (\bar{Y}_C - \bar{Y}_D) - (\bar{Y}_A - \bar{Y}_B)\\ &= (300 - 200) - (100 - 40) = \$40. \end{aligned} \tag{33}$$

As shown in Fig. 6, DD uses $\bar{Y}_E$ as the counterfactual for $\bar{Y}_C$.

Another way to understand how DD works is to consider another widely adopted but often problematic estimator, the *before-after* (BA) estimator, which uses the baseline outcome of the treatment group, $\bar{Y}_A$, as the counterfactual for $\bar{Y}_C$:

$$\delta^{BA,\ treatment} = \bar{Y}_C - \bar{Y}_A = 300 - 100 = \$200. \tag{34}$$

Despite its popularity in conventional performance-evaluation projects, the before-after estimator also has a serious drawback. The baseline-endline change in Y for the treatment group, $\bar{Y}_C - \bar{Y}_A$, may not be entirely due to the program; other factors, such as improvements in local economic conditions, may affect Y as well. As shown in Fig. 6, the mean of Y for the comparison group also changed substantially between the baseline ($\bar{Y}_B$) and the endline ($\bar{Y}_D$), even though this group was never treated.

Note that since the baseline-endline change in Y for the comparison group is not caused by the program (assuming there are no spillover effects), this change presumably captures the influence of all factors other than the program. Under the assumption that these factors affect the treatment and comparison groups over time in the same way in the absence of the program *i.e.*, the "parallel trend" assumption. DD subtracts the baseline-endline change in Y in the comparison group, $\bar{Y}_D - \bar{Y}_B$, from that in the treatment group, $\bar{Y}_C - \bar{Y}_A$, to eliminate the influence of other factors:

$$\begin{aligned}\delta^{DD} &= \delta^{BA,\text{ treatment}} - \delta^{BA,\text{ comparison}} \\ &= (\bar{Y}_C - \bar{Y}_A) - (\bar{Y}_D - \bar{Y}_B) \\ &= (300 - 100) - (200 - 40) = \$40. \end{aligned} \tag{35}$$

A quick comparison of Eq. (33) and Eq. (35) indicates that these two setups lead to the same result. Unsurprisingly, this is because both the parallel-trend assumption and the *time-invariant* selection-bias assumption imply that the influence of all factors other than the program is fixed over time and can be differenced out using repeated observations.

5.2. *Formal setup*

To see formally how DD relates to important causal parameters, consider ATT defined at the endline:

$$\begin{aligned}\Delta^{ATT,\text{ endline}} &= E(Y_1 | T=1, t=1) - E(Y_0 | T=1, t=1) \\ &= [E(Y_1 | T=1, t=1) - E(Y_0 | T=0, t=1)] \\ &\quad - [E(Y_0 | T=1, t=1) - E(Y_0 | T=0, t=1)]. \end{aligned} \tag{36}$$

The expression in the first squared bracket on the right-hand side of the last equality,

$$E(Y_1 | T=1, t=1) - E(Y_0 | T=0, t=1) \tag{37}$$

is the treatment-comparison difference in Y *observed* at the endline (*i.e.*, $\delta^{cs,\ endline}$). However, the expression in the last squared bracket in Eq. (36),

$$E(Y_0 \mid T = 1, t = 1) - E(Y_0 \mid T = 0, t = 1), \quad (38)$$

the treatment-comparison difference in Y_0 (*i.e.*, the selection bias) at the endline, is *unobservable* because $E(Y_0 \mid T = 1, t = 1)$ is unobserved. Thus, ATT cannot be directly computed using Eq. (36). Fortunately, the assumption of the selection bias being time-invariant implies that

$$\begin{aligned} &E(Y_0 \mid T = 1, t = 1) - E(Y_0 \mid T = 0, t = 1) \\ &= E(Y_0 \mid T = 1, t = 0) - E(Y_0 \mid T = 0, t = 0). \end{aligned} \quad (39)$$

This allows us to replace the *unobserved* endline selection bias in Eq. (36), $E(Y_0 \mid T = 1, t = 1) - E[Y_0 \mid T = 0, t = 1]$ with the *observed* baseline selection bias, $E(Y_0 \mid T = 1, t = 0) - E(Y_0 \mid T = 0, t = 0)$. Such a replacement yields:

$$\begin{aligned} \Delta^{ATT,\ endline} &= E(Y_1 \mid T = 1, t = 1) - E(Y_0 \mid T = 1, t = 1) \\ &= [E(Y_1 \mid T = 1, t = 1) - E(Y_0 \mid T = 0, t = 1)] \\ &\quad - [E(Y_0 \mid T = 1, t = 0) - E(Y_0 \mid T = 0, t = 0)]. \\ &= [E(Y \mid T = 1, t = 1] - E(Y \mid T = 0, t = 1)] \\ &\quad - [E(Y \mid T = 1, t = 0) - E(Y \mid T = 0, t = 0)] \\ &= \delta^{DD}. \end{aligned} \quad (40)$$

That is, δ^{DD} yields an unbiased estimate of ATT at the endline. Rearranging terms shows that DD can also be written as,

$$\begin{aligned} \delta^{DD} &= [E(Y \mid T = 1, t = 1) - E(Y \mid T = 1, t = 0)] \\ &\quad - [E(Y \mid T = 0, t = 1) - E(Y \mid T = 0, t = 0)], \end{aligned}$$ [15] (41)

which is in line with the idea behind Eq. (35).

In empirical work, one can obtain the DD estimate of the endline ATT either by computing the four means involved in Eq. (41) or by estimating the model,

$$Y = \alpha_0 + \alpha_1 T + \alpha_2 t + \alpha_3 (T \times t) + \varepsilon, \quad (42)$$

[15]The derivation of this result along the lines of Eq. (35) is a good exercise for understanding Eq. (41).

where $E(\varepsilon | T, t) = 0$ under the time-invariant selection bias/parallel-trend assumption. The parameter α_3 is the DD estimate of ATT at the endline. To see this, one need only derive the terms $E(Y | T = 0, t = 0) = \alpha_0$, $E(Y | T = 0, t = 1) = \alpha_0 + \alpha_2$, $E(Y | T = 1, t = 0) = \alpha_0 + \alpha_1$, and $E(Y | T = 1, t = 0) = \alpha_0 + \alpha_2 + \alpha_3 + \alpha_4$, and plug them into the DD formula (Eq. 41). Other covariates, especially those that are unlikely to be affected by the program, can be added to Eq. (42) to increase precision of the estimates or to check for robustness of the estimation results.

5.3. *Differences-in-differences at work*

The DD method is usually adopted when there is a policy change that affects a group of individuals but not others. For example, Card and Krueger (1994) exploited a change in the state of New Jersey minimum wage in the early 1990s to estimate the effect of minimum wage on employment in the U.S. fast-food industry. Their DD estimator compares the change in employment in New Jersey fast-food restaurants before and after the minimum-wage change with that in Pennsylvania, the neighboring state where the minimum wage stayed unchanged. To estimate the causal effect of policy-force size on crime rates, Di Tella and Schargrodsky (2004) used a DD method, exploiting a change in the allocation of police forces across districts in Buenos Aires after a terrorist attack. After the attack, police forces were increased in districts with mosques, but remained unchanged in others districts. Their DD estimator compares the differences in petty crime rates in districts with and without mosques before and after the attack. The DD case study below exploits the enactment of China's one-child policy to estimate its impact on sex-ratios in China.

Case study 5: Did the one-child policy lead to imbalanced sex ratios in China?

Sex-ratios in China increased rapidly from 106 in 1975 to 113.8 in 1990, exemplifying the "missing women" problem in Asia (Sen, 1990). While many demographers and economists argued that China's one-child policy enacted in 1979 has been the major reason for this rapid increase in sex ratios (*e.g.*, Zeng *et al.*, 1993; Das Gupta, 2005), credible evidence supporting this argument has been lacking. Li *et al.* (2011) used DD to estimate the causal effect of the policy,[16] exploiting a unique feature of it. The policy set birth quotas for all Chinese couples. However,

[16]They point out that the increase in sex ratios in China has been a result of a combination of son preference, a decrease in fertility induced by the policy, and the progress of gender selection technology, rather than the policy alone.

whereas Han couples were allowed for only one child, ethnic minority couples were allowed to have more children. This differential treatment between Han and ethnic minorities led to different time trends of sex-ratios in the post-policy period (Fig. 7), which was exploited by Li *et al.*, to identify the policy effect.

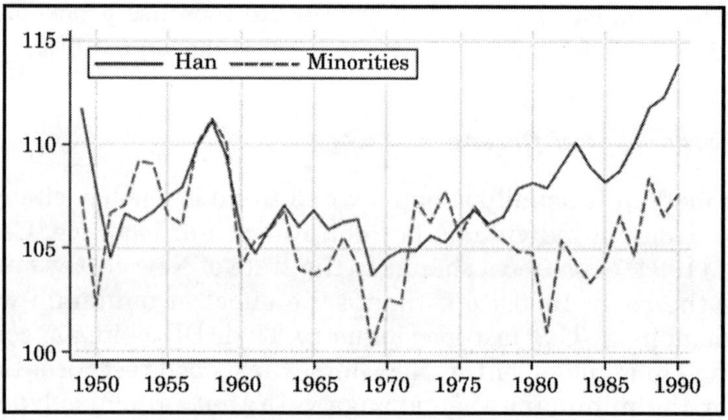

Fig. 7: Sex ratios among Ethnic Han and Ethnic Minorities.

Note: adapted from Li *et al.* (2011).

Based on the 1% sample of the 1990 Chinese Population Census, Li *et al.* estimated the effect of the policy on the probability of a child being a boy (equivalently, the proportion of boys) in the sample using the following estimator:

$$\delta^{DD} = [E(S_i | H = 1, t = 1) - E(S_i | H = 1, t = 0)] - [E(S_i | H = 0, t = 1) - E(S_i | H = 0, t = 0)], \quad (43)$$

where S_i is a dummy for child i being a boy, H is a dummy for ethnic Han, and t denotes the time period in which child i was born (t =1 if born in 1979–90; t = 0 if born in 1973–79). This estimator eliminates the influence of other factors, such as economic development in general, on sex-ratios. The DD estimate is captured by the parameter α_3 in the following regression:

$$S_i = \alpha_0 + \alpha_1 H_i + \alpha_2 t_i + \alpha_3 (t_i \times H_i) + \varepsilon_i. \quad (44)$$

Given the estimated parameters in Eq. (44), the ratio of males over females for the two ethnic groups in the two time periods can be constructed as follows: $(\alpha_0 + \alpha_1)/[1 - (\alpha_0 + \alpha_1)$ for Han before 1979, $(\alpha_0 + \alpha_1 + \alpha_2 + \alpha_3)/(1 - (\alpha_0 + \alpha_1 + \alpha_2 + \alpha_3)$ for ethnic Han after 1979,

$\alpha_0/(1-\alpha_0)$ for ethnic minorities before 1979, and $(\alpha_0+\alpha_2)/[1-(\alpha_0+\alpha_2)]$ for ethnic minorities after 1979. Then, the policy effect on sex ratio (PESR) can be calculated as

$$\begin{aligned}\text{PESR} &= 100 \times \{(\alpha_0+\alpha_1+\alpha_2+\alpha_3)/(1-(\alpha_0+\alpha_1+\alpha_2+\alpha_3)] \\ &\quad -(\alpha_0+\alpha_1)/[1-(\alpha_0+\alpha_1)\} - \{(\alpha_0+\alpha_2)/ \\ &\quad [1-(\alpha_0+\alpha_2)] - \alpha_0/(1-\alpha_0)\}. \end{aligned} \tag{45}$$

The results indicate little Han-minority difference in gender during the pre-policy period. In contrast, the difference is as large as 0.011 for the post-policy period, which is statistically significant. These differences imply that the sex ratio of Han is on average 4.7 higher than that of ethnic minorities during the post-policy period. The DD estimate of the policy effect is 0.0106 for the post-policy period (*i.e.*, the endline ATT), a statistically significant effect. Based on the estimates of α_0, α_1, α_2 and α_3, Li *et al.*, estimated that the one-child policy increased the sex ratio for Han by 4.4.

5.4. *Limitations and extensions*

The credibility of DD estimates hinges on the plausibility of the parallel-trend/time-invariant selection-bias assumption. It is possible that the baseline-endline change in Y differs between the treatment and comparison groups even in the absence of the program – after all, if these groups can be quite different at the baseline (Fig. 6), why expect their time trends to be similar? Without more data, this assumption cannot be tested. But if another pre-program dataset is available, one can use the two pre-program datasets to conduct a falsification test, *i.e.*, to estimate Eq. (42) using both pre-program datasets, treating the more recent one as the "endline" dataset. If the parallel-trend assumption is plausible, this regression should not yield a significant estimate of α_3.

More pre-program data also allow one to explicitly model the time trends. For example, Wagstaff (2010) proposed a triple-difference method that relaxes the parallel-trend assumption, using observations in the two pre-program periods to predict group-specific time trends in the absence of treatment. Also, in their study of the impact of microfinance on rural poverty in Northern Ethiopia, Berhane and Gardebroek (2011) used data covering four time periods (two pre- and two post-program periods) to allow for more possibilities to control for differences in the (untreated) time trends across groups.

6. Propensity Score Matching

6.1. *Eliminating selection bias by conditioning on observed characteristics*

When the data available do not allow one to deal with unobserved selection bias, one can only rely on *observed* information for causal inference. The task is still to find a plausible estimate of the counterfactual for the treated. The propensity score matching (PSM) method is developed based on the following idea: if we are able to find a "statistical twin" (*i.e.*, a match) from the untreated sample for a treated person, based on a set of observed characteristics, $\boldsymbol{Z}$, then we can use the observed outcome of the (matched) statistical twin of that treated person as the counterfactual for his/her treated outcome. In other words, the conditioning on $\boldsymbol{Z}$ eliminates selection bias.

To estimate ATT, our usual target, using PSM, two assumptions are needed. First, there *must* exist a set of observed characteristics, $\boldsymbol{Z}$, such that, conditional on $\boldsymbol{Z}$, the untreated outcome Y_0 is uncorrelated with a person's treatment status, P:

$$\mathrm{E}(Y_0 \mid P = 1, \boldsymbol{Z}) = \mathrm{E}(Y_0 \mid P = 0, \boldsymbol{Z}).^{[17]} \tag{46}$$

This is what eliminates selection bias. As a concrete example, suppose the set of $\boldsymbol{Z}$ variables needed for matching in our job-training example includes gender, years of schooling and income. Eq. (46) says that for persons with the same gender, years of schooling and income, the variation in their treatment status, P, is *as good as* randomly determined. Second, the probability of program participation for the treated group satisfies

$$\mathrm{Prob}(P = 1 \mid \boldsymbol{Z}) < 1, \tag{47}$$

so that matches for treated individuals can be found – after all, for treated persons whose probability of participation is always 1, no "match" based on $\boldsymbol{Z}$ can be found.

Under these assumptions, the (mean) impact of the program can be estimated by substituting the untreated outcome Y_0 observed for the matched untreated group for the missing Y_0 for treated individuals. Once the matches are found, the overall average treatment effect on the treated (ATT) can be written as:

[17] If we need to estimate parameters such as ATE and ATU, we need a stronger assumption: there exist a set of observed characteristics, $\boldsymbol{Z}$, such that, conditional on $\boldsymbol{Z}$, both of the potential outcomes, Y_0 and Y_1, are independent of individuals' participation status, P.

$$\begin{aligned}\Delta^{ATT} &= E(Y_1 - Y_0 \mid P = 1)\\ &= E(Y_1 \mid P = 1) - E_{Z|P=1}[E_Y(Y \mid P = 1, \mathbf{Z})]\\ &= E(Y_1 \mid P = 1) - E_{Z|P=1}[E_Y(Y \mid P = 0, \mathbf{Z})], \qquad (48)\end{aligned}$$

where the second term in the last line can be computed from the mean observed Y of the matched untreated group. And "$E_{Z|P=1}$" indicates that the weighted average of the observed Y is calculated based on the distribution of $\mathbf{Z}$ for the treated group.

6.2. *Dimensionality problem and the common support*

Obviously, matches can be difficult to find when the set of $\mathbf{Z}$ variables is large. Fortunately, Rosenbaum and Rubin (1983) derived a useful result for reducing the dimension of the conditioning problem. They showed that:

$$\begin{aligned}E(P \mid Y, \mathbf{Z}) = E(P \mid \mathbf{Z}) &\Rightarrow E[P \mid Y, \text{Prob}(P = 1 \mid \mathbf{Z})]\\ &= E[P \mid \text{Prob}(P = 1 \mid \mathbf{Z})], \qquad (49)\end{aligned}$$

for random variables Y, $\mathbf{Z}$, and P (which is binary). This result means that when the Y outcomes are uncorrelated with program participation, conditional on $\mathbf{Z}$, they are also uncorrelated with program participation, conditional on the *probability* of participation given $\mathbf{Z}$, $\text{Prob}(P = 1 \mid \mathbf{Z})$. Thus, rather than having to match individuals on $\mathbf{Z}$, we can match them on $\text{Prob}(P = 1 \mid \mathbf{Z})$, the so-called "propensity score".

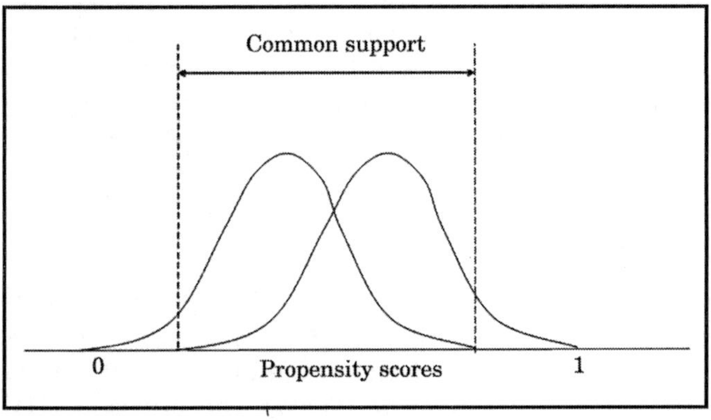

Fig. 8: Common support

With non-experimental data, there may or may not exist a set of $\mathbf{Z}$ variables for which the above two assumptions hold. And if there are certain regions where the values of Prob($P = 1 \mid \mathbf{Z}$) do not overlap for the treated and untreated groups, matching is justified only over the region of "common support" (Fig. 8). The estimated effect of the program must then be defined over the common-support region.

6.3. *Matching algorithms*

In practice, the matching procedure is implemented in two steps. The first is to estimate the propensity scores, $Ps(\mathbf{Z}) = \text{Prob}(P = 1 \mid \mathbf{Z})$, usually by a logit/probit regression of P on $\mathbf{Z}$. The second step is to match individuals on the basis of their first-stage fitted propensity scores, $Ps(\mathbf{Z})$. The match on $Ps(\mathbf{Z})$ between treated and untreated individuals does not have to be exact; it can be made between individuals whose propensity scores are deemed "close enough".

Four matching algorithms are commonly used. (1) *Nearest neighbor matching*, which matches individuals who have the closest propensity scores. (2) *Caliper matching*, which is a variation of nearest neighbor matching that avoids matching nearest neighbors whose propensity scores are far away from each other, by imposing a limit on the maximum distance allowed. (3) *Interval matching*, which partitions the common support region into a number of intervals and matches all untreated individuals to all treated individuals within the same interval. Within each interval, it estimates a separate impact, by calculating the mean difference in the observed Y between the treated and untreated groups, and then produces an overall impact estimate as the weighted average of the separate interval-impact estimates, using the fraction of treated individuals in each interval as the weight. (4) *Non-parametric matching*, which constructs a match for each treated person using a weighted average over multiple persons in the untreated group, using a kernel or local linear regression function to estimate the weights. See Becker and Ichino (2002) for more details on these algorithms.

6.4. *Propensity score matching at work*

While the assumptions needed for PSM to produce credible causal estimates (especially Eq. 46) are quite strong, it has recently been applied in many causal studies, including studies of the effect of parental death on child outcomes (Gertler *et al.*, 2004), the effect of HIV status on labor market outcomes (Levinsohn *et al.*, 2013), and the effect of migration on children's well-beings (Xu and Xie, 2015), to name a few. The following case study illustrates how PSM is used to estimate the effect of access to piped water on child health in India.

Case study 6: Does piped water improve child health in rural India?

India accounts for more child deaths due to unsafe water than any other single country. While expanding access to piped water is expected to improve child health in India, whether it improves child health in reality is unclear. For example, improper storage of piped water in the house could lead to its contamination, thereby imposing potential risks on child health.

To estimate the causal effect of having piped water on child health, one has to address the problem that the provision of piped water is not random. Since baseline data were not available, Jalan and Ravallion (2003) applied PSM to search for households with and without access to piped water that are observably comparable in their causal analysis. Based on data from a large survey conducted in 1993–94 on 33,000 rural households from 16 states in India, Jalan and Ravallion used a large set of observed characteristics such as village population, availability of high school, that of sealed road, of bus stop, telephone, bank, market, electricity, and housing quality etc. to estimate propensity scores. Then, applying a nearest-5 neighbor matching algorithm, they found that having piped water reduced diarrheal disease among Indian children – its prevalence would be 21 percent higher and its duration 29 percent longer without piped water.

6.5. *Limitations*

PSM can be performed when there is a set of observed characteristics $\boldsymbol{Z}$ to facilitate propensity-score estimation, but the credibility of the resulted causal estimates hinges on whether the researcher has a compelling argument that these characteristics satisfy Eq. (46). Unobserved selection bias is always a threat for identification. In addition, although tests have been developed to assess the performance of matching based on $\boldsymbol{Z}$, the theory of matching developed thus far still fails to provide clear guidance on which $\boldsymbol{Z}$ characteristics should be used to estimate propensity scores for matching.

7. Notes on Combining Methods

In causal studies, one may be able to apply more than one method to analyze the same data. While using more methods may mean that one has a better chance to recover something causal, it should be kept in mind that different methods usually estimate different causal parameters defined over different subpopulations/subsamples. For example, RCTs with full compliance may provide estimates of the average treatment effect on all individuals in the population of interest, RCTs with non-compliers usually provide estimates of the average treatment effect on the compliers, while RD only provide the average effect only on individuals at the eligibility cut-off. Hence, when combining different methods in causal analysis, one should clearly state and discuss what parameter is being estimated to avoid confusion or misinterpretation of estimation results.

Methods are usually combined in two ways. First, different methods may serve as complements to each other. For example, when baseline data are available, DD is usually combined with PSM. The DD part takes care of the time-invariant selection bias, while the PSM part (hopefully) eliminates some influence of the time-varying factors. Second, methods are sometimes combined to assess the robustness of estimation results. For example, Glewwe *et al.* (2004) used RCT estimates to assess the performance of a DD estimator, Buddelmeyer and Skoufias (2008) used RCT estimates to assess the performance of an RD estimator, and Chay *et al.* (2005) used a RD design to assess the performance of a DD estimator. In any case, it is always good practice to state clearly the parameter being estimated and the assumption[s] needed to estimate that parameter.

REFERENCES

Angrist, J.D. and Evans, W.N. (1998). Children and their parents' labor supply: Evidence from exogenous variation in family size. *American Economic Review*, 88: 450–477.

Angrist, J.D. and Lavy, V. (1999). Using Maimonides' rule to estimate the effect of class size on scholastic achievement. *Quarterly Journal of Economics*, 114(2): 533–575.

Angrist, J.D. and Pischke, J.S. (2009). Almost harmless econometrics: An empiricist's companion. Princeton and Oxford: Princeton University Press.

Becker, S.O. and Ichino, A. (2002). Estimation of average treatment effects based on propensity scores. *Stata Journal*, 2: 358–377.

Berhane, G. and Gardebroek, C. (2011). Does microfinance reduce rural poverty? Evidence based on household panel data from northern Ethiopia. *American Journal of Agricultural Economics,* 93(1): 43–55.

Black, D., Devereux, P. and Salvanes, K. (2011). Too young to leave the nest? The effects of school starting age. *Review of Economics and Statistics,* 93(2): 455–467.

Buddelmeyer, H. and Skoufias, E. (2008). An evaluation of the performance of regression discontinuity design on Progresa. IZA Discussion Papers 827, Institute for the Study of Labor (IZA).

Card, D. and Krueger, A. (1994). Minimum wages and employment: A case study of the fast food industry in New Jersey and Pennsylvania. *American Economic Review,* 84: 772–784.

Carrell, S.E., Fullerton, R.L. and West, J.E. (2009). Does your cohort matter? Measuring peer effects in college achievement. *Journal of Labor Economics*, 27: 439–64.

Chay, K.Y., McEwan, P. and Urquiola, M. (2005). The central role of noise in evaluating interventions that use test scores to rank schools. *American Economic Review*, 95(4): 1237–1258.

Chen, Q. (2015). Ready for school? Impacts of delayed primary school enrollment on children's educational outcomes in rural China. *International Journal of Educational Development,* 45: 112–128.

Chen, Q., Tian, G. and Okediji, T.O. (2014). Quasi-experimental evidence of peer effects in first-year economics courses at a Chinese university. *Journal of Economic Education*, 45(4): 304–319.

Das Gupta, M. (2005). Explaining Asia's 'missing women': A new look at the data. *Population and Development Review,* 31: 529–535.

Di Tella, R. and Schargrodsky, E. (2004). Do police reduce crime? Estimates using the allocation of police forces after a terrorist attack. *American Economic Review*, 94(1): 115–133.

Duflo, E., Glennerster, R. and Kremer, M. (2008). Using randomization in development economics research: A toolkit, *In:* Schultz, T.P. and Strauss, J. (*eds.*), *Handbook of Development Economics Elsevier,* 4: 3895–3962.

Elder, T.E. and Lubotsky, D.H. (2004). Kindergarten entrance age and children's achievement: Impacts of state policies, family background and peers. *Journal of Human Resources,* 44(3): 641–683.

Gertler, P. (2004). Do conditional cash transfers improve child health? Evidence from Progresa's control randomized experiment. *American Economic Review*, 94(2): 336–341.

Gertler, P., Levine, D. and Ames, M. (2004). Schooling and parental death. *Review of Economics and Statistics*, 81(6): 211–225.

Gertler, P., Martinez, S., Premand, P., Rawlings, L.B. and Vermeersch, C.M.J. (2011). Impact Evaluation in Practice. Washington DC: World Bank.

Glewwe, P., Kremer, M., Moulin, S. and Zitzewitz, E. (2004). Retrospective vs. prospective analyses of school inputs: The case of flip charts in Kenya. *Journal of Development Economics,* 74(1): 251–268.

Glewwe, P., Park, A. and Zhao, M. (2016). Better vision for development: Eyeglasses and academic performance in rural primary schools in China. *Journal of Development Economics*, 122: 170–182.

Imbens, G. and Wooldridge, J. (2009). Recent developments in the econometrics of program evaluation. *Journal of Economic Literature*, 47(1): 5–86.

Jalan, J. and Ravallion, M. (2003). Does piped water reduce diarrhea for children in rural India? *Journal of Econometrics*, 112(1): 153–173.

Khandker, S.R., Koolwal, G.B. and Samad, H.A. (2011). Handbook on impact evaluation: Quantitative methods and practices. Washington DC: World Bank.

Krueger, A. (1999). Experimental estimates of education production functions. *Quarterly Journal of Economics,* 114: 497–532.

Lee, D. (2008). Randomized experiments from non-random selection in U.S. House elections. *Journal of Econometrics,* 142: 675–697.

Lee, D. and Lemieux, T. (2010). Regression discontinuity designs in economics. *Journal of Economic Literature*, 48: 281–355.

Levinsohn, J., McLaren, Z.M., Shisana, O. and Zuma, K. (2013). HIV status and labor market participation in South Africa. *Review of Economics and Statistics*, 95(1): 98–108.

Li, H., Yi, J. and Zhang, J. (2011). Estimating the effect of the one-child policy on the sex ratio imbalance in China: Identification based on the difference-in-differences. *Demography*, 48(4): 1535–1557.

Li, H., Zhang, J. and Zhu, Y. (2008). The quantity-quality trade-off of children in a developing country: Identification using Chinese twins. *Demography,* 45(1): 223–243.

McCrary, J. (2008). Manipulation of the running variable in the regression discontinuity design: A density test. *Journal of Econometrics*, 142(2): 698–714.

Miguel, E. and Kremer, M. (2004). Worms: Identifying impacts on education and health in the presence of treatment externalities. *Econometrica*, 72(1): 159–217.

Morgan, S.L. and Winship, C. (2007). Counterfactuals and causal inference: Methods and principles for social research. Cambridge: Cambridge University Press.

Moulin, S., Kremer, M. and Glewwe, P. (2009). Many children left behind? Textbooks and test scores in Kenya. *American economic Journal: Applied Economics*, 1(1): 112–35.

Ravallion, M. (2008). Evaluating anti-poverty programs, *In*: Schultz, T.P. and Strauss, T.P.J. (*eds.*), *Handbook of Development Economics, Elsevier*, 4: 3787–3846.

Rosenbaum, P.R. and Rubin, D.B. (1983). The central role of the propensity score on observational studies for causal effects. *Biometrika,* 70: 41–55.

Rubin, D.B. (1974). Estimating the causal effects of treatments in randomized and non-randomized studies. *Journal of Educational Psychology*, 66: 688–701.

Sacerdote, B. (2011). Peer effects with random assignment: Results for Dartmouth roommates. *Quarterly Journal of Economics,* 116(2): 681–704.

Schultz, T.P. (2004). School subsidies for the poor: Evaluating the Mexican Progresa poverty program. *Journal of Development Economics,* 74(1): 199–250.

Sen, A. (1990). More than 100 million women are missing. New York review of books.

Skoufias, E. (2005). PROGRESA and its impacts on the welfare of rural households in Mexico. Research Report 139, International Food Policy Research Institute, Washington, DC.

Todd, P. (2008). Evaluating social programs with endogenous program placement and selection of the treated. *In*: Schultz, T.P. and Strauss, J. (*eds.*), *Handbook of Development Economics, Elsevier*, 4: 3847–3894.

Wagstaff, A. (2010). Estimating health insurance impacts under unobserved heterogeneity: The case of Vietnam's health care fund for the poor. *Health Economics*, 19(2): 189–208.

Wooldridge, J. (2010). Econometric analysis of cross sectional and panel data. Cambridge: MIT Press.

Xu, H. and Xie, Y. (2015). The causal effects of rural-to-urban migration on children's wellbeing in China. *European Sociological Review,* 31(4): 502–519.

Zeng, Y., Tu, P., Gu, B., Xu, Y., Li, B. and Li, Y. (1993). Causes and implications of the recent increase in the reported sex ratio at birth in China. *Population and Development Review*, 19(2): 283–302.

Zhao, M., Konishi, Y. and Glewwe, P. (2013). Does information on health status lead to a healthier lifestyle? Evidence from China on the effect of hypertension diagnosis on food consumption. *Journal of Health Economics*, 32(2): 367–385.

8

Infrastructure of Bulgarian High-Rise Estates: Realities and Hopes

Elena Kalcheva[1]*, Ahmad Taki[1] and Yuri Hadi[1]

ABSTRACT

This chapter studies the quality and characteristics of the infrastructure in several high-rise estates in Sofia, Bulgaria and evaluates to which extend it serves the residents in the tall buildings. Most of the high-rises in Sofia and their surroundings were built in the Soviet era so they represent a very old design concept and this is why it is no surprise that the quality of the public realm and the buildings is quite sub-standard. The spaces around the high-rises lack public spaces other than the streets and empty large pieces of land. There is lack of integrated natural features with the design of the high-rises. Hoping to achieve a functional and attractive built environment, the following need to be implemented: new layout of the streets, introduction of viable public spaces with strong sense of place where the high-rises act as a power symbol and development of green infrastructure.

Key words: High-rise, Infrastructure, Sofia, Mladost, Liulin

INTRODUCTION

Infrastructures, such as roads, rivers, dams, harbours, airports, waterworks, and railroads, are crucial for the national development and closely relates to the quality of life for citizens. Their presence is also an important indicator of national competitiveness and economic growth (Park, Park and Lee, 2016). Adequate infrastructure is vital for

[1]Leicester School of Architecture, De Montfort University, Leicester, LE1 9BH, UK.

**Corresponding author*: E-mail: eli_kalcheva@yahoo.com

the proper functioning of the society. High-rises present a specific challenge for the infrastructure due to the big number of people they attract, and the associated load on automobile and public transport. This is why the provision of responses to the high-rise residents' needs and aspirations should be a priority to city planners and presents an interesting research topic for scholars, academics and professionals.

Bulgarian high-rise estates were mostly built in the Soviet era when the design philosophy favoured skylines dominated by standardized blocks to temporarily solve overcrowding issues. The high-rise estates in Sofia can be described as influenced by the Modernist architecture such as those of Le Corbusier and his plans for Paris. The housing developments generally represent tower blocks in large open settings, constructed from standardized and mass-produced structural insulated panels to allow for rapid construction. The complexes are mainly located in the periphery of the capital where large empty areas make it possible to build. Luilin is the largest residential district in Sofia, the infrastructure works started in 1971 and the first condominium was built in 1973. The complex has a population of 240000 people and is notorious for being a concrete jungle. Mladost is one of the fastest developing areas in the city. In 2012 it has 114,887 residents making it the second-most-populous district in the capital.

As demonstrated by these two districts, urban infrastructure systems are characterized by long lifespans of the buildings and facilities and through that time it has a strong influence over the environment and the life of the citizens. Processes of strategic planning for urban infrastructure are thus the means to realize environmental sustainability aspirations. Thus to achieve environmental sustainability aspirations, strategic planning should be implemented. To continue investing in infrastructure with adverse environmental impacts indicates a lack of sustainability priorities in the planning process (Malekpour, Brown and Haan, 2016).

To secure long-term sustainability, infrastructure needs to be designed and operated to provide vital service delivery with radical resource use minimization. This new approach will need to: (1) incorporate the end-user demand; (2) focus on the service provided (Roelich *et. al.*, 2015).

The basic needs for the residents are spaces to interact, for leisure activities, mixed use of shopping, working and living to minimize the car dependence. Creating a pleasurable street experience is the way to enhance physical activities such as walking and cycling. In the past two decades in other countries, promoting walking and cycling has been a subject of increased policy attention in many sectors including health, transport and climate change (Chief Medical Officers of England, 2011; Department of Health and Department for Transport, 2010; THE PEP, 2009; WHO, 2002; Goodman, Sahlqvist and Ogilvie, 2013). It is increasingly acknowledged that creating a comprehensive built environment may play a crucial role in enabling the success of individual level interventions (Giles-Corti, 2006; Goodman, Sahlqvist and Ogilvie, 2013) and in promoting enduring population behaviour change (Butland *et al.*, 2007; Institute of Medicine and National Research Council of the National Academies, 2009; NICE, 2008; Goodman, Sahlqvist and Ogilvie, 2013). In other countries there has been an expanding investment in bicycle infrastructure internationally in recent years, partially to meet environmental and population health concerns created by heavy reliance on motorised transport. Disturbing levels of physical inactivity in the population, air pollution and greenhouse gas emissions from urban traffic are worsening already unsustainable transport systems, signifying that an alternative to personal motor vehicles needs to be implemented (Woodcock *et al.*, 2009; WHO, 2011; Crane *et al.*, 2016). There is also a need for facilities for children and young people. They need opportunities to be active in safe and attractive settings and to travel actively; older children should be provided with infrastructure that allows them to be independent but safe.

Successful planning acknowledges the diversity of the end-users and will not exclude anybody. Sofia can learn from the rapid development of Singapore the last 40 years. Singapore was confronted with the problems of overcrowding in the city, poor living conditions and a severe lack of infrastructure. Today, Singapore is a flourishing city and international business hub entertaining a high standard of living in a clean and green environment. The success did not come about accidently but through a process of proactive and long term planning. This shows that infrastructure is clearly central to socio-economic advancement. An efficient infrastructure secures delivery of information, goods and services, stimulates economic growth and is a base for achieving social objectives such as high living standards and educational levels (Lim, 2008). Sofia can relate to such positive examples when stepping towards regeneration of its outdated and old concept infrastructure. However, successful cities in the world invest a significant part of their GDP in improving the infrastructure by sensible, adequate big-scale projects. The most recent project in Sofia of such significance was the construction of the metro-link connecting densely populated districts of Lyulin-Mladost and Nadezhda–Lozenets. Also, since 2 April 2015, Line 1 is servicing the Sofia Airport. There is also investment in paths for cyclists but their scale and layout has left the users largely dissatisfied.

There are three locations studied for their infrastructure in conjunction with residential high-rise buildings. Kniajevo, Mladost and Liulin are chosen for the good example they represent as high-rise residential complexes. Kniajevo has the least high-rises, Mladost and Liulin are "concrete jungles" almost entirely composed of tall buildings. The chosen buildings are similar in architectural quality and situation, but furthermore they are the same as almost the whole percentage of the buildings and their surroundings in the districts.

1. KNIAJEVO

1.1. Observations

Kniajevo buildings are 18 storey tower blocks located near a main road. The surrounding infrastructure consists of streets, green areas and areas covered with asphalt (Fig. 1).

Fig. 1: Kniajevo infrastructure around the tower blocks

The road infrastructure around the high-rises is decent, there are bollards and traffic calming humps, but no cycling paths. The green patches by the road are in very bad condition, so is the pavement, there is no aesthetical sense in the pattern of the sidewalks and they are made fast and cheaply (Fig. 1). There is no anyone car street promotion. Regarding the immediate surroundings maintenance seems of low priority: shabby asphalt, large parking lots that cause visual clatter, green areas that are more like a jungle than an urban setting and allow no strolling and enjoying the natural features because they are so dense and badly maintained (Fig. 2). The open space in front of the buildings can hardly be called plaza. The numbers features, diversity of function are almost non-existent, and the observation did not show the existence of network of functions such as shopping, working or leisure. Business and commodities are not attracted to the site but can be found in the vicinity (cafe and shops). The nature is not in any way integrated with the design, the planting is monotonous, boring and trivial, there is no richness in colour and type, no change of light, textures and smells, the ground floors of the buildings are not articulated with richer architectural detail, there is not differentiation between formal and informal, or any seating, the environment is completely inappropriate for ground floor restaurants and shops (Fig. 2), there is no outdoor playground facilities, nor recreational facilities or public art. Street furniture seems like an impossible luxury considering the state of the conditions of the green patches and the pavement on the road. There are also no interesting sites to observe while seated so there is no point introducing seating except for resting in clean air outside the building, but it is very unsatisfactory experience. There are no changes in levels from the street so the access is unobstructed and the visitors can easily approach the buildings, no steps and planters to use as informal seating, but the location is not popular for a variety of people to use it. The impact on public life and the community perception altogether is quite weak and poor: the infrastructure does not engage with the users on sensual level and people do not use it actively.

Fig. 2: The ground floors of the buildings Kniajevo

1.2. Recommendations for Improvement

What the authors hope to see in such a group of buildings is some cultural activity around public art or water features, used by diversity of people. A greater number of activities such as picnicking, sleeping, reading, sunbathing, sprawling should be accommodated. The participation of the residents in the city life should be more obvious. The pedestrian layout should be encouraging pedestrian freedom, now obstructed by the wild and displeasing vegetation. The ground floors of the buildings should be suitable for retail, civic and recreational functions.

There must be area where people can meet and chat, watch and walk, stand or sit; the area should be vibrant considering the number of people the buildings shelter and the busy road with active frontage. The street is not meeting necessary conditions such as clean air, low noise levels, cleanness which are needed to support environmentally sustainable way of life. The place should be designed so represent a meaningful location, rather than asphalt desert with tall buildings on it. There must be a sense of place and reconnecting urban and natural environment with community. Variety of functions and facilities is key. Views and the clean air are drivers for selling high-rise apartments, but on ground level they absolutely do not exist, there are no landmarks to which important vistas to be orientated. There is no guidance of the pedestrian floor by bollards, planters and walls, no nooks and corners, seating orientations, the trees and bushes disturb the connections between the buildings, the area should have a strong image, not this shabby appearance, the complexity: nature, architecture, public realm should be expressed. There is enough space for nice plazas with areas for encounter and gathering, to address different needs, the places should feel safe and secure, not abandoned as in the moment. The quality of the built environment in the present situation is quite low and should be enhanced. The group of high-rises has absolutely no identity. The visiting of such a place should be leaving the visitor with meaningful experience not like now with a sense of lost time. The character of the complex should be enhanced by strong urban design intervention so the memorable skyline of the place to attract visitors to a higher quality space.

2. MLADOST

2.1. Observations

The high-rises in Mladost are located on a main road and form an array of tall buildings with unrealized potential for creating an active frontage. The situation is similar with the tower blocks in Kniajevo. The road infrastructure is decent, there is even cyclist path, but nothing more. Green features and traffic calming are missing, the road is lacking character and attractiveness to provoke positive pedestrian experience (Fig. 3).

Fig. 3: Mladost road infrastructure

Parking lots located by the road create unpleasant visual clatter. Sidewalks are crucial for the functioning of the city. The sidewalks in Mladost are wide enough (around 2 m) but the pavement is lacking aesthetic component, they are simply asphalt or unpleasant concrete tiles (Fig. 3). This is not enough to make walking more attractive. Another downside is the distance between vital services which is significant and do not encourage taking it by foot. The sidewalk is the space where people interact the most with one another and with businesses but the size, distance from buildings and the visual impact of the Mladost sidewalks do not support this. This decreases the economic strength and the quality of life of the district. The negative features of the Mladost sidewalks deprive the residents from the possibility to observe the street life and have activities in retail and commercial venues. They do not benefit from public art, human scale design features, and vendors and feel empty and lacking public life.

The road is also used for parking and there are not designated bus lanes. Dedicated median bus lanes prevent conflicts with drop-offs, deliveries, or illegal parking along the road. Where roads are wide enough it is recommended by London: The Stationery Office the bus lane to be 4.25 m wide and the minimum preferred width is 4 m; this allows buses to overtake cyclists safely and reduces the possibility for problems generated by general traffic in the adjacent lane. The minimum width of 3 m is recommended for bus lane operation in each direction and pavement markings BUS.

The situation of the high-rise surroundings is similar to the Knijevo case. Badly looking pedestrian paths, wild vegetation missing aesthetic impact, large asphalt areas for the cars, minimum of services and functions on the ground floor. The availability of a café and a shop is meaningless since there is no plaza for better visual impact and users' experience (Fig. 6). There are no seating arrangements, neither formal nor informal. There is no enclosure that clearly defines private and public areas. Rather, all the space around the buildings is public realm. There are no facilities for playing outside or active doing areas for the elderly. There is no creation of important spot for gathering and social interaction. There is not observed design that is comfortable in peak times in regards to sun, shade and windiness (Fig. 4).

Fig. 4: Mladost high-rise surroundings

Fig. 5: Interaction between buildings and infrastructure Mladost

The different functions such as shopping or relaxing are not enhanced by design. There are no links between communities and businesses.

The spaces are not welcoming and are not used and look redundant (Fig. 5). Altogether the impact on public life and community perception is quite weak. There are no cultural activities or diversity of people using the infrastructure.

Activities such as picnicking, sunbathing, reading or sprawling are not supported. There is not obvious residents' participation in the urban life. Places for lingering, walk and watch, stand and watch, sit and watch are missing since there is no creation of vistas and no orientation towards landmarks that are not existent (Fig. 4).

Fig. 6: Shop on the ground floor Mladost

2.2. Recommendations for Improvement

The authors are hoping to see places in Mladost that are meaningful locations. It is important to rebuild the sense of place in the urban environments once through reconnection with nature and next, by considerate design of amenities and facilities. Public art is a powerful mean to achieve these goals. Due to their size high-rises are prerequisite for creating a strong image by memorable design and interaction with the infrastructure.

Variety of the design and function is a key to higher utilization and appreciation of the places around the buildings. The buildings must be tied into functional and appropriate pedestrian system. The positive pedestrian activities can be enhanced by a variety of the forms, colours, surface structures, sculptures, different seating, nooks and corners, trees and bushes in maintained natural strips. There is need for creating plazas in conjunctions with the cafes on the ground floors that will serve as places for gathering. The sufficient quality in terms of materials and detail will relate to people use and get more attention. The high-rises create memorable skyline which is an advantage for the sense of place but the connection with the road is quite practical and incorporates a lot of areas for car parking, while from the spaces in-between the buildings where the natural features are fitted quite inappropriately, there is not enough incentive to appreciate it which should be change by the creation of more welcoming, considerate public realm.

3. LIULIN

3.1. Observations

The situation in Liulin does not differ significantly from the two reviewed districts. There is a wide road, but without cycling paths or bus lanes (Fig. 7). This considerably reduces the quality and opportunities for transportation from the reviewed location.

Fig. 7: Road edge with high-rise in Liulin

A segment of the road from approximately 1.5 km has been studied. At some part of the road the high-rises are long, continuous mass, at other are point references. There are limited number of shops and no cafes. The vegetation is not as abundant as in the previous examples and is definitely not part of any urban design scheme, simply exists as an addition to the public realm. Parking lots again form unpleasant visual clatter. The accessibility is good: tower entrances are visible from the road, but there are no gathering places and spaces for encounter and enjoying the environment. The sidewalks are in very bad condition. Considering the importance for pedestrian activities, missing a sidewalk on the one side of the road is unacceptable. The distances between the towers suggest enough space for plazas, pocket parks and different spaces other than parking that will add character to the place. The character of the place depends on the way the streets, the building and the landscape come together. Parks and open spaces are vital elements to local distinctiveness, creating possibilities to reflect elements of the landscape, culture and heritage through design concepts, materials, topography and planting. Often the natural features themselves may help create identity for the place, standing out as icons of the district. However, the open spaces in Liulin are dull and uninteresting, simply connecting separate buildings without any distinctiveness and social function.

Fig. 8: Road infrastructure in Liulin

When the area was relatively new, the substantial width of the roads and the height of the buildings created memorable image, but today the shabby exterior and public realm impose the notion that it is poor and underdeveloped area (Fig. 8). The vehicle speeds do not create feeling of safety and calmness, the speed limit is 50 km/h. The parking lots are persevering image damaging the legibility of the area. There is no differentiation: public areas in the front and private areas in the back of the building so the functioning of the buildings and their surroundings is not facilitated by design responses (Fig. 9).

The ground floor of the second part of the road segment do not encompasses a diversity of uses, rather is poor and indifferent interface (Fig. 9). Diversity may combine different uses within one space (*e.g.*, sports facilities, play area and quiet garden) or a series of single use spaces by the road segment. The connection open space-building is seamless, but these spaces are under used and unwelcoming which is a very negative for the quality of life of the residents and the visitors' experience. The green strips are under-maintained; there is no diversity and attractive patterns of pavements, no seating and places or objects for observation.

Fig. 9: Ground floor of the buildings Liulin

The ease of movement is supported by a number of pedestrian routes but is diminished by hindrances such as parked cars and vegetation. There is not a variety of routes and streets for convenient access. The roads are linking routes with green spaces, but they are of low quality so that pedestrians and cyclists cannot move along attractive, enjoyable routes. There are no natural desire routes just hard paths around the towers. Legibility is also low, there are no small intimate streets connecting small pocket-parks to great open park areas. The result of street layout predominantly accommodating vehicular movement is relatively bland coming first and the housing fitted along it results in bland development designed for the car. The street should cater for pedestrians too, rather than solely vehicular needs.

There is a good hierarchy, creating a rich, varied environment: a main street that runs through the heart of the development, connecting it all together; secondary streets that link to the main street, and also feed other streets and spaces; yards with natural features. The character of the street is a result of the distance between the buildings and the footway, and the treatment of front gardens: the buildings set back behind large, green front gardens enclose the street less categorically resulting in a quite different, more suburban character. However the green spaces are of very poor quality: they do not seem to include functions for playing, exercise and/or relaxation; they do not seem to fit in wider green strategy, but are rather separate opportunistic interventions (Fig. 9). In spite of that the buildings are overlooking the green space they do not make the most of existing landscape and cityscape features and assets; it doesn't seem that the green spaces provide continuous green corridors and the landscape and open space strategy for the site does not seem to aim to enhance the biodiversity of the site.

3.2. Recommendations for Improvement

The authors' aspirations are to see is traffic calming and 30 km zones, the creation of home zones: remodelling streets as spaces and giving the pedestrians priority, changing the character of the place and developing linked open space networks of meaningful places, reinforcing areas of local importance, such as a community centre or school. It is important to have streets that offer possibilities to enhance the character of the district by high quality materials and sensitive road layouts; good example of civic spaces, with simple, high quality materials, a lack of clutter and active building frontages onto plazas in between the towers; good examples of district streets, where paving materials relate to the character of the local area, and pedestrians can safely and conveniently access buses. Improving spaces (or creating new ones) should be a part of a district strategy that aims to locate spaces where they are most useful and impact is the most sensible. Designing spaces should be flexible and adaptive so that different activities to be accommodated, using robust, sustainable materials to promote longevity. The design should reunite frontages to new plazas, create new ground floor uses that complement the open space and rationalise street furniture and signage in order to supply simple, uncluttered environment easy to maintain. The new look of the district must ensure that important views (to public buildings, public art, along major streets) are not obscured. The area should connect to local facilities and different uses. Commuter and recreational cycling should be accommodated. The natural features should be design for order, specific purpose and variety. It should be designed for social sustainability: a strong sense of community and social inclusion.

Between February and July 2016 the authors interviewed 10 prominent architects in connection with the role of the infrastructure and high-rises for the placemaking process. Ashton Allan thinks there is certain sophistication to the urban environment that should be created. And the way to realize placemaking through residential buildings, larger multifamily residential buildings today are really created through what happens on that first floor and placemaking is created through retail experience or through another kind of program. It's really enlightening that ground floor it's creating the type of destination or environment that people will typically go to which activates an area that allows for this chance encounters and creating a sense of place.

Analysing Ashton Allan's answer, it makes sense that besides different uses on the ground floor, such a building needs surrounding infrastructure in terms of small plaza or pocket-park in front of the building for a finished complex of function that promote positive experience for the end-users. None of the reviewed buildings has such a complete infrastructural response for the needs of the residents which is a great drawback for the satisfaction and quality of life of the people inhabiting the buildings.

Brian Kidd thinks how the buildings stand in response to the neighbourhood is an important thing, where do you locate the lobby, where you might have retail or other functions that work with existing context, but also trying to create a sort of interesting spaces for the public area of the building. How people go through their day and trying to anticipate the needs of the many different types of people that live in these buildings.

Facilities about which Brian Kidd is talking could be combined playground and pocket-park where people can relax, watch their children play and interact with other people. None of the reviewed buildings has such infrastructure around it, but this is of great importance for the residents' satisfaction.

Brian Nichols says you build high-rises and amenities in clusters and on the first floor you have communal services. The architect again stresses on the importance of the ground floor reinforced with facilities from the public area around the building, which is implemented very poorly in the reviewed examples.

Frances Gannon says there are few aspects. First is creating a tall building in an environment that is the edge of the city centre. So the building has a presence and is visible in the skyline and expands the city centre. The building is a real marker that brings people to come and then go to the city centre. On a more local level there are connections on the ground level. If you are on your way to somewhere you can pass through the building which is an interesting experience. The architect again emphasizes the importance of the ground floor for the residents and passer-by but for this purpose the pedestrian infrastructure should be with higher quality than the one presented in the examples.

Lee Rubenstein says that it is important to look at every site and try to understand the context, how the people live, who is going to live there, and what building is really appropriate. Than the focus on a lot on things like streetscape design, what's going on the ground floor, so to be a pleasant site you need street cafes, good stores or just a place to walk, so there need to be important building services which you need to have because the building won't work without them? The reviewed examples are suffering from small to inexistent mix of uses which significantly diminishes the quality of the districts.

Anthony Markese (works for Pickard Chilton) claims that really starts at the base of the building, and how thoughtfully places the building within the context whether it's a city or more suburban conditions, that will set some of the design decisions that will define what happen with the base. In a city condition obviously ways to activate the streetscape are important, looking to have more public uses at the base of the building, looking for a way to have program features, whether it is courtyards and plazas or some sort of retail, that allow the building to engage the local citizens, invite them into the building. In a more suburban setting typically the building need to connect to the landscape and have it feel like it is part of it, naturally. Placemaking is important at the base of the building. The infrastructure around the reviewed example does not comply with what the architect says.

Scott Erdy says an urban residential hi-rise must take into account the scale, texture and demographics of its context. Then is the inserting the amenity and social spaces between these volumes. The socialization of the building is the glue holding together the masses of the building. The reviewed buildings need to include amenities and mixed use in the infrastructure around them.

Sherief Elfar says the base of the building and how it meets the street and the type of uses located at grade level are critical to creating better places. The building has to participate with the street and adjacent side walk. This is hardly done in the reviewed areas.

Mr. Sieger says activities should be provided outside of the buildings where by those people that live within the high-rises. All these are missing in the reviewed infrastructure.

In conclusion all the architects emphasized the importance of the ground floors of the towers in conjunction with facilities and amenities. There must be activities and social functions between the blocks. Clearly this is something not implemented in the old high-rise districts in Sofia but the authors hope that beautification of the old high-rises will start from there.

The reviewed examples all had decent road infrastructure but the districts were all built in the 70s' when the technological level of the construction and automotive industry was very different from today's needs of the residents. Even if the transportation infrastructure is recognized as a powerful driver for the change in urban form, it is not so often recognized for the possibility to act as a social and behavioural catalyst. With the demographic change of people inhabiting the cities and the corresponding demand for space of transportation infrastructure, as well as the introduction of new technologies to transportation, new design of such a vital urban component is crucial (Maia, Teicher and Meyboom, 2015). In the future the main roads can accommodate in the future charger for electric cars. There could be synergy between stations and other activities for ultimate convenience and usability. This alternative mode of transportation can improve the quality of the air in the district and thus positively influence the public health. Besides electric vehicles cycling is an important aspect that needs to be supported by the infrastructure. Altogether the roads are with good size but their layout is very unattractive. Different design should be proposed for better frontage and interaction with the residential component. It might include green strips, bicycle lanes, bus lanes and designated parking lots. The sidewalks should be treated with pleasing pavements and connect the street level with the ground floor of the buildings opened for shops and cafes.

Both landscape and infrastructure are now a subject of a renewed movement of urban analysis including themes such as the adaptive capacity of cities to climate change, the application of ecological ideas to urban design, or the renovation of old industrial sites (Gandy, n.d.). All the three districts have an abundance of green features, but they are not a part of a design, they are wild vegetation that is badly maintained. The goal of future improvements could be the creation of green infrastructure encompassing the three districts natural features. Even though green infrastructure is a new term, the idea is not new. It began in planning and conservation endeavours one hundred and fifty years ago. Green infrastructure originates from two important concepts: (1) connecting parks and other green spaces to the wellbeing of people, and (2) preserving and linking natural areas to support biodiversity and against habitat fragmentation. In his work in public parks in the late eighteenth and early nineteenth centuries, landscape architect Frederick Law Olmsted argues that "no single park, no matter how large and how well designed, would provide the citizens with the beneficial influences of nature". Instead parks should "to be linked to one another and to surrounding residential neighbourhoods". This idea of connecting parks for the wellbeing of people (*e.g.*, focusing on recreation, pedestrian and bicycle trails and public health) has evolved into the modern greenways movement (Benedict and McMahon, n.d.).

Many dimensions of human quality of life and economic activities depend on ecosystem functions and processes. For example, the food security relies on the existence and maintenance of fertile soil; we need the air filtered by plants; our lives and properties are protected from flooding by soil infiltration, dune systems or riparian forests; and our mental and physical health may be connected to the availability of green spaces (MA, 2005; Alcock *et al.,* 2014; Liquete *et al.*, 2015). More importantly, some nature-based technical solutions (*e.g.*, green roofs, bio-infiltration rain gardens, vegetation in street canyons) have proved in many cases to be more efficient, inexpensive, adaptable and long-lasting than the so-called "grey" or conventional infrastructure (*e.g.,* Gill *et al.*, 2007; Pugh *et al.,* 2012; Ellis, 2013; Flynn and Traver, 2013; Raje *et al.,* 2013; Liquete *et al.*, 2015). These solutions can find their way to the future renovation of the reviewed districts.

Rapid urbanisation around the world connected to exhaustive resource and energy consumption, waste generation, and environmental degradation demands a transition toward more sustainable examples of urban development (Giddings *et al.,* 2005; Girardet, 1999; UN, 2002; Li, Beeton, Sigler and Halog, 2016). Even though cities are great contributors to economic welfare, improvements to living conditions, and social progress, the growth of cities has also generated major obstacles to biophysical systems that possibly pose a threat to human health and long-term development (Bettencourt and West, 2010; Dye, 2008; Galea and Vlahov, 2005; Leon, 2008; Moore *et al.,* 2003; Shen *et al.,* 2012; Li, Beeton, Sigler and Halog, 2016). Often, however, the environmental topics and impacts on human health are marginalised in favour of economic questions (Matus *et al.,* 2012a; Li, Beeton, Sigler and Halog, 2016).

Considering this, and in conclusion, the creation of green infrastructure should become a major question when planning for renovation of the Sofia's high-rise districts along with better street layout and improved interaction between ground floors and surroundings.

REFERENCES

Benedict, M. and McMahon, E. (2016). Green infrastructure: Smart conservation for the 21st Century, [Online] Available at <*http://www.sprawlwatch.org/greeninfrastructure.pdf.*

Crane, M., Rissel, C., Greaves, S., Standen, C. and Wen, L. (2016). Neighbourhood expectations and engagement with new cycling infrastructure in Sydney, Australia: Findings from a mixed method before-and-after study, [Online] Available at<*http://www.sciencedirect.com/science/article/pii/S221414051500688X.*

Gandy, M. and N.D. (2016). Landscape and infrastructure in the late - Modern metropolis, [Online] Available at <*http://matthewgandy.org/datalive/downloadfiles/Blackwellcompanion.pdf.*

Goodman, A., Sahlqvist, S. and Ogilvie, D. (2013). Who uses new walking and cycling infrastructure and how? Longitudinal results from the UK iConnect study, [Online] Available at <*http://www.sciencedirect.com/science/article/pii/S0091743513002314*> Accessed on August 22, 2016.

Li, Y., Beeton, R., Sigler, T. and Halog, A. (2016). Modelling the transition toward urban sustainability: A case study of the industrial city of Jinchang, China, [Online] Available at <*http://www.sciencedirect.com/science/article/pii/S0959652615014377.*

Lim, H. (2008). Infrastructure Development in Singapore, [Online] Available at *<http: / / s3.amazonaws.com / academia.edu.documents / 33826670 / No.2-part2-8.Singapore.pdf?AWSAccessKeyId=AKIAJ56TQJ RTWSMTNPEA&Expires=1471965935 & Signature=%2FYpCgBhTgU7XKC9%2FS%2BxtRPXMQqk%3D&response-content-disposition=inline%3B%20filename% 3DChapter_8_Infrastructure_Development_in.pdf>* Accessed on August 22, 2016

Liquete, C., Kleeschulte, S., Dige, G., Maes, J., Grizzetti, B., Olah, B. and Zulian, G. (2015).

Mapping green infrastructure based on ecosystem services and ecological networks: A Pan European case study, [Online] Available at *<https: / / www.youtube.com / watch?v=MzMbTtgNb-I&index=140&list=PLE63A8F8448CBD1F4>* Accessed on August 22, 2016

Maia, S., Teicher, H. and Meyboom, A. (2015). Infrastructure as social catalyst: Electric vehicle station planning and deployment, [Online] Available at *<http: / / www.sciencedirect.com / science / article / pii / S0040162515002826 >* Accessed on August 22, 2016.

Malekpour, S., Brown, R. and Haan, F. (2016). Strategic planning of urban infrastructure for environmental sustainability: Understanding the past to intervene for the future, [Online] Available at *<http: / / www.sciencedirect.com / science / article / pii / S0264275115000621.*

Park, S., Park, S. and Lee, S. (2016). Strategy on sustainable infrastructure asset management: Focus on Korea's future policy directivity, operation [Online] Available at *<http: / / www.sciencedirect.com / science / article / pii / S136403211630106X >*

Roelich, K., Knoeri, C., Steinberger, J.K., Varga, L., Blythe, P.T., Butler, D., Gupta, R., Harrison, G.P., Martin, C. and Purnell, P. (2015). Towards resource-efficient and service-oriented integrated infrastructure operation [Online] Available at *<http: / / www.sciencedirect.com / science / article / pii / S004016251400328X>* Accessed on August 22, 2016.

9

Phenomenological Experience of the Architectural and Urban Identity of Nicosia (North-Cyprus)

JUBRIL ATANDA[1]*

ABSTRACT

In the world today, to understand phenomenological character of a city its urban identity has to be experienced. In phenomenology of perception, experience is a flow of time or becoming. However, it becomes a process of connecting, articulating with no ground or intent. While experiencing a place it produces new events that elaborated new concept of sense and each perception therefore opens up to its own world. To experience a space Merleau Ponty depicts the human body as an expressive space, which contributes to the significance of personal actions, the body being the soul of expressive movement, and is a medium for perception of the world. A qualitative research method would be adopted, and the urban identity, will be considered by understanding Nicosia from the perspective of North-Cyprus through its architecture, historical lineage, cultural codes, ethnicity, and geographical location, which would be interpreted through a narrative with events, details and materials. A contrast between the old and new city: cultural, political and psychological experiences in a whole context will be exhibited. The overlapping cultural codes and transformation of identities between eras and ethnic influence will also be exhibited. Geographical mapping will be highly considered while defining Nicosia's urban identity. A case study research approach was adopted. First-hand observation, documentation, maps, images, master plans, will be imposed as guides to grasp the underlining identity of Nicosia. The experience gathered

[1]Department of Architecture Cyprus International University, Nicosia, Cyprus.
**Corresponding author*: E-mail: jatanda@ciu.edu.tr

will aid to improve the environment and range better possibilities for future projects in restoring the unique identity of the city.

Key words: Nicosia, Geographical-mapping, Narrative, Experience, Urban identity, Cultural codes, Phenomenology

---

1. INTRODUCTION

Nicosia, the capital of Cyprus for the last ten centuries with it, great architectural and urban theme has passed through different historical periods.

Nicosia is situated at the middle of Cyprus and it divides the north from the south, a landlocked city with historical relevance. The history of the city dates back to the Bronze Age. In antiquity and in early Christian times it was known as 'Ledra'. Since the late Byzantine era, Nicosia has been the capital of Cyprus. The Lusignans transformed it into a splendid town, with royal palaces and 50 churches. The city centre, the old "Chora", surrounded by 16th century walls, with museums, old churches and medieval buildings, maintains the leisurely atmosphere of yesteryear. Outside the walls, the modern town with its contemporary comforts pulsates to cosmopolitan rhythms. Nicosia remains the only divided capital in the world[1].

The urban identity can be easily experienced in the walled city of Nicosia, where different architectural, cultural, political and social events occurred for yesteryears. The old Nicosia (walls) represent different identities such as a city with two ethnic groups and two different region occupying a space with physical factors as narrow streets, rhythm arrangement of housing spaces within a context of a whole. The aim of this paper is to interpretive Nicosia as a narrative using geographical mapping to understand the historical multi-layers and its natural division between two ethnic groups. The image of portrayed about Nicosia as the only divided city in Europe, however, it is a city with two ethnic groups living side by side within the green line (buffer zone) which is occupied by UN. Therefore, the aim of this chapter to discover the architecture of the city, with traces of its historical uses and meaning, cultural, economical potentials to its present usage.

2. MULTI-LAYERED NARRATIVE OF NICOSIA

Nicosia is the largest city of Cyprus as well as the main business centre[2]. Nicosia is divided into the southern Greek Cypriot and the Northern Turkish Cypriot since 1954 after the Turkish invasion. The northern part of today, a pseudo-state, unrecognized internationally only by Turkey. Nicosia holds the main business centre, and was ranked 5th in 2012 as the world richest city in terms of purchasing power[3].

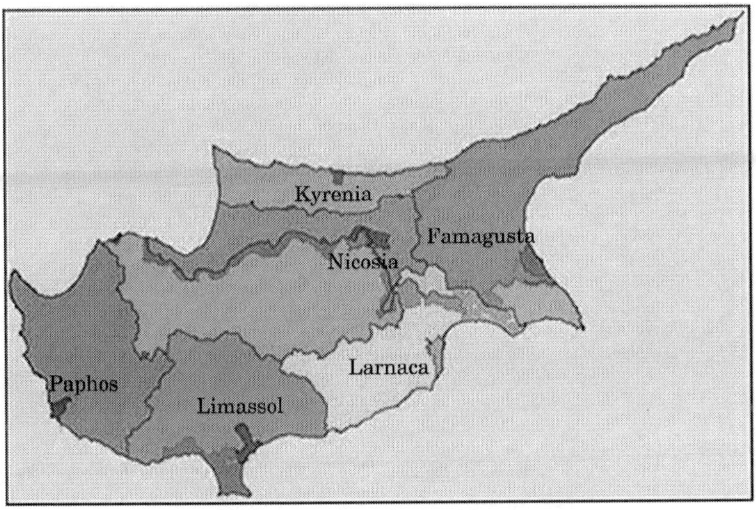

Fig. 1: Map of cyprus (Geographical location of Nicosia)[4]

Fig. 2: Map of Nicosia (1597)[5]

The walled city of Nicosia is one of the finest examples of medieval town planning, dates back to the Venetian period (1489–1571). The renaissance walls comprises of 11 bastion and three gates namely: Kyrenia gate, Famagusta gate and Paphos gate which were built to consolidate the town.

Fig. 3: Current master plan of Nicosia[6]

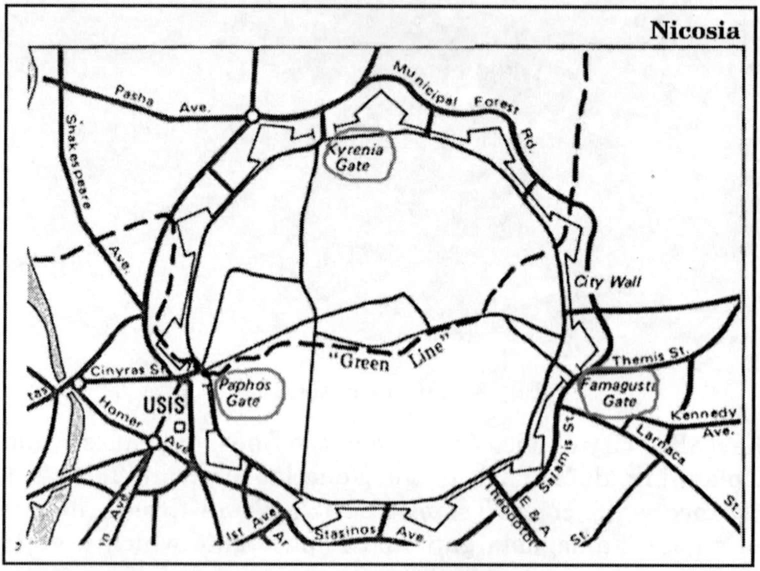

Fig. 4: Geographical location of the gates in the walled city of Nicosia[7]

The Ottoman period (1571–1878), saw the transformation of the city to a modern capital, with improvement of infrastructure and quality residential homes. However, Nicosia is not divided by this area, but by two major communities (Turks and Greeks) occupying the living areas, which were defined due to their religious centers: the Turks were located around the mosques, while the Greeks developed around the Greek Orthodox churches[8]. During the British colonial period (1878–1960), urban density in Nicosia increased[9]. The expansion of administrative, commercial and marketing functions led to the growth of suburban growth outside the city wall and along main roads[10]. Nicosia grew rapidly after the Second World War, with the population reaching 100,000 in the early 1960s. Between 1946 and 1965, the city also became more prosperous and both major ethnic communities added new residential districts outside the city walls.

Nicosia, bounded by two ethnic communities established their own independent local authorities in 1958 and work together till 1960. The political struggles in between both communities divided the city by the 'Green Line' in 1963 and the buffer zone has been established since 1974[11]. The buffer zone crosses the heart of the walled city, forming a lifeless corridor and disrupting the city's cohesion along with political, demographic and socio-economic changes, the buffer zone caused the growth of development of the outside the city wall due to the deteriorating rate of the place as a space for living. Inappropriate new function and lifestyle with different tradition started to prevail in the walled city of Nicosia. The changes greatly affected the urban identity, cultural codes of the walled city of Nicosia with physical decay, population reduction, social marginalization, loss of economic quality, wasteful land use as highlighted by Zetter[12].

Figs. 5, 6 and 7: Showing the multi-layered architecture of Nicosia

The Lusignan house of the 15th century. The British Law House of the colonial area, and the Gothic church St. Catherine which is now know has Haydar Pasha Mosque. This shows a city with a multi-layered architectural identity which spans far and wide to define the cities true identity.

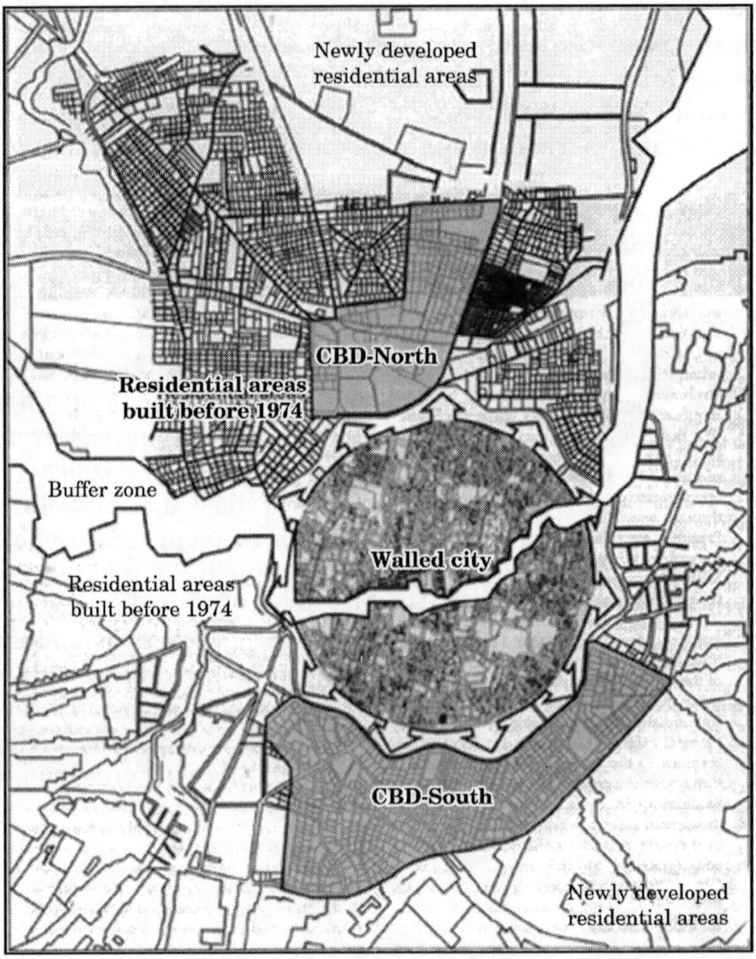

Fig. 8: The current urban structure of Nicosia[13]

3. DISCOVERING THE URBAN IDENTITY OF WALLED CITY OF NICOSIA (NORTH CYPRUS)

Nicosia has a unique architectural style, which shows different architectural period of conquerors (Byzantine, Frankish, Venetian, Ottoman and the British rule). The pattern of settlement in Nicosia around these areas (Fig. 9) are characterized by narrow streets, squares, palace, churches, mosques, rhythm of opening and closing, urban character of houses and shops, use of material (stone, yellow brick). These depicts and urban identity, where the contrast between the interior and exterior spaces, balance and instability, continuous and streamlined nature of the streetscape are expressed. As a result of this, the old city provides a clue of togetherness, belonging and wholeness, which gives the city an identity and harmony[14]. All these concepts formed a multi-layered structure of meaning which helps facilitates the reading of Nicosia as a narrative and understanding its architecture.

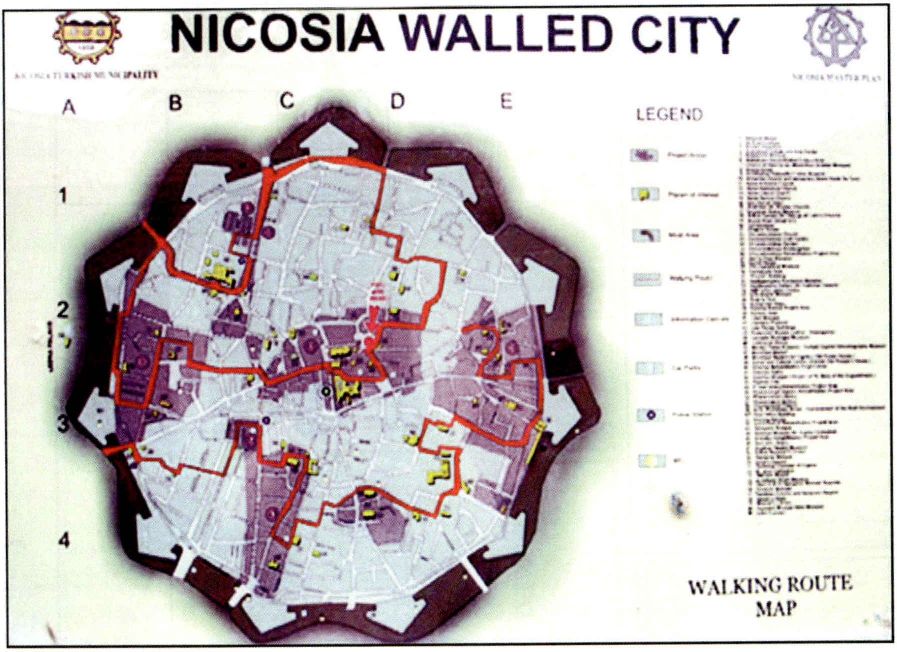

Fig. 9: Walled City Map

Utilizing geographical mapping as a method, aides the ideas of narration while experiencing Nicosia and reading its urban content and could be utilized as devices for setting up another urban map. This can convey the experience of the city with the proper stream and versatility in cooperation with diverse rates and intensities. Inside this domain, voids and stops are made, where the look cannot reach and where access is denied. Decisively in this moderate typical space, new hypothetical apparatuses can be presented, with the aspiration to catch the intricacy of contemporary urban conditions, narrative as content, picture and time arrangement.

According to De Certeau "every story reflects a spatial practice, organized by local displacements (as a moving point describes a curve), capable of constructing urban plots that transform their experience as representation – replacing the map with text, the urban narrative"[15]. Walking around the city with the sense of urban space helps compose the urban narrative and identity of the city.

While Observing and experiencing the quality of life in the walled city by analyzing it deep ecology both its urban identity and architectural and cultural patterns. The housing typologies that are of Gothic and Ottoman architecture; to name a few, Selimiye Mosque, the Bedesten, the Great Inn (Buyuk Ilan) have been renewed to serve the interest of urban regeneration. Experiencing the texture and rhythm of the walled city with historical landmarks, building that dates from 18th century, which were made of building material like wood, sandstone, and mud bricks, they are orchestrated with narrow winding streets, combing residential houses with craft shops and tavernas. Samanbahce area in the walled city was known for its growing fruits and vegetable for residents, the Samanbahce developed into a social housing complex, a unique neighborhood with defined geometric narrow roads, units are made of strong mud brick construction with red tile roofs[16].

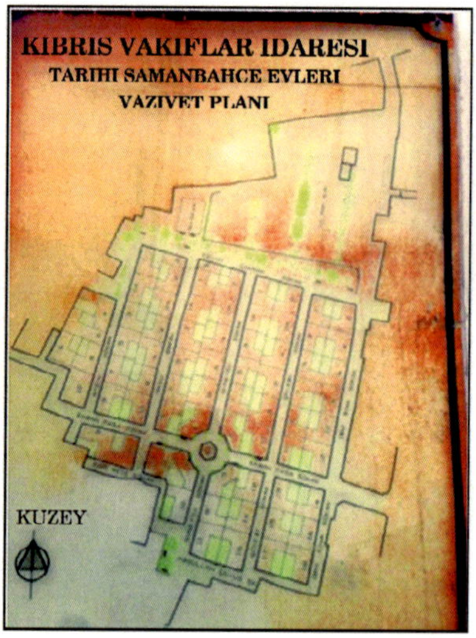

Fig.10: Map of Samanbache

Selimeye mosque originally a Roman Catholic cathedral - the oldest and one of the finest examples of Gothic architecture in Cyprus, having a monumental main door with carved stone window above it gives it a significant look. Buyuk Han a traditional market centre within the wall, originally built to provide accommodation for traveler's from Anatolia and other parts of Cyprus. After it restoration it has become a well-planned two storey building consisting of 68 rooms which are opened to the vaulted galleries surrounding a square courtyard, with an Ottoman masjid standing on marble pier, and a fountain beneath it in the centre of the courtyard[17]. The Ataturk square locally known as Sarayonu house the hub of Turkish life in Nicosia since the ottoman conquest. In the centre of the square lives a Venetian column which was move from salamis to Nicosia. The square is found of having small scale shops around it with sitting areas like a communal arrangement, it is flanked the side with a hotel (Saray) and a Mosque (Sarayonu Mosque)[18].

Fig. 11: Street of Samanbache

Fig.12: Selimeye mosque

Several restorations have occurred in Nicosia since the Nicosia Master Plan was commemorated in 1979 to help reignite the city's identity. The continuous division of the central Nicosia is central to many ongoing problems. The division restricts development and imposes common frameworks. The division stimulated a process of outward growth away from the core of the city, which leads to underlying neglect of housing area in the historic core, cultural identity, urban identity and social value are lost. However since the walled city is not integrated with newly developed section of Nicosia on either, the main public spaces in the historic core no longer serve as central plazas, and also rapid growth of urban sprawl, haphazard and scattered settlements, unused spaces improper land use and practices has created an undulating commercial, recreational, industrial and service pattern. The walled city once a vital and prosperous environment has grown to be an isolated environment by both ethnic communities with shop, wholesale unit's inhabitants with no ties with its past or tradition. However, restorations are done with the right material and technique to restore historical building within the wall.

Fig.13: Buyuk Han

Fig. 14: Venetian Column

To define the urban identity of Nicosia, it can be said to be 'kitsch' where the phenomenon of kitsch can be used to show the relationship between the subjects (people) and object (Nicosia city). According to Celikel in her paper "Kitsch as an aesthetical Category" using mediate desire "... we desire what others desire because we imitate their desire but confuse it with ours..."[19]. Nicosia can be seen as a city, which imitates its urban identity from its father-nations (Greeks and Turks) and confusing it with theirs. Therefore, "Kitsch represents falsehood...this falsehood falls back on the person in the need of it, on the person who uses this considerate mirror so as to be able to recognize himself in the counterfeit image..."[20].

4. CONCLUDING REMARKS

Due to its resources like copper and agricultural produce, as well as its geostrategic location at the crossroads of Europe, Central Asia, and the Middle East, Cyprus (Nicosia) has been attractive to a host of foreign conquerors with multiple invasions as the result which has slightly limits creating a certain urban identity. Conqueror ruled and provides different administrative, buildings, ways of life and urban character. However with this effect, the urban identity cannot be visible as a whole but can be as separate homogenous and distinctive ethnic communities occupying the city, helps modify their cultural codes, social life and identity.

In the northern part of Nicosia, with the Turks occupying the area and a small population of Turkish Cypriot, the identity of the city are being preserved with new uses accompanying them *e.g.*, Kumarcilar Han which is been restored to house 44 shop units, and will be rented to traders for selling authentic local products[21] and many more constructed and under construction.

Fig. 15: Kumarcilar front-view

Fig. 16: Kumarcilar side view

The holistic understanding on Nicosia, in light of its historical and architectural identities influenced it urban identity. Geographical mapping helped configure the city, photographic images and maps were used to show the narrative reading of the city. Thus this research creates and opened ended discussion were the study of Nicosia has no starting point nor endpoint and its open to new improved ideas in order to create a self-urban identity of the city. The narrative experience of a non-linear process, in which the city shifted from period to period created a relation to each other and formed a trace to the periodical influence of conqueror while responding to the changes in the city. One can easily see the effect of the Nicosia division with two unique ethnic communities dominating the north and south spectrums. It is possible to create a new identity by preserving Nicosia's locality and architect and urban planners reading the city as a narrative while developing new building that would be incorporated to the present identity. Revealing the city as kitsch that imbibes its urban identity from father-nations (Greeks and Turks) and confusing it with theirs, would be resolved when proper a planning and understanding of it current pattern become clear as a narration to its locals.

REFERENCES

[1] Historical analyses of Cyprus (2007). See; Cyprus tourism organization Cyprus: 1000 Years of history and civilization. The history of Cyprus organized by a group, historical text by Dr. Sofia Antoniadou, translated in English by Marina Christofidou. Ankat Publications Ltd.

[2] Oktay Derya (2005). "Cyprus: The South and the North". *In*: Ronald Van Kempen, Marcel Vermeulen and Baan Ad (*eds.*), urban issues and urban policies in the new EU countries. Ash gate Publishing, Ltd., p. 207.

[3] An analysis of most expensive and richest cities in the world (2015). "World's richest cities by purchasing power". City Mayors.2011. *www.citymayors.com/ economics/usb-purchasing-power.html.*

[4] Showing cities of Cyprus (2015). *www.wikipeida.org.*

[5] Map of Nicosia by Giacomo Franco created in (1597). *www.en.wikipedia.org/ wili/nicoisa.* Retrieved 9 January 2015.

[6] Master plan of Nicosia done by the Master plan team while rehabilitating the walled city of Nicosia, *www.akdn.org.* Retrieved 9 January 2015.

[7] Showing the gates of Nicosia which surround the walled city *http:// images.nationmaster.com/images/motw/world_cities/nicosia.jpg*

[8] Diaz-Berio, S. (1982). 'Urban Conservation' Nicosia Master Plan (Unpublished Report) Nicosia. UNDP-UNCHS.

[9] Demi, D. (1990). 'The walled city of Nicosia: A typology study', Nicosia Master Plan (Unpublished Report). Nicosia: UNDP.

[10] Zetter, R. (1985). 'City profile: Nicosia'. *Cities,* 2(1): 24–33.

[11] After the bloody ethnic violence in 1956, a barbed wire fence was erected to separate the Greek and Turkish communities in Nicosia. See Papadakis, Y. 'Nicosia after 1960: A river, a bridge and a dead zone', GMJ: Mediterranean Edition, 1, 1, Spring, 2006.

[12] Zetter, R. (1985). 'City profile: Nicosia', pp. 24–33.

[13] The current urban structure of Nicosia (2008). From, Oktay Derya' An Analysis and review of the divided city of Nicosia, Cyprus and New perspectives. *The Geographical Association*, 93(1).

[14] Reading Nicosia as a narrative, understanding its narrow street, urban character and urban identity (2014). *In*: Respect to understanding the deep urban identity of a city's social, political, cultural and global layers. See, Semra Aydinli and Avsar Karababa. Urban Identity in Globalization: Bushehr, Iran. *In*: Architecture and Globalization in the Persian Gulf Region (*eds.*), Prof. Nasser Golzari and Prof. Murray Fraser.

[15] De Certeau, Michel (1984). The Practice of Everyday Life, trans. Steven Rendall, Berkeley: University of California Press, p. 120.

[16] One of the oldest housing schemes in the walled city of the northern side of Nicosia. See, "The Samanbahce Area, Nicosia, Welcome to *Www.whatson-northcyprus.com*, A Guide to North Cyprus". Accessed January 14, 2015. *http:/ /www.whatson-northcyprus.com/interest/nicosia/north_nicosia/samanba hce.htm.*

[17] One of the most important architectural projects of the Ottoman Era. Built for travelers. See, "Buyuk Han (Great Inn), Nicosia, North Cyprus". Welcome to *www.whatson-northcyprus.com*, a Guide to North Cyprus. Accessed January 14, 2015. *http://www.whatson-northcyprus.com/interest/nicosia/north_nicosia /buyuk_han.htm.*

[18] The Centre Square in the Northern Nicosia (2015). See, "Ataturk Square and Venetian Column, Nicosia, North Cyprus. "Welcome to *www.whatson-northcyprus.com*, a Guide to North Cyprus. *http://www.whatsonnorthcyprus.com/interest/nicosia/north_nicosia/ataturk_square.htm.*
[19] Celikel, B. "Kitsch as an aesthetical Category".
[20] Broch, H. (1950). Notes on the problem of kitsch. *In*: Kitsch: The world of bad taste, (*ed.*) Gillo Dorfles. Universe Books, New York, pp. 49–67.
[21] An Ottoman era commercial Inn, been resorted presently (2015). See, "The Kumarcilar Han (Gamblers' Inn), Nicosia, North Cyprus." Welcome to *www.whatson-northcyprus.com*, a Guide to North Cyprus. *http://www.whatson northcyprus.com/interest/nicosia/north_nicosia/kumarcilar.htm.*

10

The Metrics for the Framework of Sustainable Development: The Study Case in Science and Technology Federal Institutes in Southern of Brazil[1]

Rafael Gustavo de Lima[1*], Elisete Dahmer Pfitscher[1], Vittor Soares Rocha[1] and José Baltazar Salgueirinho Osório de Andrade Guerra[1]

ABSTRACT

For the purposes of this article, the study creates and applies a sustainability assessment model for ICT's (SIAS / ICT) in Southern of Brazil combining the metric of the GRI (Global Reporting Initiative) , the A3P (Environmental Agenda in Public Administration) and ISCN (International Sustainable Campus Network). The methodology according to the objectives it's considered descriptive and exploratory. For the technical procedures was adopted in literature and multi case study for the problem of approach, qualitative and quantitative. The methodology follows three phases: theoretical framework and conceptual approaches; proposition of sustainability assessment model (SICOGEA - Accounting System Environmental Management); multicase study and comparative analysis of the results. In the end, it's possible to demonstrate the sustainability promoted by Institutes of Science and Technology (ICTs) through a qualitative and quantitative system organized in questions for assessing sustainability in ICT's, and to identify trends, rankings and importance relative to each dimension (economic, social and environmental) for the same modeling. In numbers, the ICT's national surveyed reflect the care of 58.04% for Brazil, composed of 58 contributions from ICT's national southern Brazil (IFSC, IFRS, IFPR).

---

[1]Researcher at Saint Catherine Federal University (or, in Portuguese, UFSC – Universidade Federal de Santa Catarina)

**Corresponding author*: E-mail: rafael.lima@ufsc.br

This study is very important for decision makers in ICT's and even provides subsidies for public policy makers, providing a sense of direction for new alternatives and better understanding. The index of sustainability of ICTs in southern Brazil indicates 58.04% (regular).

Key words: Institute of science and technology, IFSC, IFPR, IFRS, Sustainability, Evaluation model of sustainability, GRI, A3P, ISCN, SICOGEA

INTRODUCTION

Currently, international and national efforts of governments and companies around the world translate to a large extent, by concerns over the use of natural resources the planet is exposed continuously. Added to this, the concern for efficiency and cost-effectiveness of the measures implemented by the same actors, in favor of social objectives, processes that create or interact to achieve their goals, not forgetting to mention the growing environmental concern that is gaining space in government and corporate agendas. In this sense, the twentieth and twenty-first centuries (especially) several authors and opinion makers (Bruseke, 1994; Sachs, 1993; Coral, 2002; Brundtland, 1987) discuss new ways to improve processes and offer products in a sustainable way, integrating and making compatible the economic, social and environmental areas.

The theme of sustainable development and sustainability starts conducting a series of international studies from the mid-twentieth century (Louette, 2008). In addition to the reconfiguration of classic perceptions about development, there is the need to build reliable and internationally recognized indicators that capture the sustainability of institutions around the world. And although there are some evaluation methodologies of international sustainability few of them are complete, in the question of including the social, economic and environmental aspects (Louette, 2008; Singh, 2012; Epstein, 2004). According to Singh (2012) the majority of sustainability assessment methods emphasize on just one or two aspects of the assessment, leaving a distorted result. Ness (2007) adds that efforts should be made to combine more than one assessment tool seeking to have a more integrated and transparent model (Epstein, 2004; Ness, 2007). Supplying this gap, the method used in this study (SIAS/ICT) integrate three aspects involved on the concept of sustainability from three different metrics: GRI (Global Reporting Initiative), A3P (Environmental Agenda in Public Administration) and ISCN - (International Sustainable Campus Network).

According to Epstein (2004) large companies and organizations have sought to understand the management and control systems to implement the necessary goals. Internal communication and disclosures should be part of an integrated system that includes governance, indicators, reports, control and management systems.

This study is very important for decision makers in ICT's and even provides subsidies for public policy makers, providing a sense of direction for new alternatives and better understanding in operational terms. According to Van Bellen (2008) the main purpose of measurement is to assist decision makers in evaluating their performance against established objectives, providing basis for planning future actions.

In the first section will be briefly addressed the concept of sustainability; the second section will present the model used for assessing sustainability in ICT's (SIAS/ICT). Finally, the third section will present the results of applying the model in southern Brazil that will allow exposure our findings.

1. SUSTAINABILITY

Think the concept of sustainability is a constant challenge that makes necessary that environmentalists, businessmen, statesmen and opinion makers, researchers and scientists from various fields and interests discuss the impact of their practices and decisions on society and the environment. In this sense, in recent decades, occurs in several countries the dissemination and broad international debate of values, principles, norms and rules that assist in the process of forming a recognized and shared concept internationally.

Before start the presentation of data, it's interesting to clarify a recurring question regarding the terminology. Often the terms "sustainable development" and "sustainability" carry a very close meanings.

The literature makes few caveats regarding the differentiation of terms, but makes it clear that in most cases the first one relates to "an economic model, political, social, cultural and balanced environmental, that [meet] the needs of current generations without compromising the ability of future generations to meet their own needs" (Our Common Future, 1989). And sustainability is brought as an action that does not compromise the existence of their sources, in order to ensure their reproduction (Faria, 2011).

The two expressions deal with the integration of social, economic and environmental dimensions in order to ensure the effectiveness of their proposals through the efficient use of resources and processes. The scheme of Fig. 1, also known as *Triple Bottom Line*, and seeks to link the expressions and make visible the inter-relationship of the dimensions cited to illustrate the concept of sustainability:

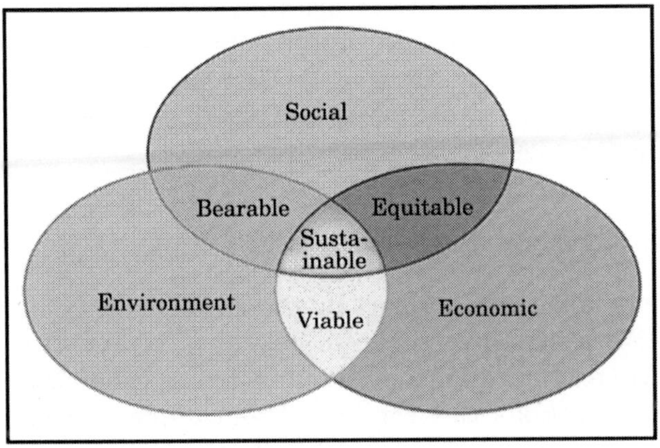

Fig. 1: Dimensions of sustainable development/sustainability. *Source*: Adams, 2006.

The theoretical framework of sustainability brings with it the need of the current civilization re-adapt to new consumption patterns. This need must take into consideration projections of future resource shortages and the productivity increases and economic efficiency (Coral, 2002), as indicated by geopolitical studies that are based on forecasts for the next few decades (Global Trends 2030, 2013). According to these studies, demographic patterns, based on aging populations in developed countries/developing and a global demand for resources could lead the planet to a general crisis (Global Trends, 2030, 2013). Prepare the individuals and institutions around the world to deal with these limitations require the need to measure the sustainability of its practical actions.

2. BUILDING A SUSTAINABILITY ASSESSMENT MODEL: SIAS/ICT

There are a considerable number of activities seeking to develop standards and indexes, monitor them and reporting social and environmental issues for stakeholders. The main purpose of the indicators is to assist decision makers about the researched object performance. This must encompass a wide range of factors that are related to sustainability, such as the ecological, economic, social, cultural and institutional apart from others. Another point is that sustainability indicators should relate to lapses last time past/present/future to have practical utility in decision making and in the choice of political alternatives (Van Bellen, 2005; Singh, 2012; Ness, 2007; Epstein, 2004).

The model to be used for assessing sustainability in selected ICT's, which we will indicate by the acronym SIAS/ICT - International System of Sustainability Assessment (in original, *Sistema Internacional de Avaliação de Sustentabilidade*) applied to Science and Technology Institutes will include contributions of GRI guidelines, A3P and ISCN as will be detailed next, plus, clarify and use the structure of SICOGEA 3 Generation.

2.1 GRI (Global Reporting Initiative)

One of the tools selected to support this research is the Global Reporting Initiative (GRI) a non-governmental organization founded in 1997 by CERES (Centre for Education and Research in Environmental Strategies) and the United Nations Environment Programme (UNEP). Currently composed by a multi-stakeholder network, the GRI has the mission of producing internationally guidelines for the preparation of sustainability reports by entities of all kinds around the world (GRI, 2013).

2.2 A3P (Environmental Agenda in Public Administration)

In addition to the contributions raised during the research and the GRI guidelines, are used some indicators related to the commitment of the Environment of the Federal Public Administration Agenda (A3P), formulated by the Ministry of Environment (MMA), for government sustainability, the ICT's in Brazil are managed by the Brazilian public initiative (MMA - A3P, 2009). The Table 2 shows the aspects considered by A3P.

2.3 ISCN

Another source of contribution to research is to consider the ISCN network - International Sustainable Campus Network which currently brings together, on five continents, sixty-seven education institutions, including Universities, Science and Technology Institutes, Polytechnics and colleges in general (ISCN, 2013, p. 04):

The idea that guides the International Network of Sustainable Campus (ISCN) is to provide a global forum to support colleges, universities, technology institutes and corporate campuses in the exchange of information and best practices to achieve sustainable operations on campus and integrate the theme of sustainability in research and education as presented in Fig. 2 (ISCN, 2013, p. 04).

Table1: Catagories and aspects in the guidelines

Category	***Economic***			***Environmental***
Aspects	• Economic Performance • Market Presence • Indirect Economic Impacts • Procurement Practices • Emissions • Effluents and Waste • Products and Services • Compliance • Transport • Overall • Supplier environmental assessment • Environmental grievance mechanisms			• Materials • Energy • Water • Biodiversity
Category	***Social***			
Sub-Categories	***Labor practices and decent work***	***Human rights***	***Society***	***Product responsibility***
Aspects	• Employment	• Investment	• Local communities	• Customer health and safety
	• Labor / management relations	• Non-discrimination	• Anti-corruption	
	• Occupational health and safety	• Freedom of association and collective bargaining	• Public policy • Anti-competitive Behavior	• Product and service labeling • Marketing communications
	• Training and education	• Child labor	• Compliance	
	• Diversity and equal opportunity	• Forced or compulsory labor	• Supplier assessment for impacts on society	• Customer privacy • Compliance
	• Equal remuneration for women and men	• Security practices • Indigenous rights	• Grievance mechanisms for impacts on society	
	• Supplier assessment for labor practices	• Assessment • Suppler human rights assessment		
	• Labor practices grievance mechanism	• Human rights grievance mechanisms		

Source: GRI 2013c –Economical, Environmental and Social Categories

Table 2: A3P guidelines

Environmental agenda in public administration	Rational use of natural resources / combating waste	Paper consumption Energy consumption. Plastic cups consumption
(A3P)	Waste management	Implementation of selective collection.
	Awareness and training	Training plan preparation and training of the management committee of A3P.
	Life quality in the workplace	Implementation of life quality programs, health and safety at work.
	Sustainable procurement	Whenever possible, purchases are made goods and materials, service contracts and environmentally sustainable projects.

Source: Adapted from MMA - A3P, 2009.

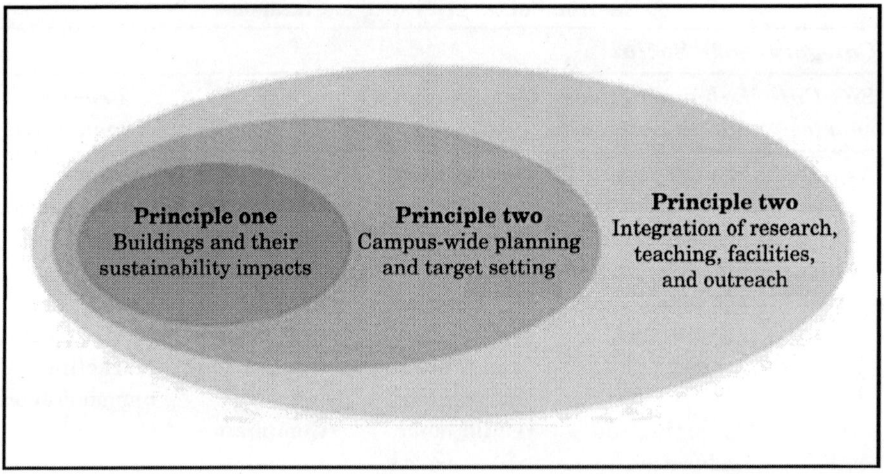

Fig. 2: Principles ISCN. *Source:* Adapted from ISCN, 2013, p. 03

2.4 SICOGEA

SICOGEA is originated by the study of Pfitscher (2004), which reflects the evolution of GAIA (Environmental Impact Aspects Management) method created by Lerípio (2001). From the SICOGEA are observed two evolutions of the model. The first one that comes up with the improvement of the evaluation model is known as SICOGEA –2 Generation, with Nunes (2010). Reshapes the model from a focus on two methods, GAIA and SICOGEA is in order to find strengths and weaknesses in a process of continuous improvement of methods and suggesting a new method. Uhlmann (2011), after analyzing the SICOGEA 2 Generation and its applications, creates the SICOGEA 3 Generation. In this version, there is no significant changes in structure itself that have appointed to changes in the indices calculation methodology environmental sustainability. However, the SICOGEA – 3 Generation shows the inclusion and reorganization of the actions, in order to enhance the results and facilitate the deployment of the system.

According Pfitscher (2004), SICOGEA - Accounting Environmental Management System, aims to operationalize the analysis of the sustainability in organizations through indicators on environmental, social and economic aspects, as well verify the environmental impacts and support decision-making by managers. The objective of SICOGEA is the environmental aspects management with a view to the sustainability of resources and processes of the organization. In this sense, SICOGEA is broad in the way it address a number of issues surrounding, since the integration of a supply chain, management, internal processes and resources used by the organization for their specific purposes. It is worth noting that the methodology being developed for ICT's focus on managing and features control process (Step 3 SICOGEA), this step is the one used for measure the sustainability of elements. Gathered at SIAS/ICT guidelines of the three metrics will be used the structure of SICOGEA Generation 3 as shows Table 3

Table 3: SICOGEA steps

Steps	*Designation*	*Observation*
Step 01	Integrating the production chain	Identify the production process, the main needs and the possible harm to the environment.
Step 02	Ecological control management	Check which parts of the organization that may be causing environmental impacts.
Step 03	Management of environmental accounting and controllership	Measure the economic, financial and operational aspects, in order to obtain new forms of contribution to the environment.

Source: Adapted from Pfitscher, 2004.

2.5 SIAS/ICT

From these contributions, Pieri *et al.* (2011) provides an evaluation framework - used by the model proposed for the evaluation of ICT's in order to establish a metric able to gather the information in the table, and establish a level of sustainability for each of the proposed criteria. Thus, it's possible to apply to local realities international guidelines arising from the GRI with the SICOGEA application methodology in order to propose a new sustainability assessment model for ICTs which falls within the quantitative level value of sustainability that lacks the methodology GRI in its windows and reporting format. This model will allow (for quantitative and qualitative means) calculate what extent and in which dimensions (economic, environmental, social) selected ICTs contribute to support the set of norms, rules and principles that are internationally disseminated in relation to sustainability.

At the end of the survey, it's possible to check what extent, in what dimensions and which ways ICT's contributes in the formation of a system of sustainability.

The SIAS/ICT is replaced in order to manage socio-economic and environmental aspects of resources and organizational processes, in order to support decision-making by managers in ensuring the sustainability of ICT.

For schematic purposes, the SIAS/ICT is divided into 301 questions to ICT's and into three stages: Economic, Environmental and Social/ Institutional. Table 4 shows the assembly steps for the SIAS/ICT, with the use of categories deriving from GRI, A3P and ISCN. As a result, you can understand how the system is structured in order to measure/ calculate quantitatively the sustainability of selected ICT's.

Schematically, the evaluation format used by SIAS/ICT establishes a metric able to combine the information in the table, and indicates a level of sustainability for each of the proposed indicators, according to the methodology of SICOGEA 3 Generation. Table 5 exemplifies the model structure in your Step 1, called Environmental Indicator, referring to the aspect of "energy".

Thus, it is possible to apply international guidelines arising from the GRI and ISCN and national (A3P) to ICT's selected, in combination with the application of methodology of SICOGEA - Generation 3, proposing a new sustainability assessment model for ICT's(SIAS/ICT) which falls within the quantitative value of the degree of sustainability.

The model has 301 questions posed to specific leaders of ICT of entity management. Furthermore, for each point there is the possibility of measuring the degree of sustainability in directions ranging from 0 to 100%, which relate to the results ranging from "Good" to "poorly". It is also possible to reverse a question, in which case the minimum (0%) corresponds to the "Great", requiring it to insert the words "S" in "Reverse Response" column. Another possibility to answer refers to the "NS" (nothing shown) that can be used when data are not available or cannot quantify an answer. The model in its entirety can be analyzed on thorough research and for now, Table 6 seeks to illustrate how to structure the evaluation of the proposed model:

Table 4: SIAS/ICT steps

Steps	***Performance indicators***		***Aspects considered***
Step 01	Economical (GRI-G4)		Economic performance; market presence; indirect economic impacts; purchasing practices.
Step02	Environmental (GRI-G4)		Materials; energy; water; biodiversity; emissions; effluents and waste; products and services; conformity; general; supplier environmental assessment; complaints mechanisms and complaints related to environmental impacts.
Step 03	Social/ Institutional	Decent labor practices (GRI-G4)	Employment; working relationships; health and safety at work; training and education; diversity and equal opportunities; equal remuneration between men and women; supplier evaluation on labor practices; complaints mechanisms and complaints related to labor practices.
		Human rights (GRI-G4)	Investment; non-discrimination; freedom of association and collective bargaining; child labor; forced or compulsory labor; safety practices; indigenous rights; evaluation; supplier evaluation in human rights; mechanisms complaints and claims related to human rights.
		Society(GRI-G4)	Local communities; combating corruption; public policy; unfair-competition further; conformity; supplier evaluation on impacts on society; complaints mechanisms and complaints related to impacts on society.
		Responsibility for product/ service (GRI-G4)	Customer health and safety; labeling of products and services; marketing communications; customer privacy; conformity.
		Institutional (A3P)	Rational use of natural/combating waste resources; waste management; awareness and training; life quality in the workplace; and sustainable procurement.
		Institutional (ISCN)	Constructions and sustainable impact; planning on campus and targets; and integration of research, teaching, and extension facilities

Source: Adapted from GRI-G4, ISCN and A3P

Table 5: SIAS/ICT questions

Performance indicator	*Aspect*	*Description*	*Questions*
Environmental (GRI - G4)	Energy	Direct energy consumption by primary energy source; Indirect energy consumption by primary source; energy saved due to improvements in conservation and efficiency; initiatives to provide low power consumption products and services;	32 Is it made maintenance and inspection of the institution's equipment in order to ensure environmental quality? 33 Is it given priority to purchase products that contribute to lower power consumption (saving light bulbs ...)? 34 There is use of alternative sources of energy? 35 The institution has electricity savings? 36 The service provides requires a high energy consumption?

Source: Elaborated by the authors and GRI data.

Table 6: SIAS/ICT measurements

Questions	*Reverse answer (S)*	*0 %* 0	*20 %* 1	*40 %* 2	*60 %* 3	*80 %* 4	*100 %* 5	*—* NS	*Possible scores*	*Obtained scores*	*Total scores*	*Sustainability Results*	*Sustainability Rating*
1 Question 15	S	X							1	0%	1	100,0%	Great
2 Question 16				X					1	40%	0,4	40,0%	Poor
3 Question 17					X				1	60%	0,6	60,0%	Regular
4 Question 18							X		3	100%	3	100,0%	Great
5 Question 19								X	3	NC	0	0,0%	–
6 Question 20			X						3	20%	0,6	20,0%	Bad
Subtotal		1	1	1	1	1	2	1	17	243%	10	58,8%	Regular

Source: Adapted from Pfitscher and Pieri *et al.,* 2011.

For the building of the evaluation model (SIAS/ICT) there is the combination of contributions coming from the Global Reporting Initiative (GRI); the principles of ISCN (International Sustainable Campus

Network); the guidelines of the Environmental Agenda in Public Administration (A3P) of Brazil, in addition to having the assessment framework proposed by SICOGEA Generation 3.

The qualitative results ranging from "Good" to "Poor" following the SICOGEA 3 Generation references as indicated in Table 7. In other words, the respondent enters your information into the model, which calculates the "degree" of effectiveness on the part of ICT's in relation to what is asked.

Table 7: Possible performances

STI status	***Degree***	***Score***
For the STI that presents *no* investment/control over the issue evaluated.	No	0 or 0%
For the STI that presents *weak* investment/control over the issue evaluated.	Weak	1 or 20%
For the STI that presents *low* investment/control, a little more than the item before, over the issue evaluated.	Low	2 or 40%
For the STI that d presents *some* investment/control, a little more than the item before, over the issue evaluated.	Some	3 or 60%
For the STI that presents *strong* investment/control, almost total, over the issue evaluated.	Strong	4 or 80%
For the STI that presents total *high level* investment/control over the issue evaluated.	High level	5 or 100%

Source: Adapted from Pfitscher and Pieri *et al.,* 2011.

Having the data collected, the SIAS/ICT requires that researchers attribute values, weights or "possible points" in order to establish a relevant metric for each question asked. According to the definitions of Pfitscher (2009) cited Pieri *et al.* (2011), these values represent the judgment of the researcher, so the author recommends to follow a single procedure to avoid deviations that compromise the work, the author also suggests establish a standard scale for assigning weights to maintain a certain degree of compatibility and comparison between categories.

The SICOGEA 3 Generation draws this standard scale and indicates numerical values of reference (0–3), keeping the connection to the following qualitative aspects relation to the verifying of sustainability as shown in Table 8:

These "possible points" are faced with the respondent's information, resulting in a "score obtained", this is the respondent information graduated by the importance that research indicates to the existing situation. The scores now, indicate, on the column "Sustainability >review" a qualitative value (as shown in Table 8) corresponding to the methodology of SICOGEA–3 Generation, with adaptations related to this research in particular, which are described in Table 9:

Table 8: Possible points

Possible scores	***Characteristic of the question***
0	Situation verified that neither impacts on the environment nor influences much on the category under analysis.[1]
1	Situation verified with low environmental impact and/or low social responsibility and/or low level of economic influence for the category under analysis[2]
2	Situation verified with medium environmental impact and/or medium social responsibility and/or medium level of economic influence for the category under analysis[3]
3	Situation verified with high environmental impact and/or high social responsibility and/or high level of economic influence for the category under analysis[4]

Source: Adapted from Pfitscher and Pieri *et al.,* 2011.

Table 9: Possible performances SIAS/ICT

Result	***Sustainability***	***Performance (control, incentive, strategy)***
Under 20%	"Terrible"	There is not practical institutional concern; great negative impact is caused on the *category under analysis*
Between 20.01% to 40%	"Weak"	There is damage for the sustainability of the *category under analysis,* but there are few positive initiatives.
Between 40.01% a 60%	"Regular"	The sustainability legislation is attended concerning the *category under analysis*
Between 60.01% a 80%	"Good"	Legislation is not the only concern; there are projects and internal attitudes that aim to value the concern with the *category under analysis.*
Over 80%	"Excellent"	High appreciation of the *category under analysis,* in the sense of predicting damage and making participants aware of sustainable conducts.

Source: Adapted from Pfitscher and Pieri *et al.,* 2011.

From this, the SIAS/ICT reaches the function to quantify the qualitative responses, and at the end indicates that institutional weaknesses situations are verified. And seek sustainability or institutional advantages that contribute to the sustainability of the analyzed category. Thus, it allows the broad concept, some qualitative and some "palpable" facts turns sustainability on a world-class discussion (structural level) and it's checked at the level of organizations (level units) in the three model steps - which relate directly to the three conceptual dimensions of sustainability (economic, environmental, social).

In this sense, and having presented the model structure, it is evident the possibility of verifying the sustainability of selected ICTs in order to meet in a unique methodology to national and international guidelines presented (GRI, ISCN and A3P) in order to check in which dimensions and which ways ICT's contribute to the formation of an international regime of sustainability, That is, if the ICT's include in their practical actions norms prescriptions proposed by an international regime on sustainability in formation.

3. ANALYSIS OF RESULTS: SOUTHERN BRAZIL

In this section, the quantitative data are available by SIAS/ICT in their application to the case of southern Brazil. The ICT's we analyzed by this survey are a part of a Federal Network of Professional Education, Science and Technology that covers all Brazilian states. According to official information, these institutes, linked to the Ministry of Education (MEC), offers technical courses, higher education in technology, graduation, master's graduation and doctoral degrees in Brazil (Rfept, 2014). For the purposes of this research are analyzed three Federal Institutes linked to this network: IFSC, IFPR and IFRS.

The analyzes based on online questionnaires sent to ICTs that divided the issues of SIAS/ICT to encourage responses. In all, 58 responses were collected of following Federal Institutes. The answer is separated by category:

It's necessary to understand that after compilation of data for each of the questions answered by the Institutes of Table 10, was created a weighted average of the answers except for the results obtained in "NS" (nothing shown). As an example, in the case of the 18 responses received to a question of economic performance, was adopted a weighted average of the answers so for the same question there's a single value that expresses the set of answers. The weighted result was included in the SIAS/ICT and analyzed.

The analysis determined by the SIAS/ICT is based on the final value of sustainability index SIAS/ICT to the case in question, which assesses the sustainability practices of ICTs in southern Brazil as "regular" (58.04%). By the methodology the ICT's from the South of Brazil, have a very relevant economic dimension, which has the highest performance index, indicated by SIAS/ICT, as "good" (64.80%), this shows that the

Institutes "demonstrate medium level of investment/control "related to the economic issue and its aspects. Interestingly, environmental and social/institutional dimensions are not far apart, each one have performances classified as "regular", but with percentages of 55.67% and 58.63% respectively.

Table 10: FI's by category

Economical performance (18 answers)	*Environmental performance (15 answers)*	*Social performance – GRI (14 answers)*	*Social performance – A3P/ISCN (11 answers)*
IFPR – Cascavel	IFPR – Foz do Iguaçu	IFPR – Foz do Iguaçu	IFPR – Curitiba
IFPR – Jacarezinho	IFPR – Palmas	IFPR – Jacarezinho	IFPR – Palmas
IFPR – Palmas	IFRS – Bento Gonçalves	IFPR – Palmas	IFRS – Bento Gonçalves
IFRS – Bento Gonçalves	IFRS – Caxias do Sul	IFRS – Bento Gonçalves	IFRS – Caxias do Sul
IFRS – Caxias do Sul	IFRS – Feliz	IFRS – Caxias do Sul	IFRS – Feliz
IFRS – Feliz	IFRS – Osório	IFRS – Feliz	IFRS – Osório
IFRS – Osório	IFRS – Restinga	IFRS – Osório	IFRS – Restinga
IFRS – Restinga	IFRS – Sertão	IFRS – Restinga	IFSC – Chapecó
IFRS – Sertão	IFSC – Chapecó	IFSC – Chapecó	IFSC – São Carlos
IFSC – Caçador	IFSC – Florianópolis -Continente	IFSC – Gaspar	IFSC – São José
IFSC – Chapecó	IFSC – Gaspar	IFSC – São Carlos	IFSC - Xanxerê
IFSC – Criciúma	IFSC – Joinville	IFSC – São José	
IFSC – Gaspar	IFSC – São Carlos	IFSC – São Miguel do Oeste	
IFSC – Joinville	IFSC – São José	IFSC – Xanxerê	
IFSC – São Carlos	IFSC – Xanxerê		
IFSC – São José			
IFSC – São Miguel do Oeste			
IFSC – Xanxerê			

Source: The authors

The average performance of ICTs, in southern Brazil, while indicate a median value of sustainability practices in the three dimensions as indicated by SIAS-ICT demonstrates that the region, by the standards internationally disseminated through tools such as GRI and ISCN, is capable, more timidly, to predict damage, to educate its employees and students about the need to have an sustainable behavior, and in particular that actions is limited only to meet the legislation regarding the sustainability.

In this sense the southern Brazil offers no overall losses, and presents financial sustainability - from the standpoint of supply assurance of higher education services without prejudice intermediate activities - and does not indicate weakness of budget constraint, since the responses indicated recent growth of their budgets.

Table 11 and Graphic 1 indicate the compiled data model application for all areas with special detailing for social/institutional dimension in which we included the concern not only of the GRI, but also the ISCN and A3P:

Table 11: Performance indexes southern Brazil

Performance index	***Sustainbility***	
	Result	***Rating***
Economical (GRI - G4)	64,80%	Good
Environmental(GRI - G4)	55,67%	Regular
Social/Institutional (GRI-G4, A3P, ISCN)	58,71%	Regular
Decent labor practices	68,78%	Good
Human rights	66,32%	Good
Society	65,60%	Good
Reponsibility by product	84,00%	Great
Institutional (A3P)	52,43%	Regular
Institutional (ISCN)	46,34%	Regular
Total ICT – Southern Brazil	58,04%	Regular

Source: The authors

Graphic 1 indicates the amounts by dimensions. The highlight is the numerical proximity of the three dimensions indicators. A capability that can be noted from the Graphic 1 data refers to the environmental

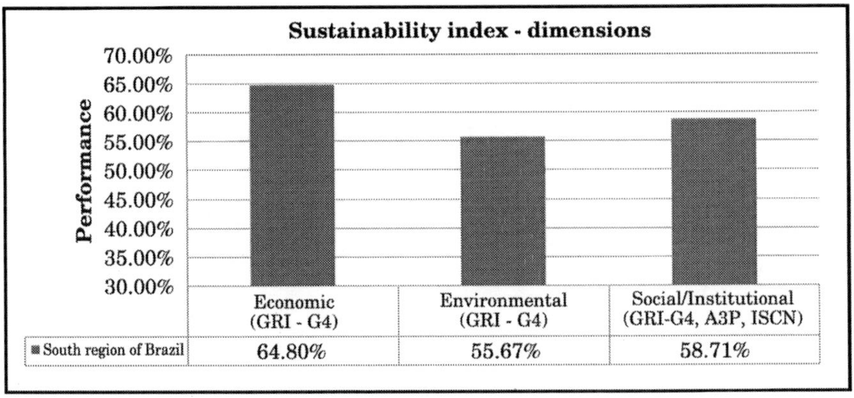

Graphic 1: Sustainability index - dimensions. *Source:* The author

dimension: this point has the worst set of performances, driven by categories related to "Water", "Energy" and "Emissions". In this sense, it is interesting that the Institutes create initiatives to combat waste of resources, and introduce new forms of waste treatment and emissions.

Table 12 shows the quantitative responses indicated to the total values ranging from 0 to 5. Thus, it's possible to observe in which range is the largest number of responses obtained, so that it can emphasize and prioritize certain areas in relation to other:

As shown in Table 12, it's observed that it's possible to explore the potential of high performance especially in the environmental and social/ institutional categories that presented little expressive values of the responses on the scale of 100%. For an example it has it's concentration in the 60 range %.

Table 12: Performance indicators

Performance index	*0%* *0*	*20%* *1*	*40%* *2*	*60%* *3*	*80%* *4*	*100%* *5*	— *NC*
Economical (GRI - G4)	0,00%	20,00%	20,00%	24,00%	4,00%	32,00%	0,00%
Environmental (GRI - G4)	7,22%	17,53%	25,77%	29,90%	17,53%	2,06%	0,00%
Social/Institutional (GRI-G4, A3P, ISCN)	0,00%	11,73%	22,91%	32,96%	22,91%	9,50%	0,00%
Decent labor practices	0,00%	7,32%	19,51%	21,95%	31,71%	19,51%	0,00%
Human rights	0,00%	15,79%	15,79%	21,05%	31,58%	15,79%	0,00%
Society	0,00%	11,54%	19,23%	23,08%	46,15%	0,00%	0,00%
Responsibility by product	0,00%	0,00%	0,00%	20,00%	40,00%	40,00%	0,00%
Institutional (A3P)	0,00%	5,41%	32,43%	56,76%	5,41%	0,00%	0,00%
Institutioanl (ISCN)	0,00%	24,39%	31,71%	39,02%	4,88%	0,00%	0,00%
Total of ICT	2,33%	14,29%	23,59%	31,23%	19,60%	8,97%	0,00%

Source: The author

For this analysis using SIAS/ICT model, it's possible to see the distance to achieve excellence in the region regarding A3P and ISCN criteria, since the answers to these indicators focus on "regular" area (60%) presenting some significant values in the "good" area (80%) and no occurrence of responses in the area of "great" (100%).

CONCLUSIONS

This article aimed to study the sustainability of Federal Institutes of Science and Technology in the Southern Region of Brazil through an evaluation model that combines internationally shared contributions of different tools (GRI, ISCN, A3P). The model was applied in 58 ICT's what allowed the measurement of weaknesses and strengths of these entities on the promotion of sustainable practices for the region.

This article meets Singh's studies (2012) and Ness (2007) at the point where it develops an international sustainability assessment model. Meets also Epstein work (2004) at the point which offers a method of evaluation to make part of an integrated system that combine all aspects of sustainable development defined by (Brundtland, 1989; Faria, 2011). It also satisfies the goal proposed by a social bookmark as defined by Van Bellen (2008).

Thus, it is stated that the answers pointed out by ICTs in the South region of Brazil also point for a corroboration of rules and procedures related to the sustainability of international order, even if they aren't fully integrated to international concerns disseminated by an interna-tional regime of sustainability. Evaluations concerning the categories "good" or "excellent" in this particular case add up to, in total, only 28.57% of total issues. Furthermore this low score, globally the South Region presents data indicating that the institutions operate with some regularity actions that are internationally promoted by sustainability in its various dimensions, as indicated in tables and graphs in this section.

It is noteworthy that there is progress to be achieved, but it's surprising that even in southern Brazil, with the ICT's away from the international networks that disseminate more strongly the rules and procedures of an international regime of sustainability, the overall indicator for sustainability of ICTs in southern Brazil indicate the 58.04% mark. Admittedly, this rating already indicates advances, however, point to areas where they can improve the indicators is critical, especially in the environmental and social/institutional dimensions, with special attention to indicators related to ISCN and A3P.

REFERENCES

Adams, W.M. (2006). The future of sustainability: Re-thinking environment and development in the twenty-first century. Report of the IUCN renowned thinkers meeting. *In:* Wikipedia. Disponível em: <*https://en.wikipedia.org/wiki/Sustainability*> Acesso em: 04 fev. 2014

Brundtland. United Nations (1987). Disponível em: <*http://www.un-documents.net/ocf-02.htmI*>. Acesso em: 02 nov. 2013

Brúseke and Franz Josef (1996). Desestruturação e Desenvolvimento. *In*: Incertezas de Sustentabilidade na Globalização. Viola, E. and Ferreira, L.C. (orgs.) Campinas, Unicamp.

Coral, Eliza (2002). Modelo de planejamento estratégico para a sustentabilidade empresarial. Florianópolis, SC, 275 f. Tese (Doutorado) - Universidade Federal de Santa Catarina, Centro Tecnológico. Programa de Pós-Graduação em Engenharia de Produção.

Epstein, Marc J. (2004). The identification, measurement and reporting of corporate social impacts: Past, present and future. *Advances in Environmental Accounting and Management,* 2(1): 1–29.

Faria, de J.H. (2011). Por uma Teoria Crítica da Sustentabilidade, pp. 15–23. *In*: Neves, Lafaiete Santos: Seminário sobre Sustentabilidade. 2010, Curitiba, Sustentabilidade: Anais de textos selecionados do V Seminário sobre sustentabilidade. Curitiba: Juruá, p. 338. ISBN 9788536235547

Global Trends 2030: Alternative Worlds. Disponível em: <*http://globaltrends2030.files.wordpress.com/2012/11/global-trends-2030 november2012.pdf*> Acesso em: 16 out 2013

Gri – Global Reporting Iniciative. Disponível em: <*https://www.globalreporting.org*> Acesso em: 02 nov. 2013

ISCN - International Sustainable Campus Network. Working Groups. Disponível em: <*http://www.international-sustainable-campus-network.org/about/iscn-working-groups.html*> Acesso em: 02 nov. 2013.

Leripio, Alexandre de Ávila (2001). GAIA – Um método de gerenciamento de aspectos e impactos ambientais. Florianópolis: UFSC, 2001. Tese (Doutorado em Engenharia de Produção) Programa de Pós-Graduação em Contabilidade, Universidade Federal de Santa Catarina, Florianópo-lis.

Louette, Anne (2008). Compêndio para a sustentabilidade: Ferramentas de gestão de responsabilidade socioambiental–uma contribuição para o desenvolvimento sustentável.

MMA – A3P (Ministério do Meio Ambiente). A3P - Agenda Ambiental na Administração Pública. 2009. 5ª ed. Disponível em: *http://www.mma.gov.br/estruturas/a3p/_arquivos/cartilha_a3p_36.pdf*Acesso em: 30 abr. 2014.

NESS, Barry *et al.* (2007). Categorising tools for sustainability assessment. *Ecological Economics*, 60(3): 498–508.

Nunes, J.P.O. (2010). Um aporte ao sistema contábil gerencial ambiental: Elaboração e aplicação parcial do novo sistema em clínica hospitalar. 2010. 241f. Dissertação (Mestrado em Contabilidade), Programa de Pós-Graduação em Contabilidade, Universidade Federal de Santa Catarina, Florianópolis.

Pfitscher, E.D. (2004). Gestão e sustentabilidade através da contabilidade e controladoria ambiental: Estudo de caso na cadeia produtiva de arroz ecológico. Tese (Doutorado em Engenharia de Produção). Florianópolis: UFSC.

Pieri, R., Pfitscher Elisete Dahmer, Frey, I.A. and Alberton, L. (2011). Gestão estratégica e ambiental: Estudo de uma universidade comunitária. *In*: XII Congreso Internacional de Costos, 2011, Punta del Este, Uruguay. Anais.

Singh, Rajesh Kumar *et al.* (2012). An overview of sustainability assessment methodologies. *Ecological Indicators*, 15(1): 281–299.

Uhlmann, V.O. (2011). Contribuições ao desenvolvimento do Sistema Contábil Gerencial Ambiental – Geração 2: Proposição da terceira geração do método. 2011. 113f. Dissertação (Mestrado em Contabilida-de), Programa de Pós-Graduação em Contabilidade, Universidade Fede-ral de Santa Catarina, Florianópolis.

11

Children's Rights and Democracy Education in Early Childhood

FÜSUN YILDIZBAS[1]*

ABSTRACT

Education given in the early childhood period provides a basis for a person to live as a successful, harmonious, healthy and happy adult. In this study, the connection between human rights and democracy is examined and basic concepts and convention on the rights of the children are analyzed within the framework of historical development of children's rights for the purpose of gaining basic knowledge, attitude and skills required for a democratic social life respectful to teachers and teacher candidates and human rights. In this context, the importance of children's rights and democracy education in the early childhood period is emphasized. Also, the importance of children gaining democratic attitude and behaviors in early childhood individually and socially is emphasized. In this regard, activities supported mostly with life experiences in terms of raising awareness about children's rights and democracy education and creating education environments to gain children democratic values such as "respect and tolerance", "taking responsibility", "cooperation and sharing" and "obeying the rules" in early childhood period in accordance with programs applied in preschool educational institutions in Turkey are included.

Key words: Early childhood, Children's rights, Child rights agreement, Democracy education, Teachers

[1]Istanbul Arel University, School of Health Sciences, Department of Child Development, Turkey.

**Corresponding author*: E-mail: fusunyildizbas8@gmail.com

INTRODUCTION

Children are the most valuable beings in a society. They are also the keystones of a society which shapes and steers its future. Education given in the childhood provides a basis for a person to live as a successful, harmonious, healthy and happy adult. During this period, educational institutions assume an important function in creating democracy awareness and protecting children's rights as the starting place of a planned, systematic and goal-oriented education.

Implementation of democracy principles effectively in preschool education institution which are social institutions the children are included after their families is of great importance in terms of children gaining democratic attitude and behaviors. By this way, children are able to gain skills and values such as respect, freedom, equality, tolerance, cooperation, decision-making and empathy starting from early ages.

First of all, societies need to apply children's right so that children can improve themselves and be useful to society in the future. Convention on the Rights of the Children is an important agreement made internationally to prepare children as healthy individuals for the future. Children to be brought up as individuals competent socially, physically and personally and to lead a qualitative life depend on them gaining experiences in this regard during the childhood period. Raising children as healthy individuals for the future is one of the responsibilities of every part of society, especially families, and administration units. These institutions should act together and make common studies to provide children's safety, protection, development and efficient contribution to the society.

CHILDREN'S RIGHTS, HUMAN RIGHTS AND DEMOCRACY

Children's rights, human rights and democracy are interlocked, interrelated concepts which complete one another. The relationship between democracy, human rights and children rights concepts is shown in Fig. 1.

Democracy includes government organization and life rules formed according to human rights. Human rights are an important part of democracy. Democracy includes subjects such as democratic regimes, development of democracy as well as human rights. Children's right is a part of human rights and it can be accepted as a form of human rights adapted to children. In this context, democracy has a quality which includes human rights and children's rights.

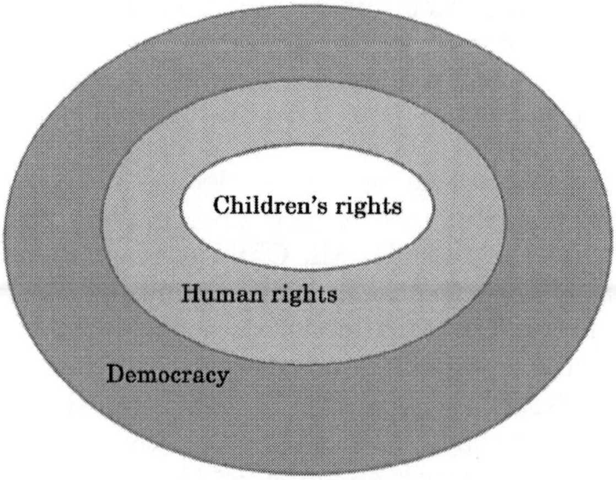

Fig. 1: Relationship between children's rights, human rights and democracy

Children's Rights

Children's rights are the whole of authorities bestowed on children in private law, social law, public law and international law. They are the rights children are endowed with due to their need of maintenance and care and for them to be individuals[1]. The rights children should have in an international level are determined and gathered in the Convention on the Rights of the Children. This agreement has the quality of children's bill of human rights. It is signed with the intent of children to be brought up as qualified humans in every respect[2]. In other words, children's rights are the adapted version of human rights for children due to the requirement of regulating them in accordance with children's developmental qualities.

The relationship between democracy, human rights and children's rights can be explained with an example. For example, the right of children to contribute to the rights which concern them is associated with humans' right to elect their own government. It is only possible for children and humans to use these rights through democratic management. In other words, human rights and children's rights represent an understanding which find meaning within democracy and develop with democracy.

Basic concepts regarding children's rights

Child concept should be known to understand basic concepts regarding children's rights. Child concept is used in various meanings in time according to economic, social and cultural change of human history. Child concept varies across societies since it is formed according to societal norms and values beyond the understanding brought by developmental periods of human history.

Today, all branches of science acknowledge the birth of the child as the beginning of the child and there are different approaches regarding the ending of the childhood's end. Child concept in psychology and medicine is classified according to development qualities and ends with the start of puberty. End of childhood depends on the person based on physical, social and emotional qualities of the individual. Child concept in law is used to describe separating children from adults and paternity of parents. Child concept in law depends on the age of the child until which the child needs protection and help. Generally, the ones who are under age 18 are accepted as children so that children's physical and moral are protected, but there are some established rules according to children's developmental periods[1].

Convention on the Rights of the Children describes child as a being which has needs developed with age and maturity as people under 18 and also as an individual. Therefore, it goes beyond other agreements by creating a balance between children's rights and rights and tasks of other people which are responsible in child support, development and protection areas and by entitling the children to participate to the rights which are about their current situation and future[3]. By taking these definitions into consideration, it is possible to define children as individuals under 18 and carry different qualities than adults. Children's rights are inherent rights of children in terms of natural law, rights ànd responsibilities entitled to children in terms of law which is in force in a government in terms of positive law.

Historical development of children's rights

Children's rights have developed in parallel with changes in economic and social life of human history. In the development of children's rights, socio-cultural movements such as economic structure of family, industrial revolution, world wars, Renaissance and the Age of Enlightenment have played an important role. The idea of establishing an organization regarding the protection of children was firstly presented by Jules de Jeune in 1894. Afterwards, the League of Nations published Geneva Declaration of the Rights of the Child on 26 September 1924 through the endeavors of "International Aid Association and International Women's Assembly." Children's Declaration of Human Rights was accepted by the United Nations General Assembly on 20 November 1959.

A bill was created by the United Nations on 20 November 1989 and entered into force as Convention on the Rights of the Children in international law on 2 September 1990[4].

Basic principles and classification of the convention on the rights of the children

Rights in the Convention on the Rights of the Children are arranged according to specific principles. These principles have the quality of being basic conditions which are considered in using all rights entitled to children and carrying out tasks imposed on governments. These can be listed as[4].

- Not discriminating,
- Right to live and develop,
- Protection of children's high benefit (safety),
- Respecting children's opinions.

Convention on the Rights of the Children describes child as a being which has needs developed with age and maturity as an individual. Therefore, it goes beyond other agreements by creating a balance between children's rights and rights and tasks of other people which are responsible in child support, development and protection areas and by entitling the children to participate to the rights which are about their current situation and future[3].

Basic principles which dominate the Convention are; *"not discriminating"* (Article 2), *"children's high benefit"* (Article 3), *"right to live and develop"* (Article 6) and *"respect for children's opinions"* (Article 12). Other principles and provisions in the Convention are under the titles of life, development, protection and participation[5].

In terms of the types of children's rights in the Convention can be gathered in four groups as vital rights, development rights, protection rights and participation rights:

a) ***Vital rights*** are the rights which set forth to meet the basic needs of children such as having the right to life and appropriate right standards, medical care, nutrition and sheltering.
b) ***Development rights*** are the rights necessary for children to realize themselves in the top level such as right to education, right to play and rest, right to information, freedom of faith, conscious and thought.

c) ***Protection rights*** are rights which provide protection for children against all kinds of neglect, abuse and exploitation.

   These are the rights which provide protection for children in subjects with regards to judicial system, armed conflict, child labor and special care.

d) ***Participation rights*** are the rights which provide children to gain an active role in their families and societies[1,6].

In this context, children's rights consists many rights in civil, political, economic, social and cultural areas. Convention on the Rights of the Children lays emphasis on institutions, establishments and the related people which serve children for them to be prepared as equipped for the future.

Children should know the rights they have and they should learn how to appreciate and use them. Learning children's rights means knowing and understanding which rights the children have. Learning experiences in children's rights education should be included in schools in a wide range to achieve it. For children to understand children's rights and to use their rights in school and daily life is an important action plan. This is an activity application about children's rights in the classroom by the teacher. For children to experience/live children's rights as basic principles in the classroom and by the school administrators should be taught through children's rights. By this way, children develop attitude, value and skills. Learning children's rights should be encouraged through the use of learnt rights in classrooms, schools and societies.[7]

Human Rights

Human rights are international principles and rules which aim at protecting and developing humans' personality and value only due to being human[8]. Human rights can be defined as rights inherited by humans and which allow humans to live as humans. Human rights enable individuals to use their skills, to become conscious and to raise their commitment to life and make the development of a peace and tranquility environment in the society possible. For this reason, human rights are important in terms of individual and societal development[9]. Even though human rights firstly started with ideas such as equality and freedom, it has obtained a qualification which includes all dimensions of life such as personal and political rights, economic, social and cultural rights at the present time. Human rights are multidimensional international rules which require that humans should be appreciated at every dimension of life and supports individual development.

Democracy

Today, governments mostly adapt democracy as their regime. Karatnyck (2002) emphasized that democracy is a developing fact in the world and stated that there was almost not a country which adapted to democracy in 1900s, 20–30 countries moved on to democratic governance in 1950s and in 2002, 121 of 191 countries adapted democracy as a regime. According to this, almost 70% of world populations live in countries which have democratic governance[10]. Of course, this situation keeps democratic education constantly on the agenda. UNESCO (2000) emphasized that democracy is a regime which values humans and enables their development in a report they published and stated that democracy needs to be taught so that it can be learnt and turned into a life style. In this context, education appears as precondition of democracy[8].

Democracy is defined in various ways according to perspectives of all branches of science. Administration science experts defines democracy as a regime, law experts lay an emphasis on its human rights dimension, pedagogy experts and other social area experts lay an emphasis on life style quality of democracy. Today, democracy is defined as a life style established on basic human values as well as being a regime[11]. Instead of having only one truth, democracy is about achieving living in peace with people who think and act differently by respecting the truth of others.

Democracy dominates all dimensions of live in the developed countries and functions as a system degraded into the level of the right to elect and be elected and the voting right and which consists of only these as presenting a systematized structure[11]. Therefore, it is possible to encounter different applications in the countries which accept democracy as a regime.

Relationship between human rights and democracy

Democracy and human rights are two intertwined concepts. Moreover, human rights are a concept which completes democracy concept. According to the understanding which spreads in our day, the development level in the democracy of the countries is determined with the importance the country places on human rights. Therefore, it is difficult to separate these two concepts from each other in terms of concept and definition.

Democracy is usually used as political regime in which the environments towards the protection of human rights are prepared and human rights makes rights and freedoms of the individual clear within the regime. These rights and freedoms are protected within the order. In this context, it is necessary to mention human rights when democracy is mentioned. Principles of democracy are actualized with human rights applications and human rights applications develop and strengthen democracies[12]. Therefore, there is a strong and intertwined relationship between democracy and human rights. The rights humans have as humans are valued and applied in democratic environments. Since democracy is a system based on the public, democracies should be based on the foundation of human rights and freedoms[11].

Democracy and human rights principles have a consistent and complementary quality between themselves. In 1993, International Human Rights and Democracy Education Congress held under the leadership of EU in Montreal made decisions in this regard. In the final declaration of the congress, the fact that democracy, human rights and basic freedoms cannot be separated from each other is emphasized with a certain statement. In the same declaration, the fact that human rights should be included in the education programs to strengthen democracy and development and human rights and basic freedoms[8].

When education applications are examined, it is seen that some resources bring citizenship education, some democracy education, some democracy and human rights education concepts into the forefront. Also, when the subject is viewed in terms of education provided in the level of preschool, elementary school and secondary school, it is seen clearly that democracy and human rights concepts are used together in studies mostly in relation to education programs and classes in relation to the field.

Developments in Relation to Human Rights and Democracy Education

The scopes of democracy and human rights concepts change constantly based on developments in the fields of rights and freedoms. Right and freedom concepts have been discussed since the first age to our day.

Democracy is usually interpreted in three different ways. First of them is the understanding which defines democracy as a regime. Second approach is the approach which is based on human rights level of democracy. Last approach is the approach which sees democracy as a way of life[11]. However, democracy to be seen as a way of life has gained importance in the recent years. According to Levin[13], democracy should be seen as a way of life. In other words, democracy should have an equivalent in human life and a meaning in daily life.

Democracy is not only a regime or basic human rights or life form. Democracy consists all elements and it is both a democratic regime respectful to human rights and a fact which humans can feel in all areas of their lives. According to what[8] quoted from San (1985), for children to understand that democracy is not only a regime, but also a way of life is directly related to providing them a chance to live in a democratic and free environment in family and school. Because democracy does not have the quality of a class which can be taught as history, geography or mathematics. Democracy is a political regime which can be learnt and adapted by applying in daily live and within the level of attitude and behaviors. Democracy can only be taught in a democratic environment. According to Ersoy[14], teaching democracy can only be realized through democracy education in democratic environments. Democracy education is a process which starts with the birth of the child and the effect of school and social environment. For this reason, the values the child develops within the scope of social development affect the development of democratic attitude and behaviors. Especially when preschool period is thought to be one of the critical stages of the development of the child, it is an important fact that democracy education given to children shapes their lives in the future years, helps them to internalize democratic attitude and behaviors and to be individuals which can use them in their lives. In the study made by Gündogdu[15], the fact that participators stated that it is necessary for democracy and human rights concept and culture to be acknowledged from early ages in Turkey which endeavors to create a democratic society and to sustain it supports this opinion.

School and family are the primary environments in which democracy education should be provided. However, according to Ersoy[14] democracy learnt by children in the family is not sufficient for them to gain a democratic attitude and behaviors. Democracy education is a concept that is to be learnt through lifelong practice. This process should start with the birth of the child and continue lifetime. Democracy education starts in the family with informal ways and it should be turned into a more purposeful and systematic state by children starting to have a more formal education.

Role of the family in human rights and democracy education

Family is one of the environments which children face starting from the time they are born and which affect children. In the development of children in the early period, the opportunities presented by families in establishing the self and personality on a solid base and in terms of children learning their rights through practice are of great importance.

Children have rights within Convention on the Rights of the Children and human rights and which strengthen themselves. The parents have rights and responsibilities such as having children. Parent's responsibilities consist of providing appropriate care and fulfilling their needs without neglecting and exploiting children[16]. Increasing understanding of children in relation to respect, recognition, participation shows itself in social interactions[17]. Children learn social values, rules, roles and standards during social development process to adapt to society and establish healthy relationships[18]. It is possible to say that children learn respect, the distribution of roles within the sense of right and justice, social roles such as cooperation firstly in family environment[11]. Relationships of children with family members underlie their attitudes with other people, objects and life as a whole. Also, family imbues children with the awareness that they are a member of the family and establishes the foundation of socialization. Democracy understanding is developed in children which experience mutual love, respect, sensitivity to each other's rights and tolerance in domestic relationships[19].

When children are allowed to learn and use their rights in family and school, to participate in decisions and works that interest them, to be entitled with competency to monitor their own rights, the purposes of democracy education are realized. Oppressive attitude which tries to control and direct children's behaviors constantly may cause children to be individuals who submit, do not trust themselves and have inferiority complex. Children should be raised with a supervision which is not over-protective and allow them to realize their own ideas[20,21]. One of the basic qualities of a democratic school and family environment is effective participation. Therefore, children's opinions should be received in terms of taking decisions about them, determining choices in different situations, discussions in different subjects and their participation should be ensured[11].

The development of self-control in children is provided through giving freedom and responsibility in terms of what they can do at every age enough to prevent them from hurting themselves and their environment. If such an attitude is not presented starting from early ages, children may find it difficult to relate between freedom, restriction, right and responsibility and self-control[22]. Entitling the right of choice to children is an important step for them to gain responsibility behavior. The right of choice expresses a limited responsibility. However, it is necessary to know the children and their limitations well to decide which responsibilities they can take. No responsibility beyond these limitations should be given to children[23]. Responsibility starts from early ages and by giving tasks in accordance with child's age and development level. In this environment, children learn to be self-sufficient and to lead themselves[24]. Taking responsibility should be considered with freedom concept for children. Being responsible requires for them to keep their promises, to care, to be careful, to take on and to be sensitive. As the age of the child increases, their rights and responsibilities should also be increased. Children like responsibilities appropriate for their level and chosen correctly for them. Expecting responsibilities from children above their capacities is as wrong as expecting nothing from them[25].

Children start to become individuals by interacting with adults and other children in their environment and also playing games with them. Children learn to be little citizens who abide by these rules, shares and collaborate and take responsibility. They learn the obligation to protect their own right, respecting others' rights, protecting themselves and reconciling by interacting with their environment[26].

In a study made by Dinç[27], the purpose is to determine opinions of parents who have children around 5–6 with regards to children's rights and reveal the applications of children's rights education and the problems faced in these applications. At the time of the study, parents mention the rights to express their opinions, to select and decide, to do as they wish as long as they do not hurt others and it is seen that they do not know enough about children's rights and they need to gain awareness. It is found out that parents use the approaches of talking with children and explaining with examples, learning by practice in family environment and posing a model in the applications realized towards children's right education in the house. Based on the results of the study, it is recommended those children's rights education programs with the family participation in preschool education are developed and spread. Also, when the subject is viewed in terms of education provided in the level of preschool, elementary school and secondary school, it is seen clearly that democracy and human rights concepts are used together in studies mostly in relation to education programs and classes in relation to the field.

Role of the school in human rights and democracy education

Main characters who provide the application and sustainment of children's rights in schools are teachers and school administrators. Studies in pedagogy show that the qualities of teachers affect the personality development of the child. Intellectual attitudes, emotional reactions, various habits of teachers affect students. Teacher behaviors are indicators of student behaviors gained at the end of education process. Teachers should make students adapt democratic understanding, attitude and ideals and make these values an inseparable part of their own lives[28]. Since teachers are the main element from whom children can receive information regarding their rights within education system, educators have an important role in this process. As expressed in article 42 in the Convention, children's rights applications to be effective and successful depends on educating teachers on children's rights and the effectiveness of learning processes planned.

Schools are institutions responsible for arranging environment to share information in an appropriate way. Regulation of information sharing process in the schools in a democratic way will contribute democracy and human rights education of students positively. The structure of education programs in regulating democratic education environment and giving human rights education in schools is determinative. The dimensions of education program such as purpose, content, education process and evaluation should be planned in accordance with the principles of democracy and human rights.

Children's rights education is an important tool in actualizing the rights projected in the articles of the Convention on the Rights of the Children. In this context, the regulation of formal education system tools and the formation of education process in accordance with children's rights with regards to children's rights are characterized as the most prominent role of teachers. In other words, teachers need to refer to international agreements in their classes in the school and education programs should be created in a quality that supports national and international publications with regards to children's rights[29].

According to Howe and Covell[30], children's rights education should be given in an environment in which rights in the Convention on the Rights of the Children are actualized and respected. In this context, it is important that the mentioned elements are applied in the education institutions so that an effective children's right education can be realized. In an environment where children's rights are not respected, giving content information with regards to children's rights is not of much importance and these different and conflicting warnings may confuse the children more.

Role of the teachers in human rights and democracy education

It is important especially for teachers to arrange activities within the scope of democracy education, to be accurate role models for children with their attitudes and behaviors in the education institutions that children first start to take formal education in preschool period. However, behaviors of teachers and how they perceive democracy effect this education process greatly.

In the study made by Neslitürk and Ersoy[31], the purpose is to determine the activities developed towards children's rights education of preschool teacher candidates and the opinions of them in relation to applications in preschool education institutions. At the end of the study, it is found out that teacher candidates mostly benefit from drama, native language and game activities in children's rights education. Teacher candidates stated that they apply the activity they plan easily even though it looks difficult to be planned at the beginning and children enjoy this activity. Also, they stated that children's rights education may be given through activities in accordance with the level of children in the preschool period.

In the study realized by Ucus and Sahin[32], the purpose was to determine the opinions of teachers and school administrators with regards to applying and carrying out the Convention on the Rights of the Children in the schools. According to the study results, teachers and school administrators do not have sufficient information about children's rights, they do not make applications directly in relation to children's rights and they share this subject with students when it is included in the curriculum.

Güder and Yildirim[33] made a study to determine the meanings attributed to democracy by candidate teachers who are the future teachers through metaphor. At the result of the study, the metaphors of teacher candidates in relation to democracy concept are divided into nine categories. The metaphors acquired are determined as freedom, combination of different ideas, cooperation, the importance of democracy, equality-justice, changes based on initiative, democracy with its impossibility aspect. Teacher candidates mostly created metaphor in equality-justice category. The most repeated metaphor is the metaphor of scales. At the result of the study, it is determined that teacher candidates do not approach democracy concept with all of its dimensions and they focus on it mostly in management dimension. Also, even though teacher candidates relate democracy concept to concepts such as politics, regime, none of them relate it to education processes.

Democracy Education in Early Childhood Period

Early childhood period is the period in which children experience important physical, social and personal developments. The education in this period covers an important time period since it creates the basis for other educational steps and in which foundation of life is formed. The quality of the education children receive in this period plays an important role in the formation of their futures.

Democracy education is also included in international documents. Teaching adults and children their rights are included in article 26 in the Universal Declaration of Human Rights, in article 42 in the Convention on the Rights of the Children and in the European Convention on Human Rights and the governments are encumbered with the responsibility in this regard. In these documents, democracy and human rights education are included as a human right for individuals and as a legal obligation for governments[8]. With the article "Children's rights must be taught to children and adults" in the Convention on the Rights of the Children, children to know their rights according to laws and conventions is defined as one of their basic rights[34]. Individuals who do not know what human rights are, what their scope and dimension are and how to use them cannot use their rights. Humans' right to know their rights is one of the basic human rights. Individuals can only acquire the right to know human rights through democracy education. Democracy education is closely related to democratic culture in the society, because democracy can only exist in societies which can protect and maintain it. Society to have democratic values depends on individuals in the society to be equipped with democratic behavior and attitude, bringing in democratic behaviors and raising individuals depend on the society having democratic values. Therefore, one of the basic elements which enable the existence of democracy in a society is democracy culture. Within this scope, we see democracy as a life style which is learnt in a democratic culture environment strengthened with education. Therefore, it is possible to say that the most important factor which enables and develops the existence of democracy is education. Since the democratic cultural structure of society has gained importance in democracy education, democracy culture in society forms democracy education and democracy education forms democracy culture[34].

Children start to learn democracy in daily life in the family before coming to school. Children learn democracy by experiencing it in their daily lives. Because children take part in society as individuals who use their rights and responsibilities from the moment they are born. However, the meaning of citizenship and democracy are different for them compared to adults. Children learn democracy by participating to different experiences and learning different roles[35].

Democracy experience children learnt in their families is not enough for them to gain democratic attitude and behaviors. Democracy education is a process which needs to be long-term and lifelong. This process starts with the birth of the child in the family and goes on during the life. Democracy education which starts in the family leads in an aimed and planned way when children start school. By this way, democracy understanding of the child is formed during the education process and supported by life experiences. Union developed by school and life in democracy education is an important factor for the child to adapt democracy and turn it into a life style. However, in countries where democracy cannot develop sufficiently as a life style, democracy education is rather under the responsibility of schools. Children gain democratic attitude and behaviors by learning that some attitudes cannot correspond with democracy in family environment and school.

Today, education process starts with preschool period and preschool period is conducted as compulsory education in many countries. Therefore, democracy education must be given gradually by activities suitable to every age during the education process which starts with preschool period and continues until higher education. Democracy education must be in all education levels without getting interrupted[36]. Within this scope, we see preschool education period as the first educational step children meet with democracy education after their families.

Importance of Democracy Education in Early Childhood Period

Education in early childhood period is the development and education process which includes the first years the child starts education from the day the child is born, the period between the ages 0–8 and in which physical, psycho motor, social, emotional, mental and language development of children are mostly completed and this period creates the foundation of children for their next lives. This period is one of the fastest periods in terms of physical, mental and social development of children[37]. Democracy education is a learning process which develops with the birth of the child and the effect of school and social environment. Therefore, social environment in which the child lives, socio-cultural structure of this environment, relationships the child form in this social environment and social skills the child gains plays an important role in the development of social conscious. In other words, the values the child develops within the scope of social development affect the development of democratic attitude and behaviors.

There is a parallelism between social development and the child gaining democratic attitude and behavior. For this reason, education institutions should support children's social development by providing them a democratic learning environment and there should be institutions which enable children to gain democracy conscious. Also, children spend time with their peers for the first time and learn how to form relationships with them. In this period, education institutions provide an environment in which children can learn social behaviors in a planned and systematic way[38]. Children gain many social skills such as collaboration, sharing, participating to group activities, expressing their opinions in public, taking responsibility for their actions and education[39]. For this reason, preschool education institutions play an important role in children gaining democratic attitude and behaviors.

Personal Gains

Democracy education in early childhood period has many contributions to the personal development of children. These can be listed as such; Democracy education

- Contributes to children to gaining self-confidence by enabling them to move in a more free way. Children start to feel more confident after their achievements they acquire through the works they do on their own. This confidence is one of the foundations of success.
- By providing a safe environment whose rules and principles are certain, it enables children to trust other people.
- It enables children to know themselves and to develop self-respect. Children understand their aspects different to those around them and develop their own self.
- It enables children to think freely and to develop their creativity at the highest level.
- Children understand that respecting themselves and others and their differences are valuable[40].
- It enables children to explain their opinions freely and to express themselves. By this way, it develops language development of children as well as thinking, analyzing and communication skills of children.
- Through democratic environment presented to children, children learn to take the responsibility of their own behaviors[40].
- It supports them to grow up as healthy individuals by forming their attitude and behaviors towards their environment.

- It contributes them to realize negative behaviors around them and to reduce child abuse.

Democracy education realized in education institutions supports children to be individuals who are at peace with themselves, have high self-respect, have self-confidence, are creative, can express themselves, take their responsibility and are sensitive in terms of evaluating themselves.

Social Gains

Democracy education is the precondition in developing healthy democratic socials. Democracy education in early childhood period has many contributions to the social development. These can be listed as such. With democracy education;

- By raising children who adapt to democratic attitude and behavior, it contributes the formation of strong and democratic societies in the future[38].
- It enables children to become citizens who know their rights in the future[41].
- It enables children to gain social skills such as abiding by rules, cooperation, participating to decisions, sharing and taking responsibility and by this way, their effective participation to the society is provided[38]. Therefore, children can take part in society as respectful individuals.
- It enables them to grow up as individuals sensitive to others by developing their empathy skills[9].
- Children to accept different qualities of others, respecting differences and developing tolerance are supported and children to contribute to social peace are provided.
- Children also contribute to universal peace as well as national peace[33].
- Preschool democracy education support children to be effective and sensitive citizens who know their rights in the future and to democratic societies to be created in the future, national and international peace to be realized.

Scope and Dimensions of Democracy Education

There are various studies in relation to in which age level and how democracy education should be provided. As a result of these studies, the scope of democracy education from preschool education period until higher education is determined step by step by UNESCO. In accordance with this, scope and dimensions of democracy education to be given between the ages of 3–7 are demonstrated in Fig. 2[9].

Democracy House (Demokrasi Evi)

Level	*Objectives*	*Basic concepts*	*Basic values and skills*
3-7 age	• Self-respect • Respect to one's teachers and family • Respect to others	• Individual (Identity) • Society • Responsibility • Duty	• Being respectful • Justice • Solidarity • Working together • Communication • Solving problems • Showing empathy • Understanding cause-effect relationships • Analyzing actions • Solving conflicts
	Applications	***Human rights problems***	***Systems***
	• Cooperation and sharing • Expressing oneself • Listening • Individual study • Small group study • Showing empathy • Solving problems	• Inequality • Harming	• Class rules • Family life ***Tools*** • Convention on the rights of the children

Fig. 2: Scope and dimensions of democracy education given in the preschool period

All education levels in democracy education must determine their own gains based on democratic attitude and behaviors that are to be gained to children in the previous education level. Individual qualities and socio-cultural structure of children are important factors in children gaining democratic attitude and behaviors. Therefore, teachers must know democratic gaining in accordance with development level of children and education on different democratic values must be included according to the needs of children.

Whatever children's ages are, children must know how to act as efficient members of society and basic values of democracy to evaluate correct and wrong behaviors around them. However, democracy education given to children in early childhood period is different than elementary school and other education levels. Democracy information is not provided to children directly in early childhood period, instead the education of democratic values is realized and children to turn democratic values into behaviors and attitudes are supported. Within this scope, children in early childhood period cannot reach information as "equality is a principle of democracy." However, children realize wrong behaviors and inequality around them. For example, a child who has gained equality democratic value realizes wrong behaviors of teachers against other children in the classroom. For this reason, education institutions must be institutions in which children can live democracy and apply democracy in daily activities.

Democracy education includes obtaining information in relation to democracy and human rights and also actualizing the information obtained. Therefore, democracy education is a multidimensional learning process that can be supported by more life experiences. Within this scope, democracy education activities in early childhood period can be realized in three ways which are democracy education activities, process and management of education institution and learning in accordance with basic democratic values[42]:

- ***Democracy education activities*:** Education programs in early childhood period should include education of objectives and gaining in relation to democracy education through activities in accordance with basic values and principles of democracy.
- ***Management of education institutions in a democratic way*:** Employees and students in democratic education institutions should participate to school studies and learning activities. These can be developed in formal and informal ways. For example, it can be formal studies such as classroom meetings or informal studies such as discussion environments in which discussions in relation to content, method and techniques of activities are realized.
- ***Development of education environments in accordance with basic democratic values*:** Basic democratic values should be realized in education institutions and these values should be based on. Basic values of democracy should be included in every environment of school. Education environments and attitude and behavior of individuals, communication between them during activity breaks, school hallways, school garden, management rooms except these environments play an important role in democracy education.

Therefore, basic attitude and behaviors teachers try to gain to children should also be basic values of preschool education institutions and create a democratic school culture. Daily activities should also be created through democratic ways. By this way, children develop responsibility conscious and include interests and needs. Basic dimensions of attitude and behaviors that should be focused on in democracy education in preschool education are explained below.

Respect and Tolerance Education

Respect and tolerance are one of the basic principles of democracy. Respect and tolerance are basic conditions of individuals who live in a society to live together by accepting their differences. In other words, union of differences in democracy is provided through respect and tolerance. Therefore, respect and tolerance consist of a major part of democracy education. Education institutions are small communities in which children with different talents, histories and genetic qualities come together. Therefore, these education institutions should be a democratic environment which answer to and support their differences as well as giving education according to their individual differences[40].

Studies on understanding of children in relation to differences around them show that children can understand differences around them starting from age 1 and can demonstrate behaviors towards differences arising from appearances. Also, it is determined that children in preschool period compare their own qualities with the ones people around them have, they realize that they are respected more by establishing a relationship between strength and some differences and they conclude some differences as "good" or "bad"[43]. According to these results, it is possible to say that children in preschool period give meaning to differences around them. During this interpretation, children may be affected by the negative effect of the environment. Respect and tolerance education should be provided in preschool period so as to reduce negative effect of the environment and to enable them to accept differences as a natural richness. By this way, children can respect differences and approach them with tolerance through education process.

Activity Example 1: Teacher, why do they not play with me?

Sevgi is a child who talks and moves slowly because of an inflammatory disease. Sevgi's situation is accepted by her family and her close environment, but her friends do not adopt it when she starts preschool. Her friends do not want her to participate when they play games. Sevgi gets upset about it and asks her teacher: "Teacher, why do they not play with me?"

Her teacher watches Sevgi and determines the children that do not tolerate Sevgi. She reads them a story in which what a

> *disabled child experiences is told and asks them if there is a person like that around them. She mentions Sevgi's situation and asks them to think themselves in her place and makes them feel that whey they do is wrong. She also asks for support from their families. Afterwards, children gradually accept Sevgi's differences and learn to be tolerant, thus their personality qualities develop*[44].

In the education process, children should communicate with different people and empathize with them. Children should realize bias of themselves and people around them, consider them critically and defend themselves and others against these bias. Respect to differences education should be a part of daily activities in preschool. Teachers should provide information to children first in terms of respect education towards differences and then enable children to use these information in their lives. Children should communicate and empathize with individuals who have differences. Lastly, teachers should evaluate respect and tolerance behaviors of children towards difference with observation forms. Teachers can include the following applications in the education process of children for them to gain respect and tolerance[43]:

- Self and group identities of each child based on information and self-confidence should be supported,
- Children should communicate with people with different experiences and qualities,
- Children should be supported to look at different attitudes and biases critically,
- Children's abilities to face different attitudes and biases towards themselves and others should be developed.

In teaching respect and tolerance to children, teachers have an important role, but it is not enough on its own. Respect and tolerance education should be reflected on teacher's applications, programs, school environment and process. The role of family should not be forgotten during this process and the family should be involved. Respect and tolerance understanding of children towards the differences of others should be observed and the results should be evaluated[45]. Also, children who are not respected and tolerated because of their differences in school and negative attitudes of other children in this regard should be observed and various precautions should be taken for this purpose. Children should feel that they are respected by every employee in every environment of preschool education institutions.

Taking Responsibility Education

Sense of responsibility is tried to be gained to children starting from preschool period. Children who start elementary school should have already gained the responsibilities in relation to self-maintenance skills such as wearing his/her clothes, washing his/her hands and going to toilet. Because a child who starts elementary school should be ready to take new responsibilities such as learning how to read and write, preparing his/her bag besides these responsibilities.

In the education of responsibility, children seeing the consequences of their behaviors are an important factor. Therefore, adults should allow children to see the result of what they have done. Also, teachers should allow children to make a choice, support them to solve the problems they face on their own, award the behaviors that children demonstrate responsibility and enable them to evaluate the consequences of the behaviors they show.

Children to start a work on their own can be the first stage of responsibility behavior. Children should be supported when they show such wishes as long as they are not harmed. By this way, children can take new responsibilities[46].

Activity Example 2: Why does Ahmet not gather his toys?

Ahmet is an energetic and joyous boy. However, whenever it is time to gather the toys, he goes to the toilet or someplace else. His friend Gamze realizes it. She says to their teacher: "Teacher, we always play with these toys together, but Ahmet does not gather them at all. Please tell Ahmet to gather them." Teacher calls Ahmet to her side and says: "If we want to live together, there are responsibilities we all must be careful about. We would like to see you by our side while we gather toys." Ahmet tells that gathering toys is boring. Teachers turn on an energetic music as they gather toys and makes students dance as they tidy up. When the work becomes fun, Ahmet joins his friends and they gather the clothes while having fun. By this way, gathering toys is now fun for Ahmet[44].

In preschool, children should take personal responsibility in actions children take towards themselves and the people around them for the purpose of qualitative social development, children should be supported to develop democracy values by giving them decision-making and cooperation opportunities.

Starting from preschool period, children can develop a sense of responsibility by giving them gathering duties such as gathering their toys and stuff, maintenance of plants and animals in the classroom, control of lights in the classroom. Before these, the following studies can be made in developing a sense of conscious in preschool[46]:

- All children can be assigned towards their skills in protecting class order.
- By creating daily attendance panel, children may be asked to mark the sections which belong to themselves every day.
- The pages of the calendar may be collected by them in turn.
- They may be asked to place the activities they do in their files on their own.
- The duties in relation to the protection of order in their activity corners may be carried out in turn.
- They may be asked to repair the worn-out books.
- The responsibility to wearing and taking off their clothes may be given to them.
- They may be responsible of their own bags.
- They may be asked to transmit the note that needs to be transmit to the house orally on their own.

Developing social responsibility in preschool period plays an important role in the development of democracy conscious. Children can take responsibility for their close environments as well as their responsibilities in the classroom. For this purpose, children may realize learning activities by serving the community. Learning by service approach recommended firstly for middle school and higher education is also realized by preschool and elementary school students in our day. Preschool students can participate to these activities whose purpose is service to community under the guidance of their teachers[47]:

- Greening works in the gardens of the schools
- Gathering toys for the children of families with low income
- Gathering clothes for children who are in need of clothes
- Gathering school materials for children who are in need
- Preparing food basket for children who are in need
- Participating to cleaning works in school such as gathering garbage
- Preparing cards for children who say in orphanages such as birthday cards or cards for special days

Cooperation and Sharing Education

Cooperation and sharing is important in terms of development and settlement of democracy in a society since it is one of the top level social skills. Children who have cooperation and sharing skill adapt to society more easily and they can carry out responsibilities they have to carry out in their future lives in a more efficient way. Children start to gain cooperation behavior firstly in preschool education period. Group activities and games they play with their friends in this period is efficient for them to gain cooperation and sharing behaviors[38].

Cooperation works realized based on group activities help children to gain cooperation and moving together conscious. It creates group identity by pulling away from egoistic thinking. Group activities help children to develop participation skills and to take part in society as individuals. Also, children learn to make decisions, to respect various opinions and to compromise with group activities. Preschool teachers should emphasize the importance of cooperation and sharing for them to gain cooperation and sharing behavior and should enable children to make group activities in which they can develop common products by working together. Children have the sense of achieving great success by working together.

Activity Example 3: This picture we have made together is more beautiful, teacher!

Esra and Murat were happy on that day since they were going paint. Teacher said:

"We will make a different painting today" and hung a paper on the two walls that consisted of four cardboards. Teacher divided them into two groups. There were ten children in each group. Teacher said: "You will make this painting together. Decide what you want to do." Groups talked amongst themselves and they started working by choosing one of their various opinions. One group made a painting of the sea and other group painted a park. Children enjoyed this work which they did while listening to music. They were happy since they achieved something together and they said to their teachers: "This picture we have made together is more beautiful, teacher!"[44].

Working with group supports the development of communication skills and sense of responsibility of children. Preschool teachers can make these applications as group study:

- Playing games together
- Singing songs together
- Drama
- Producing projects together etc.

Participation to Decisions Education

One of the basic qualities of democracy is for individuals to participate to decisions about themselves and their close environment. Individuals participate to decisions in democratic societies whether they are being directed or they direct[38]. Because all individuals have to take responsibility in works made in democracy. Therefore, after opinions are expressed, all decisions must be taken through taking a vote.

By democracy education in early childhood period, children should trust that they can take decisions about their own lives. Children to take their own decisions develop their sense of self-confidence. These qualities are of great importance in creating self-confidence value[40].

Children to participate to decisions in societies in which they take part as individuals are also a children's right. Children to participate to decisions that are related to them are in article 12 in the Convention on the Rights of the Children. Children who have the behavior to participate to decisions make correct decisions in their future lives and they can participate to life as more efficient individuals. Therefore, education process should provide children to gain behavior of participation to decisions.

Participation to decisions firstly develops in family environment together with the process of them starting to talk. Education institutions are the first institutions in which children can participate to decisions in their social lives after family. Teachers to try to develop participation to decisions behavior of children while applying educational programs, taking children's opinions in selecting activities and games play an important role for them to learn the behavior of participation to decisions[38].

Activity Example 4: Should we sing or make drama?

Mother's day was close. Teacher Ayla thought of calling mothers to the classroom and prepare a surprise for them with children. Teacher Ayla asked children: "Should we prepare a surprise for your mothers?" All children said "Yes." Teacher Ayla wanted this to be activity to which all children participated and loved. She asked to children: "Should we sing or make drama on mother's day?" She aimed children to take their own decisions in this regard. Some children wanted to do drama and some wanted to sing. Teacher clarified the situation: "Do you want to sing 'My dear mother' song or do you want to play mothers and children?" This time, drama group was superior. Teacher Ayla designed an activity in which a group of children can do drama and the other group can sing. Mother's Day activities were successful. Meral told her mother on that evening: "Mom, do you know that today's activities were the idea of my class?" She told about it by feeling proud[44].

In the preschool, teacher may provide children to participate to decisions and be prideful of these decisions by giving them options. Teacher may provide the participation of children to decisions with these applications in the preschool period[40].

- Teacher may want children to choose one of the two activities. For example, "Should we paint or play a game?"
- Teachers may ask children to give their own decisions without offering them options.

For example, "We are not going to play in the garden since the weather is cold. What can we do?" By this way, teachers may enable them to give their own decisions by making them think that they have various options.

Participation of children to decision-making processes is important for them to develop self-respect. Because children who see that their decisions are asked and these decisions are reflected on their applications feel that they are valued and they become more participative in the application of the decisions taken. In the preschool period, children to gain the behavior of participation to decisions provide them to be more enthusiastic in participation to decisions taken in societies and enables them to be gain more efficient personalities.

Obeying the Rules Education

Obeying the rules which is one of the basic qualities of democracy is among the responsibilities of all citizens. Obeying the rules is based on the behavior of accepting the supremacy of law in democratic countries.

In democratic societies, individuals participate to the creation of rules and obey the rules. In early childhood period, obeying the rules education is realized by obeying class and school rules.

Creating class rules with children becomes a driving force them to obey the rules. Children who participate to the process of creating classroom rules understand why they need rules and realize which rules will help them to arrange behaviors in the classroom. Also, they understand the necessity of following and obeying the rules, they adopt the process of rules and learn to share the responsibility in relation to the events in the classroom[48].

Children learn the behavior of obeying the rules in the preschool period firstly with games. Children learn rules in an easy and harmless way through games. In a similar way, they learn to cooperate by participating to group activities. These activities play an important role for them to create rules and to gain the behavior of obeying the rules[36].

Activity Example 5: "Let's not break our games"

Seyda tried to make the biggest apartment in her imagination in block learning center in the free game time. But she could not succeed. Like always, Tolga came and crashed the apartment Seyda made with long efforts. Seyda could not take it any longer and started to cry. She sobbed. Because she told Tolga every time that he should not do it, but Tolga did not listen to her. Everybody gathered around Seyda. They tried to learn what happened. Tolga watched them from afar. Teacher suggested them to hold a meeting and asked everyone to sit in a circle. They made a rule: "Let's not break our games." Everybody made a picture in relation to this rule. Tolga drew a crying child in his picture. Teacher wrote "Let's not break our games" beneath it. Tolga's picture was hung on the panel for classroom rules. After that day, children played more comfortably[44].

Teacher should emphasize the necessity of rules in developing classroom and school rules to children. Especially necessities and problems provide important environments in developing classroom rules. Classroom rules should be made with children, teachers should lead children so that they act in accordance with rules. In creating classroom rules, children to make rules with their own words and paintings increase the efficiency of rules. Also, classroom rules should be hung to places where children can see them[47].

Activities that can be used in Democracy Education in Early Childhood Period

In education institutions which make full day, half time and dual education, two kinds of activities as routine activities and group activities are made. These activities can be used for children to gain democratic behavior and attitude. How democracy education can be included within these activities is as follows.

Routine Activities

Activities that are realized in certain times of day such as arrival to and departure from school, cleaning, toilet, sleeping and meal times. In these activities, children eat together and tidy up the classroom together. Children realize responsibilities such as carrying food try and gathering toys and they also obey the school roles such as queuing up for cleaning. Teachers should observe children during these activities, help them to carry out their responsibilities and make them obey the rules. Teachers should produce sound and productive solutions for problems children may face in this regard.

Group Activities

These are the activities children realize in small or big groups under the guidance of the teacher. Teachers include various activities according to the schedule. These activities consist of language, science and mathematics, game and movements, music, preparation to reading and writing, drama, art activities and field trips.

Teachers may benefit from these activities in terms of democracy[44]:

- ***Language activities*:** Basic values of democracy can be taught to children through language activities. In the activities before story, conversations with children about basic values of democracy may be had. Afterwards, stories about responsibility, respect, tolerance, sharing, cooperation, participation to decisions and obeying the rules may be read. After the story, children may be asked to play what happens in the story through dramatization, role playing and pantomime. For example; after a conversation about why there are rules in society, what happens to a child who do not obey the rules is told through story and after the story, what happens to this child may be dramatized.
- ***Game and movement activities*:** Game activities with rules are activities created by teachers or children and played by the group.

In the game activities, children move according to certain rules. Teachers should help children to create game rules and follow these rules. Also, themes such as peace, sharing and cooperation may be treated in the games. For example; children who represent different countries turn hand in hand in a circle. They tell the qualities of the countries and they pull up the world model together.

- ***Science and mathematics activities*:** These are the activities which steer children to make observation, research and examination. In science activities, children are introduced to their physical qualities and respect may be developed for self-identity by introducing others' physical qualities. Also, lives and feelings of people who do not have an arm or a leg, have problems in their various organs such as their eyes and ears or with disabilities which prevent them from moving may be included. For example; children may be asked to play a game with blindfolds. In science and nature activities, the right of children to live in a healthy environment may be included. Responsibilities that children need to realize for a healthy environment may be told.
- ***Studies for preparation to read and write*:** Preparation studies to read and write are the studies realized to increase the level of being prepared in the passing process to elementary school of children. In these studies, study papers which enable children to recognize, differentiate their own physical qualities and similarities and differences with others may be used. Also, different behavior samples may be pictured and children may be asked to mark correct and wrong situations in these paintings.
- ***Music activities*:** With music activities, music of different countries may be included to enable children to perceive different music. By this way, it can be demonstrated that music change by societies. Also, the fact that people can like different music may be explained. Within the scope of democracy education, studies with stories with music that are about democracy may be realized. For example; a music piece about classroom rules may be created.
- ***Drama activities*:** Drama is a frequently used method in democracy education. With drama, children may be asked to play different democratic values. Drama creates life like situations and enables them to understand the situation more closely. Children may reflect problems about their friends who are disrespectful, break cooperation and games.
- ***Art activities*:** Art activities may be used on their own or as complementary for the other activities. For example; after a story activity about children who are not fed about, children may be asked to paint a picture how to help these children. Children may

be asked to paint a picture or play dough blindfolded to enable them to feel the emotions of and empathize with a visually impaired person.

- ***Field trips*:** Children may be provided to visit cultures with different qualities. For example; families with high socio-economic level can visit schools with low socio-economic level as field trips. By this way, children realize that there are different lives.

In the preschool period, since children are in the pre-process period, democracy, human rights education of should be provided through various activities in accordance with the level of children. Also, principles such as provision of efficient participation, benefitting from daily life and creation of democratic learning environment should be considered. In this period, it must be considered that children are emotionally sensitive and materials and activities that may affect them negatively should be avoided[30].

CONCLUSIONS

Nations to maintain democracy life depends on individuals who believe in democracy and who adapt basic values of democracy as a lifestyle. Therefore, all countries should teach democracy to their children and provide them to gain a democratic personality. The early childhood period in which a part of personal development is realized is an important process for individuals to gain democracy conscious.

Children to gain democratic attitude and behaviors in early ages are of great importance individually and socially. Introducing and teaching children the basic rights of children and basic freedoms that they should have is one of the necessities of our age. In this context, the Convention on the Rights of the Children is the most important document prepared in relation to children's rights and it brings in an international quality and dimension to children's rights. Children's rights are human rights unique to children and children's rights are intertwined with democracy education. The most important place in which children can learn about their rights and use the right of education is school. They go to school starting from early ages and start to use the right of education.

In education institutions, in terms of children taking effective children's rights and democracy education, teacher has an important role in acting in accordance with democracy and human rights, not distinguishing between nation, belief and socio-culture, respecting students' opinions in the classroom.

Democracy education given in the preschool period creates the foundation of democracy conscious given in the elementary school and the following education steps. In other words, other education steps should be based on the democracy education given in the preschool period and follow it gradually.

REFERENCES

[1] Akyüz, E. (2000). Ulusal ve Uluslar Arasi Hukukta Çocuk Haklarinin ve Güvenliginin Korunmasi. Ankara: Milli Egitim Basim Evi.

[2] Çilga, I. (2001). "Demokrasi, Insan Haklari Kültürü ve Çocuk Haklari". Milli Egitim. 151: 69–73.

[3] Ballar, S. (1998). *Çocuk haklari*. Istanbul: Beta Basin Yayin Dagitim.

[4] Akyüz, E. (2001). "Çocuk Haklari Sözlesmesi'nin Temel Ilkeleri Isiginda Çocugun Egitim Hakki". Milli Egitim. 151: 3–24.

[5] Aras, H., Birinci, F. and ve Uluç, F. (2001). Ikinci uluslararasi egitimde çocuk haklari konferansi, Milli Egitim Dergisi, 151, Available from *http://yayim.meb.gov.tr/dergiler/151/aras_*

[6] Franklin, B. (1993). Çocuk Haklari, Istanbul: Ayrinti Yayincilik.

[7] Gollob, R. and Krapf, P. (2007). Exploring children's rights - nine short projects for primary level. Council of Europe Publishing. V.

[8] Gülmez, M. (2001). Insan Haklari ve Demokrasi Egitimi. (2. Baski). Ankara: TODAIE Yayinlari.

[9] OHCHR (The Office of the High Commissioner for Human Rights) (2003). ABC, Teaching Human Rights: Practical Activities for Primary and Secondary Schools. (cited 2016 November 10) Available from *http://www.unhchr.ch/html/*

[10] Patrick, J.J. (2003b). Teaching Democracy. (ED.480420). (cited 2016 November 10) Available from *http://www.eric.gov*

[11] Yesil, R. (2002). Okul ve Ailede Insan Haklari ve Demokrasi Egitimi. Ankara: Nobel Yayin Dagitim.

[12] Selvi, K. (2004c). "Ilkögretim Programlarinda Demokrasi ve Insan Haklari Egitimi". XI Egitim Bilimleri Kongresi, Cilt I, 193–211, Ankara: 2004.

[13] Levin, B. (1998). The Educational Requirement for Democracy. *Curriculum Inquiry*, 28(1): 57–79.

[14] Ersoy, A.F. (2008). Okulöncesinde demokrasi egitimi ve çocuk haklari. *In*: Deveci, H. (*ed.*), Okulöncesinde demokrasi egitimi ve çocuk haklari. Eskisehir: Anadolu Üniversitesi Yayinlari. pp. 70–92.

[15] Gündogdu, K. (2004). Ilkögretimde Demokrasi ve Insan Haklari Egitimi Üzerine Bir Durum Çalismasi. Yayinlanmamis doktora tezi. ODTÜ, Ankara.

[16] Baker, J. (2004). Parenting, childhood studies an introduction. Oxford: Blackwell Publishing.

[17] Smith, A.B. and Bjerke, H. (2009). Children's citizenship. *In*: Taylor, N. and Smith, A.B. (*eds.*), Children as citizens. New Zealand: Otago University Press.

[18] Craig, W. (1999). Childhood social development. London: Blackwell Publisher.

[19] Büyükkaragöz, S.S. and Kesici, S. (1998). Demokrasi ve Insan Haklari Egitimi. Ankara: Türk Demokrasi Vakfi Yayinlari.

[20] Cirhinlioglu, F.G. (2001). Çocuk ruh sagligi ve gelisimi: Okul öncesi dönem (1. Basim). Ankara: Nobel Yayin Dagitim.

[21] Oktay, A. (1999). Yasamin Sihirli Yillari: Okulöncesi Dönem. Birinci baski. Istanbul: Epsilon Yayincilik.
[22] Oktay, A. and Unutkan, Ö.P. (2003). Okulöncesi Egitim Programi Uygulama Rehberi: Ne Yapiyorum? Neden Yapiyorum? Nasil Yapmaliyim? Istanbul: Ya-Pa Yayinlar, pp. 65–66.
[23] Altinköprü, T. (2000). Çocugun Basarisi Nasil Saglanir? Istanbul: Hayat Yayinlari.
[24] Yavuzer, H. (2006). Çocuk Psikolojisi (29. Basim). Istanbul: Remzi Kitabevi.
[25] Aydin, M.Z. (2008). Ailede çocugun ahlak egitimi (6. Baski). Ankara: Nobel Yayin Dagitim.
[26] Basal, H.A. (2007). Geli°im ve psikoloji: Nasil mutlu bir çocuk yetistirebilirim? (4. Baski). Istanbul: Morpa Kültür Yayinlari.
[27] Dinç, B. (2015). Okulöncesi egitim kurumuna devam eden çocuklarin ebeveynlerinin çocuk haklari egitimi konusundaki görüsleri. Egitimde Nitel Arastirmalar Dergisi - *Journal of Qualitative Research in Education*, 3(1): 7–25. [Online]: Available from http://www.enadonline.com
[28] Gözütok, D. (2007). Ögretim Ilke ve Yöntemleri. Ekinoks Yayincilik: Ankara.
[29] Jenkins-Parker, M. (1999). Sparing the Rod: Discipline and Children Rights, London: Trentham Books.
[30] Howe, R.B. and Covell, K. (2005). Empowering children: Children's rights education as a pathway to citizenship. London: University of Toronto Press.
[31] Neslitürk, S. and ve Ersoy, A.F. (2007). Preschool Teacher Candidates' Opinions on The Teaching of Children's Rights. *Journal of Theory and Practice in Education,* 3(2): 245–257. (cited 2016 October 6) Available from http://eku.comu.edu.tr/index/3/2/snesliturk.afigenersoy.pdf
[32] Uçus, S. and Sahin, A.E. (2012). Çocuk Haklari Sözlesmesi'ne Yönelik Ögretmenlerin ve Okul Yöneticilerinin Görüsleri. Adnan Menderes Üniversitesi Egitim Fakültesi Egitim Bilimleri Dergisi, Haziran 2012, 3(1): 25–41 Available from *http: / /dergi.adu.edu.tr / egitimbilimleri /*
[33] Güder, S.Y. and Yildirim, A. (2014). Adiyaman Üniversitesi Sosyal Bilimler Enstitüsü Dergisi, 7(16): 151–170
[33] Karaman-Kepenekçi, Y. (2000). Insan Haklari Egitimi. Ankara: Ani Yayincilik.
[34] Gözütok, D. (1999). "Vatandaslik ve Insan Haklari Egitimi Projesi". 4. Ulusal Egitim Bilimleri Kongresi. Cilt 1. Eskisehir: Anadolu Üniversitesi Yayinlari, pp. 55–67.
[35] Korhonen, R. (2005). "Teaching Citizenship in Pre-School Educational Process". *In*: Ross, A. (*ed.*), Teaching Citizenship. London. CiCe, 443–448.
[36] Patrick, J.J. (2003a). A Global Perspective on Human Rights Education. (ED.421447). Available from *http: / /www.eric.gov*
[37] Poyraz, H. and Dere, H. (2001). Okulöncesi Egitimin Ilke ve Yöntemleri. Ankara: Ani Yayincilik.
[38] Yasar, S. (2002). "Okulöncesi Egitimde Temel Aliskanliklar ve Sosyal Davranislarin Kazandirilmasi". Okulöncesi Egitimin Ilke ve Yöntemleri. (*ed.*), Yasar, S. Eskisehir: Anadolu Üniversitesi Açik Ögretim Fakültesi Yayinlari, pp. 87–98.
[39] Hopkins, G. (2002). Teaching Citizenship's Five Themes. (cited 2016 October 6) Available from *http: / /www.education world.com / acurr008. html*
[40] Erwin, E.J. and ve Kipness, N.A. (1997). "Fostering Democratic Values in Inclusive Early Childhood Settings". *Early Childhood Education Journal*. 25(1): 57–60.

[41] NCSS (National Council for Social Studies) (1998). Social Studies for Early Childhood and Elementary School Children Preparing for the 21st Century. (cited 2016 October 6) Available from *http://socialstudies.org/positions/elementary*

[42] Skolverket (2005). Democracy and Fundamental Values. (cited 2016 October 12) Available from *http://www.skolverket.se/content/1/c4/12/57//en_demokrati.pdf*

[43] KDEV (Kadin Emegini Degerlendirme Vakfi) (2006). Erken Çocuklukta Farkliliklara Saygi Egitimi El Kitabi. Birinci basim. Istanbul: Kadin Emegini Degerlendirme Vakfi Yayinlari.

[44] Deveci, H (*ed.*) (2008). Okulöncesinde demokrasi egitimi ve çocuk haklari. Eskisehir: Anadolu Üniversitesi Yayinlari.

[45] Adams, L.D. and Ebbeck, M. (1997). "The Early Years and the Development of Tolerance". *International Journal of Early Years Education,* 5(2): 101–106.

[46] Unutkan, Ö.P. (2005). "Okulöncesi Dönemde Sorumluluk Egitimi". Okulöncesi Egitimde Güncel Konular. Ayla Oktay and ve Özgül Polat Unutkan (*eds.*), Istanbul: Morpa Yayinlari, pp. 189–197.

[47] Gaye, B. (2003). "Teaching Citizenship and Social Responsibility". Childhood Education. 22. Available from *http://www.thefreelibrary.com/_/print/PrintArticle.* aspx?id=112165892

[48] DeVries, R. and Zan, B. (1994). Moral Classrooms, Moral Children: Creating A Constructivist Atmosphere in Early Education. New York: Teacher Collage Press.

12

Women Empowerment Through Micro Financing in India

NAZIA JAMAL[1]* AND FARHANA. JAMAL[2]

"Geeta took out a bank loan to pay for the materials for her loom. She sells her products in the local market –empowering through micro financing"

ABSTRACT

The concept of microfinance is described by F.A.J. Bouman's in his (1990) book, "Small, Short and Unsecured" - microfinance is the provision of very small loans that are repaid within short periods of time, and is essentially used by low income individuals and households who have few assets that can be used as collateral. Availability and access to credit by low-income families is the most important pre-condition for development, as it helps in increase in the income-earning activities and opportunities of the poor, further it also improves their living conditions, particularly through housing and infrastructure provision. Problems associated with access to loans from banks and other formal institutions, and the low-income / asset-holding position of the poor themselves are two factors that require a drastic restructuring in the mechanism of the existing systems of credit delivery, as it creates a demand-supply mismatch and results in inefficient and insufficient transformation of the policy efforts in to results. In this article an attempt

[1]Institute of Management Science, University of Lucknow, Sultanpur village, Jankipuram extension, Lucknow, Uttar Pradesh, India.

[2]Institute of Co-operative and Corporate Managment, Research and Training, 467, Sector=21, Institutional Area, Ring Road, Indira Nagar, Lucknow, Uttar Pradesh-226016, India.

**Corresponding author*: E-mail: naziajamal786@gmail.com

has been made to assess and analyse the concept and further role played by microfinance in empowering women in India.

***Key words*:** Microfinance, Microinsurance, Micropension Women Empowerment

---

The prime challenge India facing today is balanced and inclusive economic growth. The profits from the economic growth are mostly with the creamy layer of the society while the poorer struggles to reap the benefits. In the hierarchy from top most to lower bottom, it's quite hard to keep the lower society that too women especially in the same lane as that of the creamy layer. Due to societal suppression women are most likely to refrain themselves from the economic activities. To encourage more and more women enrolments or empower more and more women for economic activities is quite necessary to provide appropriate access to financial services of banking sector in rural areas which has always remained a formidable task owing to several supply side constraints including poor branch network in remote areas, lack of appropriate financial products and demand side constraints like financial illiteracy etc. Engaging these sections of society to mainstream economically is essential to achieve equitable growth. Microfinance sector has responded to these challenges admirably in the last 20 years. Microfinance is a mechanism for economic prosperity that provides savings and investment facility to the underprivileged. Microfinance includes services ranging from credit facilities, savings, insurance, remittance and also covers non - financial services like training and counselling. Microfinance plays a major role in the financial inclusion which is considered as a major policy objective in the country. Varied schemes and microfinance programmes are initiated by the government with a focuses on mitigating poverty and to improve the lives of rural poor with the help of income generating economic activities. Creating self employment opportunities is one way of attacking poverty and solving the problems of unemployment. There are over 24 crore people below the poverty line in the country.

The Scheme of Micro-Credit has been found as an effective instrument for lifting the poor above the level of poverty by providing them increased self-employment opportunities and making them credit worthy. Total requirement of micro-credit in the country has been assessed at Rs. 50,000 crore. Micro-credit programme works through NGOs/SHGs and the merit lies in weekly monitoring and refund of instalments. The rate of recovery under SIDBI's Micro credit programme is as high as 98%. Though there are various Departments and Organisations implementing micro-credit schemes in the areas of activity falling under their purview but their total reach is very low *i.e.*, not more than Rs. 5,000 crore. Thus the existing programmes cater to only 5 to 10% of total requirements and there is considerable scope for expansion of such programmes.

In India, Micro-credit programmes are run primarily by NABARD in the field of agriculture and SIDBI in the field of Industry, Service and Business (ISB). The success of Micro-credit programme lies in diversification of services. Micro Finance Scheme of SIDBI is under operation since January, 1999 with a corpus of Rs. 100 crore and a network of about 190 capacity assessed rated MFIs/NGOs. Under the programme, total amount of Rs. 191 crore have been sanctioned upto 31st December, 2003, benefiting over 9 lakh beneficiaries. Under the programme, NGOs/MFIs are supposed to provide equity support in order to avail SIDBI finance. But they find it difficult to manage the needed equity support because of their poor financial condition. The problem has got aggravated due to declining interest rate on deposits. The Office of the Development Commissioner (Small Scale Industries) under Ministry of MSME is launching a new scheme of Micro Finance Programme to overcome the constraints in the existing scheme of SIDBI, whose reach is currently very low. It is felt that Government's role can be critical in expanding reach of the scheme, ensuring long term sustainability of NGOs/MFIs and development of Intermediaries for identification of viable projects.

What is empowerment? There are several interpretations. Krishna (2003) defines empowerment as "the process of increasing the capacity of individuals or groups to make choices and to transform those choices into desired actions and outcomes. Central to this process is actions that both build individual and collective assets, and improves the efficiency and fairness of the organizational and institutional context which govern the use of these assets." Thus, as a report from the World Bank confirms (World Bank, 2001), societies that discriminate on the basis of gender pay the cost of greater poverty, slower economic growth, weaker governance and a lower living standard for their people.

The World Bank also identifies four key elements of empowerment to draft institutional reforms: access to information; inclusion and participation; accountability; and local organisational capacity. Empowerment is also related to the concepts of social capital and community-driven development, with which it is sometimes confused. As Krishna (2003) points out, empowerment by nature is a process and/or outcome. Social capital, on the other hand, features social organisation such as networks, norms and inter-personal trust, which facilitate coordination and cooperation for mutual benefit. And Community

Driven Development (CDD) is a methodology for undertaking development organisations that give control of decisions and resources to community groups. Thus it is an activity by nature. Connecting these three, Grootaert (2003) points out that building social capital facilitates empowerment. Social capital and empowerment are multi-level concepts and facilitate the link to poverty reduction, whereas CDD is a manifestation of social capital and empowerment.

Microfinance is a basket of financial services, which are used in addressing issues related to poverty alleviation, financial support to micro entrepreneurs etc. who have no collateral and wouldn't otherwise qualify for a standard bank loan. These are available through institutions, non-profit organizations and larger banks. Microfinance is a one of the tool for fighting women empowerment on a large scale. It provides small loans, to poor people, mostly women, to start or expand very small, self-sufficient businesses. Through their own ingenuity and drive, and with the support of the lending microfinance institution (MFI), poor women are able to start their journey out of poverty.

Micro financing by non-formal financial organisations already had tentative beginnings by the time NABARD initiated the pilot project for Self Help Group-Bank Linkage in 1992. The earliest instance of microfinance in India can be traced to the initiatives undertaken for providing banking services to the poor women employed in the unorganised sector of Ahmedabad city in Gujarat through the SEWA Bank, set up as an urban cooperative bank in early seventies. Since then the bank has been providing banking services to the poor and self employed working as hawkers, vendors, domestic servants etc. This model has not been replicated elsewhere in the country, though the Working Women's Forum (WWF) started promoting working women's cooperative societies in Tamil Nadu since 1980. Annapurna of Pune and Shrey as in Kerala were other similar initiatives. The Savings and Credit Groups experiment of MYRADA was later supported by NABARD and emerged as the crucible of its pilot project for linking banks with self - help groups (SHGs) This pilot evolved into a regular lending programme as an outcome of the recommendations of the RBI's Working Group on NGOs and SHGs (RBI,1996). The number of SHGs expanded exponentially with governments poverty alleviation programmes using them as the base as in Mahalir-thittam in Tamil Nadu, Kudumbashree of Kerala or Velugu in Andhra Pradesh. Thus the SHG - Bank Linkage Programme has expanded at a fast pace in India to evolve into the largest microfinance programme in the world, and undoubtedly, it is the main microfinance programme in India.

REVIEW OF LITERATURE

There are lot of literature on opportunity and challenges of micro finance institution across the world, though only few studies have been carried out on the related topic, Emerson Moses, has studied that micro finance has emerged as a catalyst of rural development, especially in the overpopulated country like India. S. Sarumathi and Dr. K. Mohan found that microfinance brought psychological and social empowerment than economic empowerment. Impact of micro finance is appreciable in bringing confidence, courage, skill development and empowerment. Devraja T.S. has studied the India's achievement of the MDG of halving the population of poor by 2015 as well as achieving a broad based economic growth also hinges on a successful poverty alleviation strategy. In this backdrop, the impressive gains made by SHG-Bank linkage programme in coverage of rural population with financial services offers a ray of hope. In a similar study Mr. Nikhil considered that the microcredit movement has proved that it is possible to deliver financial services to poor people living in rural areas at a large scale, free from any reliance on subsidies. Manisha Raj, in his research paper entitled "Microfinance Institutions in India and its Legal Aspects" states that Microfinance institutions have been proved a very important financial wing to incorporate the poor in the financial sector. Now on the other aspect like the challenges faced by the microfinance institutions Mr. Badrudduza found the positive results shown by MFIs in many countries but still there are a number of challenges before the microfinance industry, he has shown in his paper. Rajesh and Ravi states in their paper, despite the role of microfinance is very good in poverty alleviation but the unethical and extortionist practices by MFIs led to arguably a draconian measure in its home turf Andhra Pradesh halting the industry in its tracks. In the line of challenges Dr. Sidhatha and their co authors found that the Microfinance delivery involves macro and micro challenges. The macro challenges faced by MFIs include the inaccessibility of the micro finance services to the rural poor, the capital inadequacy of the MFIs, the demand supply gap in provision of microcredit and micro savings and the lack of women orientation in marketing, evaluation and delivery of microfinance. The micro challenges include the inability to reduce the high transaction cost involved in delivering microfinance, the non-availability of documentary evidence and collateral among majority of rural poor, difficulty in reducing the dependency of the rural poor on money lenders and lastly the problem of repayment tracking where lending is not based on documentary evidence. K. Muralidhar Rao found in his paper that Private MFIs in India, barring a few exceptions, are still fledgling efforts and are therefore unregulated. Jonathan Morduch and Stuart Rutherford in his study "Microfinance: analytical issues for India" states that the microfinance movement is thus striving to match the convenience and flexibility of the informal sector, while adding reliability and the promise of continuity and in some countries it is already doing this on a significant scale. "It appears that what microfinance means is well understood, but to clearly articulate". However, microfinance is term that refers to the provision of a broad range of financial services such as deposits, loans, payment services, money transfers and insurance to poor and low-income households and their micro-enterprises. The needs of microfinance comes from the disadvantaged sections of the society - who are unable to access to services of formal sector financial intermediaries - and are typically excluded from the formal banking system for lack of survival collateral, in short the poor and the very poor. The definitions of these groups vary from country to country. The clients of the microfinance institutes are normally employed in the informal sector, with closely interlinked household and business activities and earning low income. In a much narrower sense though, microfinance is often referred to as microcredit for tiny informal businesses of micro entrepreneurs, the services being mainly delivered by socially oriented non-governmental organizations (NGOs).

WOMEN EMPOWERMENT

Certain definitions of Empowerment from report on "Empowering women through Micro finance" "enabling each person to reach his or her God - given potential". According to UNIFEM, "gaining the ability to generate choices and exercise bargaining power", "developing a sense of self - worth, a belief in one's ability to secure desired changes, and the right to control one's life" are important elements of women's empowerment, In order for a woman to be empowered, she needs access to the material, human, and social resources necessary to make strategic choices in her life.

Not only have women been historically disadvantaged in access to material resources like credit, property, and money, but they have also been excluded from social resources or insider knowledge of some businesses. In a nut shell, women empowerment through microfinance has aim to make them economically able to contribute in their life and in their family income so that they would have self-esteem and opportunity to develop as well as important role in decisions with respect to life related to them.

Following five dimensions of women empowerment are used to measure overall empowerment:

1. Household decision making;
2. Economic decision making;
3. Freedom of movement;
4. Ownership of property and
5. Political and social awareness, etc.

Higher income increases women's ability to contribute more to the household expenditure, and eventually improve their empowerment.

MICRO FINANCE AND WOMEN EMPOWERMENT

Micro Finance is usually understood to entail the provision of financial services to micro-entrepreneurs and small businesses, which lack access to banking and related services due to high transaction costs associated with services these client categories. The two main mechanisms for the delivery of financial services to such clients are (1) relationship-based banking for individual entrepreneurs and small businesses and (2) group-based models, where several entrepreneurs come together to apply for loans and other services as a group.

There are some 500 million low income entrepreneurs in the world and about 5% have access to financial services. It is a tool for empowerment of the poor low income persons that do not have access to formal financial institutions. Micro-finance targets poor women because they have good track records. When they have the financial means, they invest that money back into their families, resulting in better health and education, and stronger local economies.

Research has shown that investing in women offers the most effective means to improve health, nutrition, hygiene, and educational standards for families and consequently for the whole society. Thus, a special support for women in both financial and non-financial services is necessary.

IMPACT OF MICROFINANCE

Micro finance programmes for women are increasingly seen by development agencies as effective poverty alleviation intervention, High repayment rates are interrelated to mean that women are using loans productively and controlling credit. It is widely assumed that is a clear and direct relationship between access to credit and an increase in the status of women within their households and communities.

Bank linkage programme, which is the largest microfinance programme in the world, today touches 101 million households through 7.9 million SHGs with thrift and deposits of about INR 1,36,914 million, annual loan off take of INR 3,72,869 million and loan outstanding of nearly INR 5,71,192 million. Despite these milestones, a large section of the poor population still remains unreached and even majority who are in the SHG fold face the issue of inadequate credit. Bridging the last mile gap and forging partnerships to meet the myriad needs of the poor and to ensure sustainable livelihoods to them are the biggest challenges being faced today. Recently, NABARD and NRLM collaborated in a meaningful way to bring greater synergy in efforts and in taking SHG Bank linkage programme to a higher plane.

Microfinance: A Little goes a Long Way

Microfinance involves extending small loans, savings and other basic financial services to people that don't currently have access to capital. It's a key strategy in helping people living in poverty to become financially independent, which helps them become more resilient and better able to provide for their families in times of economic difficulty. Considering nearly half the world survives on less than $2 day, microfinance is a vital solution. Here are six benefits of microfinance:

1. ***Access:*** Banks simply won't extend loans to those with little or no assets, and generally don't engage in the small size of loan typically associate with micro-financing. Micro-financing is based on the philosophy that even small amounts of credit can help end the cycle of poverty.
2. ***Better loan repayment rates*:** Microfinance tends to target women borrowers, who are statistically less likely to default on their loans than men. So these loans help empower women, and they are often safer investments for those loaning the funds.
3. ***Extending education*:** Families receiving micro-financing are less likely to pull their children out of school for economic reasons. Sita serves tea in her grocery and snack shop in Nepal. Sita received skills training and a business loan from Plan.
4. ***Improved health and welfare*:** Micro-financing can lead to improved access to clean water and better sanitation while also providing better access to health care.

5. ***Sustainability***: Even a small working capital loan of $100 can be enough to launch a small business in a developing country that could help the benefactor pull themselves and their family out of poverty.
6. ***Job creation***: Micro-financing can help create new employment opportunities, which has a beneficial impact on the local economy.

SHG-BANK LINKAGE PROGRAMME

SHG-Bank Linkage Programme through its innovative model of linking informal SHGs with the formal banking system had brought in a paradigm shift in expanding the credit penetration and financial inclusion of the marginalized and excluded sections in society. The community based microfinance approach under SHG-BLP, which centered on bringing the poor onto the frontline in terms of thrift, credit linkage, livelihood activities, income generation, financial management and overall socio-economic empowerment was well accepted by the financial institutions, NGOs, civil society organizations, governments as well as other stakeholders. Despite the positive trend being exhibited there is a lurking fearregarding overheating of the sector, multiple financing to the poor clients, poor financial literacy and some grey areas in regulation. SHG-BLP is rather uncharitably being compared by many with MFI led Micro-finance programmes ignoring its contribution in terms of thrift and savings, handholding to inculcate financial literacy, provision of credit besides bringing community participation and building social capital etc. Efforts of NABARD during the year had paid off and can be seen in the turnaround made.

SPECIAL INITIATIVES

Scheme for Promotion of Women SHGs in backward districts of India NABARD, in association with the Department of Financial Services, Ministry of Finance, Govt. of India continued to implement a scheme for promotion and financing of Women Self Help Groups in 150 identified backward districts of the country. The USP of this scheme is that it provides for selection of an anchor NGO in each of the district not only for promoting and enabling credit linkage of these groups with banks (like any other SHPIs under SHG-BLP of NABARD) but also serving as a business facilitator for extending outreach of the banks, regular monitoring of the SHGs promoted and also being responsible for repayment of loans by SHGs to banks. For these services the Anchor NGO is entitled for service charges @5% of the outstanding loan amount. This approach is expected to facilitate sustained financial inclusion by extending banking services to women members of SHGs, promote sustainable livelihood opportunities to the members and facilitate effective implementation of other social development programmes for women through SHGs.

Swarnajayanti Gram Swarozgar Yojana (SGSY) and National Rural-Livelihoods Mission (NRLM) SGSY was effective from 1st April 1999 as a self employment programme introduced by union government to provide assistance to poor families living below the poverty line in rural areas to take up self employment by forming SHGs. Persons taking up self-employment are called Swarozgaris. They may take up the activity either individually or in group. Swarozgaris earn '2,000 per month, exclusive of bank loan repayment. SGSY was restructured as NRLM. Aajeevika or National Rural Livelihoods Mission (NRLM) was introduced by Ministry of Rural Development with the assistance from World Bank for addressing poverty alleviation with greater focus and momentum and to achieve Millennium Development Goals.

MICRO INSURANCE

To increase awareness regarding micro insurance among SHG members and to enhance their enrolment under the scheme Religare Health Insurance has been sanctioned two pilot projects, one in Alwar district of Rajasthan and another in Ramgarh district of Jharkhand. The projects envisages: provision of Health Insurance and Personal Accident Cover; issuance of a Master Policy in the name of the SHPI and individual cover in the name of SHG member and his/her spouse (the couple being treated as one unit); that the insured must be at least 18 years and not more than 70 years of age; that insurance cover will be provided for a period of one year to each beneficiary from the date the policy comes into effect; and will enable SHG members/families to avail cashless treatment in a hospital for any illness/injury/disease (that is not specifically excluded) and also for maternity treatment needs upto a maximum limit of 50,000/.

MICRO PENSION

International Network of Alternative Financial Institutions (INAFI) has been sanctioned a micro pension pilot project to be implemented in the tribal district of Dungarpur in Rajasthan. The project envisages educating SHG leaders, federation leaders and NGOs on the micro pension products, through pension literacy/mobilization meetings and workshops for NGO staff members and technical workshops for finalizing the pension products. The project targets coverage of minimum 1000 SHG members under micro pension.

Microfinance is a developmental approach towards alleviating poverty and vulnerability. It is also acknowledged as a cost effective tool to provide financial services to the underprivileged. Microfinance through self help group model results in greater impact in transforming the lives of poor. SHG model has emerged as largest and fastest growing successful community based organisation in the developing world. The SHG bank linkage model provides the cheapest and most direct source of funds. However, this has to be set against the low volume of funds that can be made available through this channel in view of the linkagc of credit with savings. As in other financial services models the microfinance model also has evolved over the last two decades. India is a country in which stone-age tribal communities and 21st century condominiums cohabit. Bullock carts and bullet trains are contemporaries. Likewise even in the financial services sector, despite expansion taking place with increased outreach of mainstream institutions through a range of technology platforms and novel institutions like small finance banks and payments banks cominginto being, the niche area for microfinance will continue to exist, not only till the complete eradication of poverty, but even beyond that. In the nook and corner of the country NGO-MFIs, Self Help Groups will keep up their activities, providing services to the needy as long as they are demanded. In this gigantic effort, the spectrum of stakeholders is contributing its mite to nurture and strengthen this institutional infrastructure so that financial services reach the last person in the remotest corner of the country.

REFERENCES

Ackerly, Brooke A. (1995). "Testing the tools of development: Credit programmes, loan involvement and women's empowerment". *IDS Bulletin*, 26(3): 56–68.

Amin, R., Becker, S. and Bayes, A. (1998). "NGO-promoted micro credit programs and women's empowerment in rural Bangladesh: Quantitative and qualitative evidence". *The Journal of Developing Areas*, 32(2): 221–36.

Batliwala, Srilatha (1994). "The Meaning of Women's Empowerment: New Concepts from Action" *In*: Sen, G., Germain, A. and Chen, L.C. (*eds.*), Population Policies Reconsidered: Health, Empowerment and Rights, Harvard University Press, Cambridge, pp. 127–38.

Chambers, Robert (1997). Whose Reality Counts? Putting the First Last London.

Goetz, Anne Marie and Gupta, Rina Sen (1996). "Who takes the credit? Gender, power, and control over loan use in rural credit programs in Bangladesh". *World Development*, 24(1): 45–63.

Hashemi, Syed M., Schuler, Sidney Ruth and Riley, Ann P. (1996). "Rural credit programs and women's empowerment in Bangladesh". *World Development*, 24(4): 63553.

Human Development Report (1995)

Mayoux, Linda (2000). "Micro-finance and the Empowerment of Women - A Review of the Key Issues". International Labor Organization, Geneva.

13

Restructuring Indian Economy Through Economic Reforms

Nazia Jamal[1*]

ABSTRACT

The reform process in India was initiated with the aim of accelerating the pace of economic growth and eradication of poverty. The process of economic liberalization in India can be traced back to the late 1970s. However, the reform process began in earnest only in July 1991. It was only in 1991 that the Government signaled a systemic shift to a more open economy with greater reliance upon market forces, a larger role for the private sector including foreign investment, and a restructuring of the role of Government. In this paper attempt has been made to evaluate the process of restructuring in Indian economy through various economic reforms initiated in India.

***Key words*:** Demonetisation, GST, FDI, Black money, Economic liberalisation

The economic reforms initiated in 1991 introduced far-reaching measures, which changed the working and machinery of the economy. These changes were pertinent to the following:

- Dominance of the public sector in the industrial activity
- Discretionary controls on industrial investment and capacity expansion
- Trade and exchange controls
- Limited access to foreign investment

[1]Institute of Management Science, University of Lucknow, Sultanpur village, Jankipuram extension, Lucknow, Uttar Pradesh, India.

**Corresponding author*: E-mail: naziajamal786@gmail.com

- Public ownership and regulation of the financial sector

The reforms have unlocked India's enormous growth potential and unleashed powerful entrepreneurial forces. Since 1991, successive governments, across political parties, have successfully carried forward the country's economic reform agenda.

REFORMS IN INDUSTRIAL POLICY

Industrial policy was restructured to a great extent and most of the central government industrial controls were dismantled. Massive deregulation of the industrial sector was done in order to bring in the element of competition and increase efficiency. Industrial licensing by the central government was almost abolished except for a few hazardous and environmentally sensitive industries. The list of industries reserved solely for the public sector – which used to cover 18 industries, including iron and steel, heavy plant and machinery, telecommunications and telecom equipment, minerals, oil, mining, air transport services and electricity generation and distribution was drastically reduced to three: defense aircrafts and warships, atomic energy generation, and railway transport. Further, restrictions that existed on the import of foreign technology were withdrawn.

REFORMS IN TRADE POLICY

It was realized that the import substituting inward looking development policy was no longer suitable in the modern globalising world. Before the reforms, trade policy was characterized by high tariffs and pervasive import restrictions. Imports of manufactured consumer goods were completely banned. For capital goods, raw materials and intermediates, certain lists of goods were freely importable, but for most items where domestic substitutes were being produced, imports were only possible with import licenses. The criteria for issue of licenses were non-transparent, delays were endemic and corruption unavoidable. The economic reforms sought to phase out import licensing and also to reduce import duties.

Import licensing was abolished relatively early for capital goods and intermediates which became freely importable in 1993, simultaneously with the switch to a flexible exchange rate regime. Quantitative restrictions on imports of manufactured consumer goods and agricultural products were finally removed on 1 April 2001, almost exactly ten years after the reforms began, and that in part because of a ruling by a World Trade Organization dispute panel on a complaint brought by the United States.

FINANCIAL SECTOR REFORMS

Financial sector reforms have long been regarded as an integral part of the overall policy reforms in India. India has recognized that these reforms are imperative for increasing the efficiency of resource mobilization and allocation in the real economy and for the overall macroeconomic stability. The reforms have been driven by a thrust towards liberalization and several initiatives such as liberalization in the interest rate and reserve requirements have been taken on this front. At the same time, the government has emphasized on stronger regulation aimed at strengthening prudential norms, transparency and supervision to mitigate the prospects of systemic risks. Today, the Indian financial structure is inherently strong, functionally diverse, efficient and globally competitive. During the last fifteen years, the Indian financial system has been incrementally deregulated and exposed to international financial markets along with the introduction of new instruments and products.

The economic ecosystem of India has undergone extreme overhaul at all levels since the time it gained Independence on 15 August 1947.

The reforms commonly known as economic reforms has completely changed the way Indian economy is now being perceived by other nations. The economic reforms kick-started in 1991 brought about changes and expansion of the services sector. The economy received a massive boost after it was liberalised and changes were brought in the trade regime. It must be noted that the moves gave more power to the consumers and reduced poverty significantly. The economy became more customer-centric with prime focus on services. Further in the very recent times specifically in 2016 passing of GST Bill and demonetisation of Rs. 500 and Rs. 1000 currency notes have been introduces to improve the economic efficiency of the Indian economic system. There are eight major reforms that have changed the Indian economy:

1. Demonetisation of ₹500, ₹1000: November 8, 2016

Prime Minister Narendra Modi's demonetization announcement on 8 November took the entire country by surprise. The move was initiated to curb black money, bring in cash into the banking system to the greatest possible extent, put an end to fake currency and plug all funding that could be used for terrorism.

The govt instructed people that whatever money they have in ₹500 and ₹1,000 denomination notes should be deposited into their bank accounts. At the same time, Finance Minister Arun Jaitley also made it very clear that the demonetisation move will in no way create any form of immunity.

After 8 November public cannot deal with high denomination currency notes and sales invoices cannot be issued by accepting high denomination notes. If anyone deposits undisclosed money in banks, then this may invite the Income Tax Department to act against him/her. With the I-T department keeping an eye on suspicious transactions, the person involved could be slapped with 30 per cent tax and a huge penalty. Any person making transactions above ₹10 lakh in a year into any savings bank account might get issued a notice from the I-T Department.

2. GST Constitutional Amendment Bill: August 3, 2016

The Rajya Sabha on 3 August 2016, passed the Goods and Services Tax (GST) Constitutional Amendment Bill which the Lok Sabha had already approved last year. The exact rate of the tax has been decided itemwise. The legislation was approved by the Rajya Sabha with 203 votes in favour and none against, in the 243-member House. The bill was passed after a seven-hour debate.

The main objective of the GST is to eliminate excessive taxation. GST is a uniform indirect tax levied on goods and services across a country. Many developed nations tax the manufacture, sale and consumption of goods using a single, comprehensive tax mechanism.

3. FDI in Several Sectors: 2015-Till Date

From the beginning of 2015, the government announced fresh liberalisation of FDI rules throwing open food retail, airlines, private security firms, and defence companies to higher overseas investment.

Other sectors in which FDI norms have been relaxed include e-commerce in food products, broadcasting carriage services, private security agencies and animal husbandry.

Here's a look at the changes in FDI

- Up to 100% FDI in defence sector.
- Up to 74% FDI in brownfield pharmaceuticals under automatic route.

- 100% FDI in brownfield airport projects under automatic route.
- 100% FDI in civil aviation.
- FDI up to 49% in civil aviation under automatic route, beyond 49% through govt approval.
- Local sourcing norms for FDI in single brand retail for products having "state of art" and "cutting edge" technologies.
- 100% FDI under automatic route for cable networks, DTH and mobile TV.

Foreign investment is considered crucial for India, which needs around $1 trillion for overhauling its infrastructure sector such as ports, airports and highways to boost growth. A strong inflow of foreign investments will help improve the country's balance of payments situation and strengthen the rupee value against other global currencies, especially the US dollar.

4. Black Money Bill: May, 2015

On 11 May 2015, the Lok Sabha passed a bill to deal with black money stashed abroad, even as the government announced that a separate Benami Bill to deal with domestic black money was being prepared. The bill provides for rigorous imprisonment of up to 10 years for offenders. Earlier, piloting the Undisclosed Foreign Income and Assets (Imposition of Tax) Bill, 2015 Finance Minister Arun Jaitley said there would be short compliance window for persons having undisclosed income abroad to come clean by paying 30 per cent tax and 30 per cent penalty.

Once the compliance window closes, anyone found having undeclared overseas wealth would be required to pay 30 per cent tax, 90 per cent penalty and face criminal prosecution.

5. Economic Liberalisation in 1991

The economic liberalisation process that began in 1991, had the goal of making the economy more market-oriented and expanding the role of private and foreign investment.

Specific changes were incorporated which include–reduction in import tariffs, deregulation of markets, reduction of taxes, and greater foreign investment.

Liberalisation has been credited by its proponents for the high economic growth recorded by the country in the 1990s and 2000s.

Ever since the liberalisation process, the Indian markets opened to both private and public sector companies. India started carrying out businesses with foreign establishments as well.

6. End of Licence Raj: 1991

Putting an end to "Licence Raj" was one of the chief goals of the 1991 economic liberalisation process.

The Licence Raj was a system of licences, regulations and accompanying red tape that were needed in order to set up and run businesses in India between 1947 and 1990.

The Licence Raj was a result of India's decision to control the economy and give out licences to only a select few. During that period, nearly 80 government agencies had to be satisfied before private companies could produce something and, if a licence is granted, the government would regulate the production.

However, reforms since 1991 significantly reduced these regulations and the business houses could work without having to worry about unnecessary "red tapism."

7. Abolishing Privy Purse in India: 1971

Privy Purse was a form of payment made to the royal families of all erstwhile princely states as it was made a part of their agreement in order to integrate with India in 1947, and later to merge their states in 1949, whereby they lost all ruling rights.

Privy Purse was discontinued under Prime Minister Indira Gandhi's regime, after the 26th Amendment in 1971, by means of which all their privileges and allowances from the Centre were rendered invalid.

If Privy Purse continued, our tax money would have gone to the royal families for no reason.

8. Nationalisation of Banks (Banking Reforms): 1969

Owing to growing demand to nationalise banks in 1969, Prime Minister Indira Gandhi took a major step in the history of independent India by nationalising 14 banks. Due to unavailability of enough credit, and the sector was not working rapidly enough, the decision was taken.

Because of nationalisation of banks, today, we are witnessing a surge in private players entering the banking sector and setting up Non-Banking Financial Institutions (NBFCs) and Banking Financial Institutions (BFIs).

CONCLUSIONS

The reforms of the last decade and a half have gone a long way in freeing the domestic economy from the control regime. An important feature of India's reform programme is that it has emphasized gradualism and evolutionary transition rather than rapid restructuring or "shock therapy". This approach was adopted since the reforms were introduced in June 1991 in the wake a balance of payments crisis that was certainly severe. However, it was not a prolonged crisis with a long period of non-performance and because of series of reform steps the situation and economic efficiency of the Indian economic system has improved a lot and with the new economic reforms the path has further be smoothened.

SUGGESTED READINGS

Economic Survey various issues.
Indian Economy by Uma Kapila.
Articles –TOI, THE HINDU.

14

Gender and Tobacco Use in India

Rohini Ruhil[1]*

"Millions hold to its prudent use. How much more difficult, then, must it be to convince men that there is any danger in the gentle, soothing powers of this loved narcotic! Fashion too unites with appetite in throwing a kind of spell over the tobacco consumer, which, however absurd and wicked the habit may appear to some, yet binds its victims in iron fetters. Arguments used to such, too often seem as powerless as they would in breaking up the spell of a rattlesnake."[1]

ABSTRACT

Good health allows women the opportunity to find their way out of poverty towards prosperity which in-turn determines good health and thus both prosperity and good health reciprocate each-other. Healthy, happy and prosperous women form healthy, happy and prosperous families which are building blocks of a healthy, happy and prosperous nation. There is no dearth of evidence to reflect on harmful health consequences of tobacco use. Not only health issues, but tobacco has been discussed widely as a threat to sustainable development. The following paper discusses tobacco use from a gender perspective. Various themes which have been discussed include trends in tobacco use among women, determinants of tobacco use among women, involuntary exposure of women and children to tobacco smoke, exploitative employment of women and children in tobacco industry, and the need to include tobacco use by men in Gender discussions. The paper concludes with a need to empower and educate women and to support women representation in tobacco control initiatives especially in leadership roles.

[1]Jawaharlal Nehru University (JNU), New Delhi, India
**Corresponding author*: E-mail: drrohiniruhil@gmail.com

Key words: Gender, Tobacco control, Gender analysis, Tobacco, Second hand smoke, Smokeless tobacco, Gender equity

---

INTRODUCTION

The subject of tobacco use is most important for thousands and millions of the human race who form artificial appetites for tobacco and gratify it at the expense of health and life. In India, the prevalence of total tobacco use in any form, among women was 14.2% in 2016–17.[2] The prevalence of smokeless tobacco use among women was 12.8% in 2016–17.[2] While the smoking rates among men were constantly on decline since 1995–96 till 2016–17; the smoking rates among women were rather constant around 2–3 percent since 1995–96 till 2016–17.[2] Although tobacco use rates among women in India are found to be less as compared to men, but the women also suffer when men spend household incomes in purchasing tobacco instead of food and other basic needs.[3]

Women also lose their health by inhaling second hand smoke as male members of the household smoke in crowded living spaces and women are unable to express an objection to it.[3] The second-hand smoke is also harmful for the pregnant women and may lead to miscarriage, premature delivery, still birth, low birth weight or congenital abnormalities. Women may also suffer from other reproductive consequences like infertility and ectopic pregnancy. Lactating mothers may produce less milk or may release the toxins in milk.[3]

The tobacco companies are now targeting women of developing countries by introducing newer and cheaper products like flavoured chewing tobacco in small pouches. Tobacco companies mislead women by projecting cigarette smoking by women as being modern, fashionable and being equal to men. Specific products like "Slim- cigarettes" and "flavoured- tobacco" are made to attract women.[3]

Women are also employed in large numbers in tobacco industry and get exploited. Bidi industry and smokeless tobacco industry in India is highly unorganised and is based on home-based work done by women and their children.[4]

TOBACCO USE AMONG WOMEN ACROSS DIFFERENT STATES OF INDIA

The regional and state/UT level differentials in the prevalence of tobacco use for females are presented in Map 1. There is a large variation in the prevalence of tobacco use all across different regions and states/UTs.

The highest prevalence of tobacco use among females is reported in East (31%) and North-east and the lowest prevalence is reported in the North (4%).[5] The highest prevalence of tobacco among females is reported in Mizoram, where 62 percent of females use tobacco, in contrast to less than 1 percent tobacco use in Punjab.[5] Similarly, in Chandigarh, Delhi, Himachal Pradesh and Goa, less than 5 percent of adult females use tobacco in any form.[5]

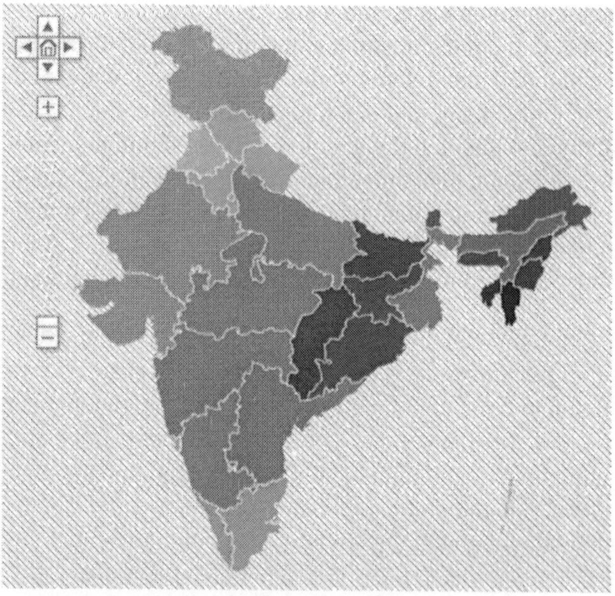

Map 1: Distribution of women tobacco users across India and its states/ UTs: GATS India 2009–10.

The prevalence of smoking among females also varies widely across states/UTs which are shown in Map 2. Highest prevalence of smoking among females is reported from Mizoram (19%).[5] In 10 out of 31 states/ UTs surveyed, less than one percent females reported smoking. It is only in the six states of North-East region *i.e.*, Mizoram (19%), Sikkim (16%), Nagaland (12%), Manipur (11%), Arunachal Pradesh (11%) and Tripura (10%), that 10 percent or more females currently smoke tobacco.[5]

Map 3 present regional and state/ UT level variation in the prevalence of smokeless tobacco use among females. Prevalence of smokeless tobacco use among females is highest in Mizoram (49%) and lowest in Punjab (0.2%).[5] In all the seven states of North and Goa, less than 5 percent females use smokeless tobacco. The gender differentials evidenced in smokeless tobacco use in most of the states are narrower compared to those in case of smoking.[5]

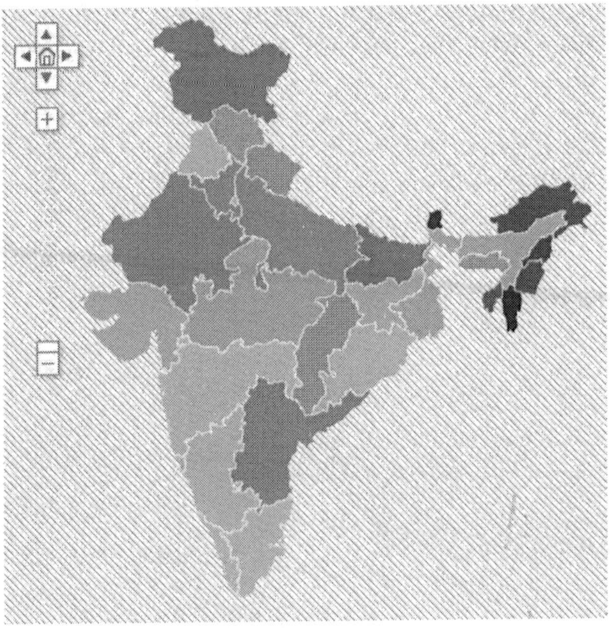

Map 2: Distribution of women smokers across India and its states/ UTs: GATS India 2009–10.

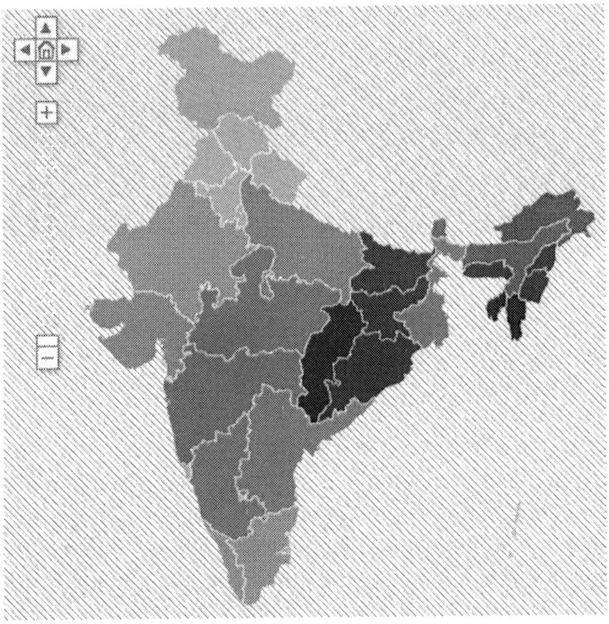

Map 3: Distribution of women smokeless tobacco users across India and its states/UTs: GATS India 2009–10.

The use of smokeless tobacco among women in India has always been much more than the smoking prevalence among them (Fig. 1). Cultural norms prohibit smoking by women, whereas smokeless tobacco use is widely accepted among both sexes in India. In the year 2009–10 there was a sharp rise in the prevalence of smokeless tobacco use among women (Fig. 1). However, the prevalence of smokeless tobacco use among women has declined from 18.4% in 2009–10 to 12.8% in 2016–17 (Fig. 1).

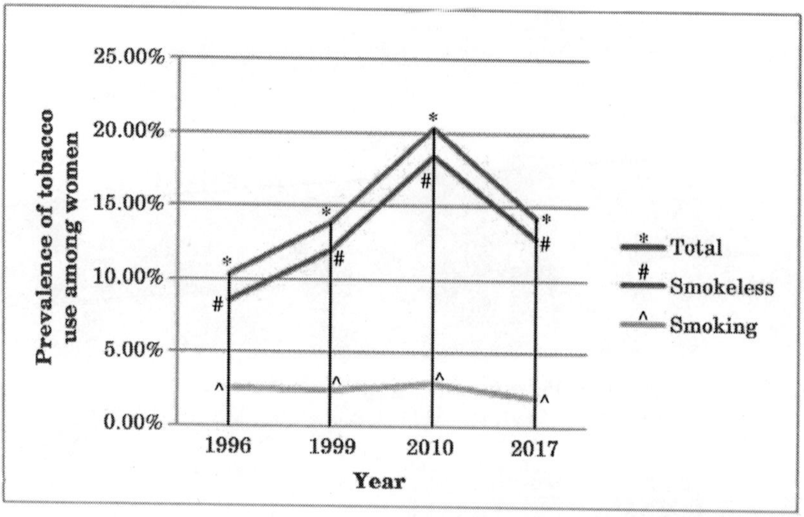

Fig. 1: Trends in the prevalence of tobacco use (smoking and smokeless) by men in India over a period of two decades *i.e.*, from 1995 to 2017

Smokeless tobacco products contain almost 4000 chemical constituents which are very harmful for human body.[6] Smokeless tobacco has been classified as a Group I carcinogen (carcinogenic to humans) by IARC (International Agency for Research on Cancer).[7] Table 1 summarises the evidence about harmful health effects of smokeless tobacco use (Table 1). There is evidence to show that women who use tobacco face greater risks for some diseases as compared to men.[8]

Smokeless tobacco is prepared by harvesting the yellow tobacco leaves with brownish spots. Leaves are then left in the field for uniform drying, and then they are tied in to bundles and moistened with water or molasses and stored for few weeks to allow fermentation.[9] Various smokeless forms of tobacco used in India include Pan (Betel Quid) with tobacco, Kaddipudi, Hogesoppu, Kadapan, Zarda, Pattiwala tobacco, Kiwam, Pan Masala, Mainpuri tobacco, Mawa, Khaini, Mishri, Gudhaku, Creamy Snuff, and Areca nut preparations.[9]

Table 1: Harmful Health Effects of Smokeless Tobacco (Chewing Tobacco): The Evidence

Disease	***Evidence***	***Notes***
Oral cancer	IARC, 2007; Boffetta *et al.*, 2008; Lee and Hamling, 2009; Idris *et al.*, 1995; IARC, 2007	The early age of initiation of tobacco use results in more severe consequences
Pre-cancerous lesions (Leuko-plakia, erythro-plakia); Oral sub-mucous fibrosis	IARC, 2004, 2007; Lee *et al.*, 2011	The pre-cancerous lesions could resolve after stopping the use of tobacco
Oesophageal cancer	Lee and Hamling, 2009; Boffetta *et al.*, 2008	
Pancreatic cancer	IARC, 2007; Boffetta *et al.*, 2008; Sponsiello-wang *et al.*, 2008; Pednekar *et al.*, 2011	
Lung cancer	Boffetta *et al.*, 2008; Pednekar *et al.*, 2011	
Cervical cancer	USDHHS, 2010; IARC, 2007; Gajalakshmi *et al.*, 2012; Simen-Kapeu *et al.*, 2009	
Cardiovas-cular effects	Piano *et al.*, 2010; USDHHS, 2010; Benowitz, 2003; Granberry *et al.*, 2003	Smokeless tobacco leads to the development of endothelial dysfunction, atherogenesis and atherosclerosis
Hypertension	Piano *et al.*, 2010; Benowitz and Gourlay, 1997; Pandey *et al.*, 2009; Gupta *et al.*, 2007	Hypertension could be aggrava-ted by nicotine, sodium and licorice present in tobacco
Stroke	Piano *et al.*, 2010; Benowitz and Gaurlay, 1997; Boffetta and Straif, 2009; Zhang *et al.*, 2010	Smokeless tobacco also badly affects prognosis after a cardio-vascular event
Diabetes	IARC, 2007; Piano *et al.*, 2010	Smokeless tobacco increases the risk of developing insulin resistance and thus type 2 diabetes
Adverse foetal outcomes	IARC, 2004; USDHHS, 2010; European Commission, 2008; Gupta *et al.*, 2007; Wikstrom *et al.*, 2010a, b; Gupta and Subramoney, 2006	Carbonmonoxide exposure may lead to foetal hypoxia and metals may cause oxidative stress in cells and thus impair foetal nutrition
Conditions of nasal cavity	Sapundzhiev and Werner, 2003	Smokeless tobacco that is inha-led nasally develop mucosal edema of nose; submucosal ede-ma of conjunctival tissue of the turbinates; atrophy of middle and inferior turbinates; inhibi-tion of nasal mucociliary cleara-nce and thus chronic rhinitis

Table 1: *(Contd...)*

Table 1: (*Contd...*)

Disease	*Evidence*	*Notes*
Dental effects		
Gingivitis, periodontitis and mouth ulcers	Greer, 2011; IARC, 2007	Gingiva begins to recede within a year of use of smokeless tobacco.
Dental decay and caries	Greer, 2011	

The smokeless tobacco use across populations is associated with similar circumstances which are socially and economically patterned and often clustered. The smokeless tobacco use behaviour is complex like other behaviours and has its interactions with social and physical environments of women. There are many local beliefs and cultural practices. For example, some Indian women believe that chewing tobacco can cure toothaches or can be useful during childbirth.[8]

Table 2 shows that socio-demographic characteristics of women are very significant in determining their smokeless tobacco use habit. The table shows that older women had higher odds of using smokeless tobacco as compared to younger age-groups with highest odds in the age-group of 65+ and such an inference remains valid when other factors also play their role *i.e.*, in multivariate analysis (Table 2). Being residing in urban areas had fewer odds of using smokeless tobacco as compared to rural areas. In other words Rural Women were more likely to use smokeless tobacco as compared to urban Women. This may be because poverty is more prevalent in rural areas as compared to urban areas. There is a need for further research in this area because urban areas are not homogenous and there will be contrasts among urban slums and urban middle-class and urban elites. Education also plays a very significant role in determining smokeless tobacco use behaviour among women. Higher was the education fewer were the odds of using smokeless tobacco. A pattern had emerged where higher the educational levels of women lower were the likelihoods of using smokeless tobacco by them. Thus there is a need to educate and empower women to protect them from menace of tobacco use.

Material Disadvantage as a Determinant of Smokeless Tobacco Use Among Women

The material and social world around women plays a very important role in susceptibility or resistance to smokeless tobacco use. There are situations that place women "at risk of risks". Tobacco use behaviour is not solely a matter of "individual choice". Rather, "environment place constraints on individual choice and incentivize particular choices with promises of social, psychological, financial or physical rewards"[10]

Table 2: Socio-demographic characteristics of women as determinants of smokeless tobacco use among them: Global Adult Tobacco Survey (GATS) India 2009-2010.

Socio-demographic characteristics	***N 35529***	***(%) 100%***	***Smokeless tobacco users***		***Univariate logistic regression analysis***		***Multivariate logistic regression analysis***	
			n 6560	***(%) 18.5%***	***OR (95% CI)***	***P Value***	***OR (95% CI)***	***P Value***
Age (In years)								
15–24	7254	20.4%	716	9.9%	1	Ref	1	Ref
25–44	18309	51.5%	3385	18.5%	2.071 (1.901–2.256)	<0.001	1.710 (1.551–1.884)	<0.001
45–64	7753	21.8%	1844	23.8%	2.850 (2.596–3.128)	<0.001	2.031 (1.826–2.258)	<0.001
65+	2213	6.2%	615	27.8%	3.514 (3.114–3.966)	<0.001	2.337 (2.039–2.679)	<0.001
Residence								
Rural	21627	60.9%	4833	22.3%	1	Ref	1	Ref
Urban	13902	39.1%	1727	12.4%	0.493 (0.464–0.523)	<0.001	0.643 (0.604–0.685)	<0.001
Education								
No formal education	12709	35.9%	3339	26.3%	1	Ref	1	Ref
Less than secondary school	13188	37.2%	2502	19%	0.657 (0.620–0.697)	<0.001	0.839 (0.788–0.894)	<0.001
Secondary school completed	3880	10.9%	368	9.5%	0.294 (0.262–0.330)	<0.001	0.438 (0.388–0.495)	<0.001
Higher secondary school completed	2620	7.4%	195	7.4%	0.226 (0.194–0.262)	<0.001	0.358 (0.305–0.420)	<0.001
College/ university completed	2124	6%	104	4.9%	0.144 (0.118–0.177)	<0.001	0.195 –0.240) (0.158	<0.001
Post-graduate degree completed	915	2.6%	23	2.5%	0.072 (0.048–0.110)	<0.001	0.084 (0.055–0.129)	<0.001

Table 2: *(Contd...)*

Table 2: (*Contd...*)

Socio-demographic characteristics	*N 35529*	*(%) 100%*	*Smokeless tobacco users*		*Univariate logistic regression analysis*		*Multivariate logistic regression analysis*	
			n 6560	*(%) 18.5%*	*OR (95% CI)*	*P Value*	*OR (95% CI)*	*P Value*
Occupation								
Unemployed	861	2.4%	251	29.2%	1	Ref	1	Ref.
Retired	143	0.4%	27	18.9%	0.566 (0.363–0.882)	0.012	0.750 (0.472–1.191)	0.222
Home-maker	23153	65.3%	3816	16.5%	0.480 (0.412–0.558)	<0.001	0.589 (0.503–0.691)	<0.001
Student	2738	7.7%	172	6.3%	0.163 (0.132–0.202)	<0.001	0.521 (0.412–0.660)	<0.001
Self-employed	4305	12.1%	1260	29.3%	1.006 (0.856–1.181)	0.945	1.125 (0.949–1.333)	0.176
Non-govt. employee	3241	9.1%	853	26.3%	0.868 (0.735–1.025)	0.096	1.066 (0.894–1.271)	0.479
Govt. employee	996	2.8%	153	15.4%	0.441 (0.352–0.553)	<0.001	1.198 (0.937–1.531)	0.149

The smokeless tobacco use habit has also been seen to get influenced by material and cultural disadvantage and deprivation. Table 3 shows that various material disadvantages play a very significant role in determining smokeless tobacco use behaviour amongst women. The various material disadvantages analysed include absence of electricity, absence of flush toilet, absence of television, absence of refrigerator, absence of washing machine, absence of fixed telephone, absence of cell telephone and absence of radio in their households. In case of smokeless tobacco use among women; even in multivariate analysis each of the material disadvantages emerged as a strong determinant of smokeless tobacco use habit (Table 3). Here absence of radio in India is not a sign of poverty instead middle and higher income groups also may not have radios but other music systems in their households. Absence of radio showed fewer odds of using smokeless tobacco. To conclude Table 3, women living in poverty without any material comforts and sources of recreation were more likely to use smokeless tobacco.

There is a need to alleviate human deprivation while ensuring distributive justice. The country is spending less and less towards development sector and towards fulfilment of developmental goals. On the other hand spending on defence sector is increasing which shows the priorities set by policy makers. Public sector spending on health is also on decline. The budget allocation for education and health is highly inadequate. The government is withdrawing from public health and promoting private health sector. The new budget 2017–18 has given tax subsidies to private insurance companies and pharmaceutical industries in the name of public-private partnership. In addition to this, the human resource employed in government's flagship programmes such as NRHM are on contractual basis and do not even get minimum wages, pension, social security and health insurance.

Table 3: Various material disadvantages amongst women as determinants of smokeless tobacco use among them: Global Adult Tobacco Survey (GATS) India 2009–2010.

Type of material disadvantage	*N 35529*	*Smokeless tobacco users*		*Univariate logistic regression analysis*		*Multivariate logistic regression analysis*	
		n	*(%)*	*OR (95% CI)*	*P value*	*OR (95% CI)*	*P value*
Absence of electricity	4879	1537	31.3%	2.326 (2.174–2.489)	<0.001	1.158 (1.068–1.255)	<0.001
Absence of flush toilet	19382	4911	25.3%	2.961 (2.787–3.145)	<0.001	1.659 (1.543–1.784)	<0.001
Absence of television	11601	3297	28.3%	2.492 (2.359–2.632)	<0.001	1.301 (1.209–1.400)	<0.001
Absence of refrigerator	24748	5760	23.2%	3.746 (3.464–4.050)	<0.001	1.808 (1.634–2.002)	<0.001
Absence of washing machine	30743	6259	20.3%	3.855 (3.410–4.358)	<0.001	1.303 (1.124–1.510)	<0.001
Absence of fixed telephone	29395	6102	20.7%	3.156 (2.857–3.487)	<0.001	1.441 (1.287–1.613)	<0.001
Absence of cell telephone	10418	2905	27.7%	2.250 (2.129–2.378)	<0.001	1.273 (1.191–1.362)	<0.001
Absence of radio	26587	4879	18.3%	0.950 (0.893–1.011)	0.105	0.754 (0.707–0.805)	<0.001

Tobacco Industry as a Determinant of Tobacco Use (Smoking and Smokeless) Among Women

Cigarette smoking was initially adopted by men in industrialised countries and was later taken up by women in those countries and men in developing countries. With the decline in smoking in industrialised countries in 1990s, the multinational tobacco companies moved aggressively into the developing nations. The high percentage of non-smoking women in these countries makes them an attractive target for the industry.[8]

Tobacco industry was fully equipped with comprehensive social research. It gained a thorough understanding of their cultures, gender norms and psycho-social aspirations; and the industry cashed on this knowledge by incorporating it within massive promotional efforts to seek new markets and sustain existing ones. In this way, the industry targeted both sexes. It also used product differentiation and marketing segmentation to maximise customer base and thus profits.[8]

Using seductive but false images of vitality, slimness, emancipation, sophistication and sexual allure; the industry targets women. Liberation, autonomy, and even female friendship feature in developed countries advertising, and, increasingly, in regions where female roles have begun to change. The Tobacco Reporter, an industry document, optimistically discussed its prospects in Asia in 1998: "Rising per capita consumption and an increasing acceptance of women smoking continue to generate new demand". Slender, so-called "light", cigarettes packaged in pastel colours convey femininity and slimness. The industry has sponsored fashion shows in shopping malls linked to magazine promotion. Such sponsorship and public smoking by super-models and film stars associate tobacco with glamour.[8]

Exposure to Second Hand Smoke (SHS) Among Women

Although tobacco use prevalence among women is low in India; but a large number of women get exposed to second hand smoke (SHS) at home and at workplace. Women and children are the most vulnerable group exposed to second hand tobacco smoke particularly at home environments. According to GATS India survey approximately 39.3 percent women reported being exposed to second hand smoke at home.[2] Also about 17.9 percent women reported being exposed to second hand smoke at workplace.[2] However the numbers have come down since 2009–10 when the prevalence of SHS exposure at home was 50.4 percent and the prevalence of SHS exposure at workplace was 21.7 percent.[5] There is plethora of studies that established association between second-hand smoke exposure and several diseases.[11] As early as 1600, King James wrote on passive smoking, "The wife must either take up smoking or resolve to live in a perpetual stinking torment".[12] Table 4 summarises the evidence about harmful health effects of second hand smoke exposure among women (Table 4).

Table 4: Harmful health effects of SHS (Second Hand Smoke): The evidence

Disease	***Evidence***	***Notes***
Cancers	Hecht, 1999; Hemminki *et al.*, 1994; Geacintov *et al.*, 1997; IARC, 1990, 1994	The mechanism of carcinogenesis of second hand smoke is similar to that of mainstream smoke. Exposure to SHS leads to uptake of various harmful chemicals by human body, which undergo metabolic process and in this process some molecules form DNA adducts and thus induce mutations and finally cancer.
Tumours of upper respiratory tract and lungs	Shimkin and Stoner, 1975; IARC, 1973, 1983; Culp *et al.*, 1998	Polycyclic aromatic hydrocarbons (PA Hs) present in second hand tobacco smoke, induce tumours of the upper respiraratory tract and lung.
Tumours of oesophagus and nasal cavity	Preussmann and Stewart, 1984; Hecht, 1998	N-Nitrosamines are also carcinogenic and could cause tumours of oesophagus, nasal cavity and lungs.
Lung cancer	Hole *et al.*, 1989; Jee *et al.*, 1999; Nishino *et al.*, 2001; Garfinkel, 1981; Hirayama, 1981; Butler, 1988; Cardenas *et al.*, 1997; Hackshaw *et al.*, 1997; Zhong *et al.*, 2000; USDHHS, 2006.	Several epidemiological cohort studies have found increased incidence and mortality from lung cancer amongst those exposed to second hand smoke as compared to unexposed group.
Cancer of urinary bladder	IARC, 1973, 1974; Garner *et al.*, 1984	Aromatic amines are proven human bladder carcinogens
Respiratory tract tumours	Kerns *et al.*, 1983; IARC, 1999	Formaldehyde and acetaldehyde may induce respiratory tract tumours
Leukaemia	IARC, 1982, 1992, 1999	Benzene present in side-stream smoke causes leukaemia in humans
Respiratory illness	Martinez *et al.*, 1988; Young *et al.*, 1991; Janson *et al.*, 2001; Joad *et al.*, 1995; Coleridge and Coleridge, 1994; Saria *et al.*, 1988; Lee *et al.*, 1992; Coleridge *et al.*, 1993; Bonham *et al.*, 2001; Geng *et al.*, 1995; Edwards *et al.*, 1999; Fainstein and Musher, 1979; Dye and Adler, 1994; Wanner *et al.*, 1996	The underlying mechanism by which SHS causes respiratory illness has been explained by many researchers. Exposure to second hand smoke induces bronchial hyper-reactivity in both children and adults. SHS also stimulate C-fibres central nervous system (CNS) reflex which causes bronchoconstriction, mucous secretion, increased microvascular leakage. It also enhances bacterial adherence to respiratory epithelium and impairs mucociliary clearance.
Asthma	Wahlgren *et al.*, 2000	
Lung function impair-	Cook and Strachan, 1999; Samet and Lange, 1996;	Especially in children

Table 4: (*Contd...*)

Table 4: (*Contd...*)

Disease	***Evidence***	***Notes***
ment	Kerstjens *et al.*, 1997	
Lower respiratory tract infection in children	Strachan and Cook, 1997; Colley *et al.*, 1974; Harlap and Davies, 1974	
Imapired lung growth in children	USDHHS, 1986; USEPA, 1992; NCI, 1999; WHO, 1999; Collins *et al.*, 1985	
SIDS (Sudden Infant Death Syndrome)	Cook and Strachan, 1999	
Chronic obstructive pulmonary disease (COPD)	Jaakola, 2002	
Otitis media with effusion (OME)	Kraemer and colleagues, 1983	
Other ENT (Ear, Nose, Throat) diseases	USEPA, 1992; Gulya, 1994; Blakley and Blakley, 1995; NCI, 1999; Di-Franza and Lew, 1996; Uhari *et al.*, 1996; Strachan and Cook, 1998; Thornton and Lee, 1999	
Nasal or sinus diseases	Barr *et al.*, 1992; Moyes *et al.*, 1995; Benninger, 1999; Willes *et al.*, 1998	
Cardiovascular diseases	Hirayama, 1984; Garland *et al.*, 1985; Lee *et al.*, 1986; Svendsen *et al.*, 1987; Butler, 1988; Hole *et al.*, 1989; Sandler *et al.*, 1989; Humble *et al.*,1990; La Vecchia *et al.*, 1993; He *et al.*, 1994; Muscat and Wynder, 1995; Steenland *et al.*, 1996; Kawachi *et al.*, 1997; Ciruzzi *et al.*, 1998; Mc Elduff *et al.*, 1998; Rosenlund *et al.*, 2001; USDHHS, 2006; Pittilo *et al.*, 1982; Sinzinger and Kefalides, 1982; Burghuber *et al.*, 1986; Davis *et al.*, 1989; Sinzinger and Virgolini, 1989; Steinberg *et al.*, 1989; Elwood *et al.*, 1991;	Second hand smoke exposure activates blood platelets and makes them sticky which increases the risk of thrombus formation. Also activated platelets lead to atherosclerotic lesions in coronary arteries and thus an increased risk of ischemic heart disease. The epidemiological studies have also shown that second hand smoke exposure would increase the likelihood and severity of Myocardial Infarction (MI). The adverse effects of SHS exposure are more profound in children. The children of smoking parents were found to exhibit low HDL levels and thus were at increased risk of cardiovascular diseases later in life.

Table 4: (*Contd...*)

Table 4: (*Contd...*)

Disease	***Evidence***	***Notes***
	Prentice *et al.*, 1989; Zhu *et al.*, 1994, 1996; Moskowitz *et al.*, 1990; Feldman *et al.*, 1991	
Reproductive outcomes		Second hand smoke exposure adversely affects reproductive system development and function at every stage of life.
Female fertility	Mattison, 1982; Daling *et al.*, 1987; Mattison and Thomford, 1987	During preconception period, second hand smoke exposure causes imbalance of hormones in women and affects female fertility.
Spontaneous abortion and congenital malformations	NCI, 1999; WHO, 1999; Sadler, 1990; Koo *et al.*, 1988; Windham *et al.*, 1992; Longo and Anderson, 1970; Mattison *et al.*, 1989	Maternal exposure to second hand smoke during pregnancy badly affects development of foetus.
Compromised physical and cognitive development in infants and children	USDHHS, 1990; Lambers and Clark, 1996; Ernst *et al.*, 2001; Gospe *et al.*, 1996	
Increased risk of neonatal mortality	Cnattingius, 1988; Malloy *et al.*, 1988; Schramm, 1997; Yerushalmy, 1971	
SIDS (Sudden Infant Death Syndrome)	Anderson and Cook, 1997; Bergman and Wiesner, 1976; Mc Glashan, 1989; Schoendorf and Kiely, 1992; Mitchell *et al.*, 1993, 1997; Klonoff-Cohen *et al.*, 1995; Ponsonby *et al.*, 1995; Blair *et al.*, 1996; Brooke *et al.*, 1997; Dwyer *et al.*, 1999	
Pre-term delivery	Ahluwalia *et al.*, 1997; Hanke *et al.*, 1999; Windham *et al.*, 2000; Jaakkola *et al.*, 2001	
LBW (Low Birth Weight) Babies	MacMahon *et al.*, 1965; Comstock and Lundin, 1967; Underwood *et al.*, 1967; Terris and Gold, 1969; Yerushalmy, 1971; Mau and Netter, 1974; Borlee *et al.*, 1978; Misra and Nguyen, 1999; Windham *et al.*, 1999; Lindbohm *et al.*, 2002.	

The women in Indian society have been designated a sub-ordinate status where head of household is always man. At the first place, nobody wants a female to be born in their family but all of them want "other" people's daughters to reproduce with their sons and carry the lineage forward. The world of a female revolves around marriage and home and they rarely have any decision making powers. Even economically earning females are not economically independent and cannot take decisions regarding their lives and lives of their children. The women are always at disadvantaged position whether at home or at workplace. In such a scenario, women do not have bargaining powers to protect themselves and their children from involuntary exposure to second hand tobacco smoke. Any woman living in a patriarchal household knows the problems she faces in asking her husband to quit smoking in the home. Threats of domestic violence are common, yet these are seldom considered relevant to tobacco control.

Tables 5 and 6, show that socio-demographic characteristics of women are very significant in determining SHS exposure to them both at home as well as at workplace. Being residing in urban areas had fewer odds of SHS exposure both at home as well as at workplace. Education emerged out as a most important determinant of SHS exposure to women. Higher was the educational attainment of women fewer were the odds of SHS exposure to them at home and at workplace.

Table 5: Socio-demographic characteristics of women as determinants of Second Hand Smoke (SHS) exposure at home: Global Adult Tobacco Survey (GATS) India 2009–2010.

Socio-demographic characteristics	*N 35529*	*(%) 100%*	*Second Hand Smoke (SHS) exposure at work place*		*Univariate logistic regression analysis*		*Multivariate logistic regression analysis*	
			n 17646	*(%) 88.2%*	*OR (95% CI)*	*P Value*	*OR (95% CI)*	*P Value*
Age (in years)								
15–24	4095	20.5%	3646	88.6%	1	Ref	1	Ref
25–44	10446	52.2%	9269	88.3%	0.964 (0.861–1.080)	0.531	0.875 (0.766–0.998)	0.047
45–64	4277	21.4%	3818	88.2%	0.959 (0.839–1.096)	0.538	0.782 (0.670–0.913)	0.002
65+	1196	6.0%	1043	85.6%	0.763 (0.633–0.920)	0.005	0.580 (0.470–0.717)	<0.001
Residence								
Rural	13688	68.4%	12293	89%	1	Ref	1	Ref

Table 5: *(Contd...)*

Table 5: *(Contd...)*

Socio-demographic characteristics	***N 35529***	***(%) 100%***	***Second Hand Smoke (SHS) exposure at work place***		***Univariate logistic regression analysis***		***Multivariate logistic regression analysis***	
			n 17646	***(%) 88.2%***	***OR (95% CI)***	***P Value***	***OR (95% CI)***	***P Value***
Urban	6326	31.6%	5483	86.5%	0.794 (0.726–0.869)	<0.001	0.882 (0.803–0.969)	0.009
Education								
No formal education	8362	41.8%	7581	90.3%	1	Ref	1	Ref
Less than secondary school	7813	39.0%	6856	87.4%	0.749 (0.679–0.827)	<0.001	0.707 (0.636–0.785)	<0.001
Secondary school completed	1752	8.8%	1520	86.6%	0.697 (0.597–0.814)	<0.001	0.666 (0.563–0.786)	<0.001
Higher sec. school completed	1082	5.4%	951	87.8%	0.776 (0.638–0.944)	0.011	0.740 (0.600–0.913)	0.005
College/university completed	752	3.8%	609	80.9%	0.456 (0.375–0.554)	<0.001	0.448 (0.364–0.552)	<0.001
Post-graduate degree completed	253	1.3%	198	78.3%	0.388 (0.285–0.528)	<0.001	0.408 (0.295–0.564)	<0.001
Occupation								
Unemployed	551	2.8%	479	86.3%	1	Ref	1	Ref
Retired	69	0.3%	58	84.1%	0.837 (0.420–1.665)	0.612	1.085 (0.541–2.177)	0.819
Home-maker	13128	65.6%	11600	88.0%	1.161 (0.906–1.487)	0.237	1.134 (0.878–1.464)	0.337
Student	1358	6.8%	1179	86.8%	1.045 (0.783–1.395)	0.765	1.048 (0.764 –1.436)	0.773
Self-employed	2599	13.0%	2347	89.8%	1.400 (1.065–1.840)	0.016	1.298 (0.979–1.720)	0.070
Non-govt. employee	1891	9.4%	1699	89.8%	1.404 (1.057–1.866)	0.019	1.284 (0.958–1.721)	0.094
Govt. employee	418	2.1%	345	82.5%	0.750 (0.529–1.064)	0.107	0.982 (0.680–1.418)	0.922

Table 6: Socio-demographic characteristics of women as determinants of Second Hand Smoke (SHS) exposure at work-place: Global Adult Tobacco Survey (GATS) India 2009–2010.

Socio-demographic characteristics	*N* 35529	*(%)* 100%	*Second Hand Smoke (SHS) exposure at work place*		*Univariate logistic regression analysis*		*Multivariate logistic regression analysis*	
			n 843	*(%)* 25.9%	*OR* (95% CI)	*P* Value	*OR* (95% CI)	*P* Value
Age (In years)								
15–24	574	17.6%	146	25.4%	1	Ref	1	Ref
25–44	1973	60.7%	507	25.7%	1.013 (0.819–1.254)	0.905	0.777 (0.605–0.997)	0.048
45–64	633	19.5%	157	24.8%	0.967 (0.745–1.255)	0.800	0.666 (0.491–0.905)	0.009
65+	73	2.2%	33	45.2%	2.418 (1.470–3.978)	0.001	1.137 (0.660–1.960)	0.644
Residence								
Rural	1684	51.8%	572	33.9%	1	Ref	1	Ref
Urban	1569	48.2%	271	17.3%	0.406 (0.344–0.479)	<0.001	0.527 (0.440–0.631)	<0.001
Education								
No formal education	708	21.8%	258	36.4%	1	Ref	1	Ref
Less than secondary school	954	29.3%	343	36%	0.979 (0.800–1.199)	0.838	0.994 (0.796–1.240)	0.955
Secondary school completed	391	12.0%	80	20.5%	0.449 (0.336–0.599)	<0.001	0.560 (0.408–0.769)	<0.001
Higher sec–ondary school completed	310	9.5%	55	17.7%	0.376 (0.271–0.523)	<0.001	0.534 (0.370–0.769)	0.001
College/university completed	501	15.4%	73	14.6%	0.297 (0.222–0.398)	<0.001	0.454 (0.327–0.631)	<0.001
Post-graduate degree completed	389	12.0%	34	8.7%	0.167 (0.114–0.245)	<0.001	0.281 (0.184–0.428)	<0.001
Occupation								
Unemployed	58	1.8%	27	46.6%	1	Ref	1	Ref
Retired	2	0.1%	1	50%	1.148 (0.068–	0.923	1.328 (0.076–	0.846

Table 5: (*Contd...*)

Table 6: (*Contd...*)

Socio-demographic characteristics	*N 35529*	*(%) 100%*	*Second Hand Smoke (SHS) exposure at work place*		*Univariate logistic regression analysis*		*Multivariate logistic regression analysis*	
			n 843	*(%) 25.9%*	*OR (95% CI)*	*P Value*	*OR (95% CI)*	*P Value*
					19.251)		23.176)	
Home-maker	393	12.1%	126	32%	0.540 (0.309–0.943)	0.030	0.563 (0.318–0.995)	0.048
Student	192	5.9%	26	13.5%	0.180 (0.093–0.348)	<0.001	0.249 (0.123–0.503)	<0.001
Self-employed	865	26.6%	368	42.5%	0.850 (0.499–1.449)	0.551	1.074 (0.621–1.856)	0.799
Non-govt. employee	994	30.6%	164	16.5%	0.227 (0.138–0.390)	<0.001	0.378 (0.216–0.662)	0.001
Govt. employee	749	23.0%	131	17.5%	0.243 (0.141–0.422)	<0.001	0.544 (0.306–0.969)	0.039

Tables 7 shows that various material disadvantages played a very significant role in determining SHS exposure to women at home. Here again, just like determinants of tobacco use, women living in poverty without any material comforts and sources of recreation were more likely to get exposed to Second Hand Smoke at home. Absence of electricity emerged out as an exception where women in households without electricity were less likely to get exposed to SHS. This may be because men remain outside their homes when electricity is not available in the homes.

Generally it is argued by smokers that they have a right to smoke. After all it is their body and their smoking habit is something very personal and it is nobody's business to tell them not to smoke. But do they really have a Right to Smoke? When a smoker smokes in presence of others especially women and children, they also inhale the mixture of side-stream smoke given off by smouldering cigarette/Bidi and mainstream smoke exhaled by smoker called "Second Hand Smoke" or "Environmental Tobacco Smoke" or "Passive Smoking".

The concerns about passive or involuntary smoking were first raised in 1972 US Surgeon General's report.[13] In 1992 Second Hand Smoke was classified as group A carcinogen by US Environment Protection Agency.[14] It has been studied that chemical compounds emitted at the level of side-stream smoke are 10 times greater than the chemical compounds in mainstream smoke[15] and at least 250 of these chemicals were known to be carcinogenic.[16] Few of these chemicals are polycyclic aromatic hydrocarbons (PAHs), heterocycles, heterocyclic aromatic amines, nitro compounds and other organic compounds[16] which causes cancer.

Table 7: Various material disadvantages amongst women as determinants of Second Hand Smoke (SHS) exposure at home: Global Adult Tobacco Survey (GATS) India 2009–2010.

Type of material disadvantage	*N 35529*	*Second Hand Smoke (SHS) exposure at home*		*Univariate logistic regression analysis*		*Multivariate logistic regression analysis*	
		n	*(%)*	*OR (95% CI)*	*P Value*	*OR (95% CI)*	*P Value*
Absence of electricity	3527	3070	86.7%			0.693 (0.606–0.793)	<0.001
Absence of flush toilet	12548	11260	89.5%			1.253 (1.120–1.403)	<0.001
Absence of television	8165	7256	88.6%			0.927 (0.818–1.051)	0.237
Absence of refrigerator	15591	13963	89.3%			1.112 (0.969–1.276)	0.131
Absence of washing machine	18395	16378	88.9%			1.383 (1.178–1.623)	<0.001
Absence of fixed telephone	17593	15770	89.4%			1.896 (1.665–2.160)	<0.001
Absence of cell telephone	6889	6118	88.4%			0.955 (0.853–1.070)	0.430
Absence of radio	15212	13400	87.8%			0.794 (0.714–0.883)	<0.001

Tobacco companies have now come up with Electronic Nicotine Delivery Systems (ENDS), which are battery-operated devices designed to heat a liquid (which contains nicotine) into an aerosol for inhalation by the user (also known as e-cigarettes). The use of ENDS has been noted in places where smoking is not allowed. Its use results in increased exposure to exhaled aerosol toxicants of potential harm to bystanders. The typical use of unadulterated ENDS/ENNDS produces aerosol containing many toxicants that have known health effects resulting in a range of significant pathological changes. ENDS aerosol contains nicotine, the addictive component of tobacco products. In addition to dependence, nicotine can have adverse effects on the development of the foetus during pregnancy and may contribute to cardiovascular disease. Health risks from passive exposure to exhaled aerosol from

ENDS/ENNDS users – or second-hand aerosol – are also well documented.[3]

There is another danger of "Third Hand Tobacco Smoke" in indoor environments. Third hand smoke is tobacco smoke contamination on all exposed surfaces and also toxic gases that remain in indoor air, long after a bidi/cigarette has been extinguished. The term was first used by Szabo in 2006. This residual form of tobacco smoke adheres to carpets, clothing, furnishings, hairs etc. from where dermal uptake and ingestion takes place. Third hand tobacco smoke may remain in the indoor environments for months. It is particularly harmful for small children who play on the ground and put everything in mouth. Third hand tobacco smoke reacts with nitrous acid in the air and TSNAs (Tobacco Specific Nitrosamines) are formed which are very potent carcinogens.[17] Ozone is another air pollutant which reacts with almost 50 components of residual smoke to form some nano-particles which are taken up by human body and gets distributed throughout the body including some sensitive sites like bone marrow, lymph nodes, spleen, heart and central nervous system.[18] Thus residual tobacco smoke could be even more harmful than mainstream smoke.

The victim blaming approach is widely prevalent in society especially for women. Generally women are held responsible for their reproductive health. Tobacco cessation programmes also focus on pregnant women to quit tobacco use during pregnancy; less attention is paid to the paternal smoking cessation. The negative health effects of paternal smoking on fertility and the health of the foetus are generally overlooked.[8] Thus tobacco cessation programmes should also focus on paternal smoking.

Women Empowerment is imperative for achieving smoke-free homes. First of all, women and girls need to be better informed about the hazards of second hand smoke to themselves, as well as to foetus, children and other family members.

Important Trade-offs of Family Income When Men Use Tobacco

Tobacco use directly fuels poverty. It channels resources away from other basic needs like food, education and health. The evidence shows that tobacco use is highest among the poor.[3] The cultivation of tobacco is done at the cost of other food crops which might be grown at the utilised agricultural land. Ultimately, the main benefits of tobacco cultivation goes to transnational companies whose annual profits are more than even GDP of many low and middle income countries. The tobacco farmers just act like pawns in the hands of billion dollar tobacco industry. In the long-run tobacco farmers remain entrapped in the chronic cycle of poverty where the short-term earnings from tobacco crop only make them hand to mouth. Tobacco consumption is especially high among the poor and large proportion of their income goes in purchasing tobacco products thereby reducing the household disposable income.[3] For low income families, even a small trade-off of resources to buy tobacco products can have a significant impact on their health, nutrition and education. As a consequence, the inequalities in society increases further *i.e.*, the gap between rich and the poor increases. Also the health services will be overstretched as they attempt to meet the tobacco health burden, which may further jeopardise primary health care delivery aimed at women and children.

Illnesses caused by tobacco use also lead to loss of productivity and thus loss of family income. Men who fall sick due to adverse effects of tobacco use cannot go to work and thus the family bear the costs of treatment and care. Family members stay at home or in hospital for the care of the diseased. Also, money is spent for buying expensive medicines and for paying huge hospital bills. Most of the time, families have to sell property or take loans for the treatment of cancers caused by tobacco use. Thus families of tobacco users become poorer and get burdened over huge debts.[3]

Children whose parents are tobacco-users get deprived of good educational opportunities because of two reasons: The household income which should be spent on the education of children gets diverted to buy tobacco products. Secondly, premature death of any of the parents due to tobacco use leaves the children unsupported and deprived of education.

Tobacco-farming and tobacco industry involve child-labour, thus depriving educational opportunities to those children. Right from tobacco-farming, curing tobacco leaves to bidi rolling and smokeless tobacco industry; children work as labourers at every step. Instead of going to school, children of tobacco- farmers help their parents in farming activities which also expose them to pesticide- related as well as tobacco-related diseases such as cancers.

Tobacco consumption in our country only benefits multinational and transnational tobacco companies.[3] This money could be channelized towards providing basic necessities to our people like food, education, housing, and healthcare; and could benefit the national economies in the long run. If people stop spending on tobacco; then the saved money will not disappear from the economies, rather it will be circulated to other more important sectors like food, education and health. The money saved by stopping tobacco consumption will come in economic circulation rather than going in the pockets of rich MNCs and this money will ultimately generate employment in the countries.

Women Employed in Tobacco Industry

Women are also employed in large numbers in tobacco industry and get exploited. For example, Bidi industry and smokeless tobacco industry in India is highly unorganised and is based on home-based work done by women and their children. There are bidi rolling villages in India where women and children in each house roll bidis most of the day and earn their bread. Panchamukhi and others have mentioned that, "Women integrate bidi rolling with their household chores and get assistance from their children and other family members".[19] The packaging of smokeless tobacco is also done by women in their homes. Thus bidi and smokeless tobacco industry is very exploitative for women and children who work in this industry.

The conditions of labour employed in bidi industry were always exploitative especially in feudal set-up where they hardly had any bargaining power.[20] Bidi companies hire contractors for supply of Bidis, who then subcontract household bidi workers, particularly women and pay them per batch of about 750 or 1000 bidis.[19] Female labourers and child labour have always played an important role in bidi industry especially in bidi-rolling. According to National Sample Survey (NSS) 50th round (1993–94), an estimated 26 lakh people were employed in Bidi sector. It was a much lower estimate as majority of unreported bidi workers work at home. According to same survey reports, an estimated 74 percent of the tobacco employment was in bidi industry and about 76 percent of bidi workers were women.[21] The studies have indicated that children have been engaged in bidi industry as bonded labours, particularly girls, from an age as early as four.[19]

The government has introduced various welfare measures for the bidi workers through the Bidi Workers Welfare Fund Act (1976). These include financial assistance for their housing, healthcare, educational needs for children and recreational needs. Besides, the Minimum Wages Act was enacted in 1948 to protect the interest of the workers engaged mostly in the informal sector. Under the provisions of the Act, both central and state governments are the appropriate authority to fix, revise and enforce payment of minimum wages in scheduled employments falling under their respective jurisdictions. Bidi making is a scheduled employment only in the state sphere. The wages are generally on piece rate basis. Hence, erosion of bidi sales could lead to reduce work per person and should not result in unemployment. Research has also shown that on 22 percent of households involved in bidi making are fully dependent on bidi income and bidi work is largely a supplementary income among most of the women.[22]

The appalling condition of women bidi workers despite the government passing several legislations is worth mentioning. Women constitute a majority of the bidi industry's workforce. Since, most women bidi workers operate from their homes, they are isolated from the rest of the industry workforce and therefore are easy targets for exploitation. There are a large number of cases where acute poverty has forced bidi rolling women to mortgage their children to repay debts. In some districts of Tamil Nadu women have pledged their yet to be born children to bidi employers in order to repay debt.[22]

Employers consistently deny minimum wages to bidi workers even the government has fixed these for them. Female and girl child workers are mostly preferred in bidi rolling because of the limitation of alternative job opportunities for them and moreover, they can be easily exploited by the contractors in paying a lower wage rate.[22]

The female bidi workers had to manage simultaneously their own household task. They had to combine wage work with their domestic responsibilities. It is found that in addition to bidi rolling, the workers had to do sundry work for their own family. The workers had nearly full responsibilities on the activities like washing clothes and utensils, water collection, food preparation and childcare. Apart from the large bulk of sundry task, often some workers had to help their husbands in agriculture activity.[22]

The women involved in tobacco industry also get exposed to harmful chemicals and develop occupational diseases. The health hazards are too many with diseases like back-pain, rheumatic pains, respiratory diseases like asthma etc. and there are no proper medical facilities, As each worker prepares lakhs of bidis in a month, over years their fingers get worn out into thin shapeless bones as a result of which they cannot perform heavy work. The children sleep amidst tobacco leaves and hence they are also exposed to various health risks.[22]

GENDER DISCUSSION ALSO INCLUDE MEN

The term Gender is generally used in Feminist perspective to develop policies that can best promote the interests of women. Gender equity focuses almost exclusively on the disadvantaged conditions of women and in respect to tobacco use women get affected badly both as users as well as non-users. It is important to talk about role of gender in health risks among boys and men. Research has shown that risk behaviours such as tobacco use are also viewed as expressions of masculine identity.[23] Verma and Mahendra, in their examination of gender and sexual health risk in the setting of India, found that "Masculinity is an overwhelming construct... providing a framework to determine (male) self-concept and also the cultural roles relating to their actions" (p. 73).

Masculine norms also discourage 'feminine' behaviours such as caring for one's health.[23] Courtenay laments the fact that even in studies that 'address health risks more common to men than women, the discussion of men's greater risks and of the influence of men's gender is often conspicuously absent'.[24] Courtenay's review also found that men and boys experience more pressure than do females to conform to gender stereotypes; health-related norms include 'independent, self reliant, strong, robust and tough'.[24] One study, entitled 'If I don't smoke, I'm not a real man', used focus groups to explore smoking norms and values with boys aged 13–17 in Java, Indonesia.[25] For these boys, smoking was a sign of achieving manhood, with attached notions of potency and bravery.

"If we don't follow our peers and smoke, they will call us feminine" (24, p.798).

Smoking was also a way of cementing connections with peers within a very communally oriented society. It represented aspects of male social and cultural life, like the giving of cigarettes to men at weddings and funerals. The informants perceived smoking as a symbol of distinction between the sexes.

Smoking among women and girls was abnormal and represented poor manners, or worse: "Smoking is only common among hookers and bad girls" (24, p.799).

Based on the evidence, being a man appears to be the strongest predictor of tobacco use. However, this strong statistical association has prompted relatively little interest in the role of masculinity in mainstream tobacco control literature. Where gender is mentioned it almost invariably refers to sex-linked differences, or to women.[23]

Tobacco industry has very skilfully incorporated gender norms in its marketing strategies. To target men it used the images invoking norms of risk-taking such as horse-riding (Marlboro Man). Tobacco industry used to sponsor the motor-racing and other sports events.[23] Brand images may appeal to consumers' social insecurities by appearing to propose solutions to identity problems.

The first harmful consequence of tobacco use for males is that tobacco kills one-third to one-half of lifetime users, on average 15 years prematurely; the vast majority of deaths in India are among men. Tobacco is expected to kill 80 million Indian men now aged 0–34.[26] It also contributes to chronic and acute illnesses that reduce quality of life, and impair productivity. Second, tobacco use particularly hurts poor men, as it is concentrated among low-income and less-educated populations of the country.[27] The poor are far likelier than the rich to become ill and die from tobacco.

Tobacco use among men hurts women in number of ways. First, through passive smoking, women have higher rates of both acute and chronic diseases. Women exposed to second-hand smoke are more likely to have adverse pregnancy outcomes, including pre-term and low-birth-weight infants.[27] Second major negative consequence is that when men fall ill due to tobacco related illnesses, it propels families into poverty. In addition, women and girls tend to be carers, and thus disproportionately burdened by looking after husbands or fathers who develop tobacco-induced illnesses. If the major breadwinner dies, survivors can be pushed into extreme poverty. Catastrophic impoverishment for women is known to be associated with entry into sex work and other risky occupations, as well as migration and human trafficking.[28]

Figure 2 shows that prevalence of tobacco use (total, smoking, and smokeless) among men in India has decreased since 2009–10 (Fig. 2). The prevalence of total tobacco use in any form, among men, has declined

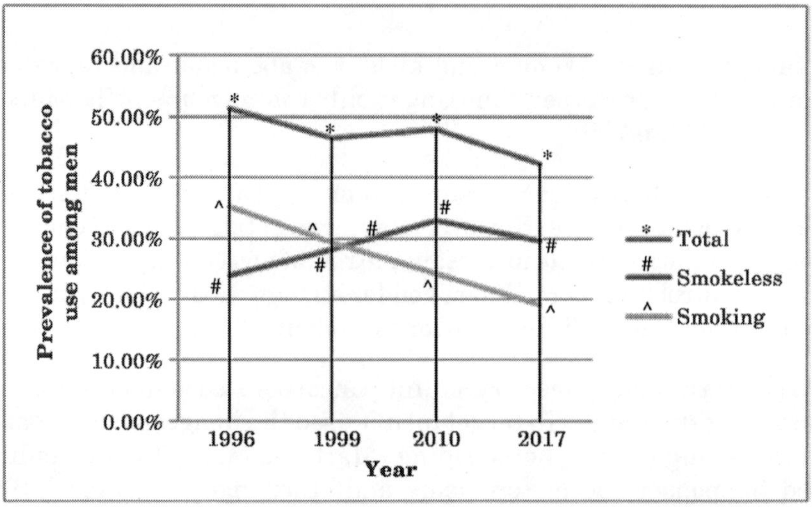

Fig. 2: Trends in the prevalence of tobacco use (smoking and smokeless) by men in India over a period of two decades *i.e.*, from 1995 to 2017.

from 47.9% in 2009–10 to 42.4% in 2016–17 (Fig. 2). However before 2009–10, there was a sharp rise in the prevalence of smokeless tobacco use among men, the smoking rates among men were constantly on decline since 1995–96 till 2016–17 (Fig. 2).

CONCLUSIONS

Thus we have seen that Gender is a key determinant of tobacco use in India. The Gender linked differences in prevalence rates of tobacco use are very high; at the same time there are other significant social issues revolving around, such as exposure to second-hand-smoke and employment of women in exploitative bidi industry. While gender equity focuses almost exclusively on the relative disadvantage of girls and women that exists in most societies, disproportionate male use of tobacco has profound negative consequences for men (as users) and for women (as nonusers). Consequences for women are also exacerbated by prevailing gender inequalities. A life-course approach is needed to fully comprehend the impacts of tobacco on the health of girls and women of all ages. There are implications of tobacco smoke exposure from childhood, through adolescence, during the reproductive years, and beyond to old age. Women leadership in tobacco control and women role models must be supported to achieve better health of both men and women that will allow them the opportunity to find their way towards prosperity.

REFERENCES

[1] Baldwin, R.D. (1853). Evils of tobacco as they affect body, mind and morals. Fowlers and Wells Publishers, New York, p. 4. Available from, *www.forgotten books.com*.

[2] GATS 2 (Global Adult Tobacco Survey – 2) Factsheet. India 2016–17. Ministry of Health and Family Welfare, Govt. of India; World Health Organisation; Tata Institute of Social Sciences. Available from, *http://www.searo.who.int/india/mediacentre/events/2017/gats2_india.pdf?ua=1*, [Accessed 14 June, 2017].

[3] WHO-SEARO (World Health Organisation – South East Asia Regional Office) (2017). Tobacco control for sustainable development. New Delhi: World Health Organization, Regional Office for South-East Asia, Licence: CC BY-NC-SA 3.0 IGO.

[4] Aghi, M.B. and Gopal, M. (2001). Exploiting women and children-India's bidi industry. *Lifeline*, 6: 8–10.

[5] International Institute for Population Sciences (IIPS), Mumbai and Ministry of Health and Family Welfare (MoHFW). Government of India: Global Adult Tobacco Survey (GATS) – India, 2009–10. New Delhi: MoHFW, Govt. of India; 2010. ISBN 978-81-920192-0-8. Available from: *http://mohfw.nic.in/WriteReadData/l892s/1455618937GATS%20India.pdf*, [Last accessed 15 July 2017].

[6] Rodgman, A. and Perfetti, T. (2009). The chemical components of tobacco and tobacco smoke. Boca Raton, FL: CRC Press, 2009. doi: 10.1201/97814200 78848.

[7] International Agency for Research on Cancer (IARC) (2007). Smokeless tobacco and some tobacco-specific-N-nitrosamines. IARC monographs on the evaluation of carcinogenic risks to humans. Vol. 89. Lyon, France: World Health Organisation, International Agency for Research on Cancer.

[8] World Health Organization (WHO) (2010). Gender, Women and the Tobacco Epidemic. Geneva: WHO.

[9] Bhonsle, R.B., Murti, P.R. and Gupta, P.C. (1992). Tobacco habits in India. *In*: Gupta, P.C., Hamner, J.E. and Murti, P.R. (*eds.*), Control of tobacco –related cancers and other diseases. International symposium. Bombay: Oxford University Press.

[10] Berkman, L.F. and Kawachi, I. (2014). A Historical Framework for Social Epidemiology. *In*: Berkman, L.F., Kawachi, I. and Glymour, M.M. (*eds.*), Social Epidemiology (Second Edition). New York: Oxford University Press. p. 8.

[11] US Department of Health and Human Services (2006). The Health Consequences of involuntary exposure to tobacco smoke. A report of the Surgeon General. Atlanta, GA: US Department of Health and Human Services, Centers for Disease Control and Prevention, Co-ordinating Center for Health Promotion, National Center for Chronic Disease Prevention and Health Promotion, Office on Smoking and Health.

[12] JHSPH (Johns Hopkins Bloomberg School of Public Health) (2007). *In*: Samet, J. (*ed.*), The Tobacco Epidemic. History: "Discovery and early use of tobacco and the foundations of the modern epidemic.

[13] US Department of Health, Education and Welfare (1972). The Health Consequences of Smoking: A Report of the Surgeon General: 1972. Washington: US Department of Health, Education and Welfare, Public Health Service, Health Services and Mental Health Administration, 1972. DHEW Publication No. (HSM) pp. 72–7516.

[14] US Environmental Protection Agency (1992). Respiratory health effects of passive smoking: Lung Cancer and other disorders. Washington: US Environmental Protection Agency, Office of Research and Development, Office of air and radiation. Publication no. EPA/600/6-90/006F.

[15] National Research Council (1986). Environmental Tobacco Smoke: Measuring exposures and assessing health effects. Washington: National Academy Press.

[16] US Department of Health and Human Services (2000). 9th Report on Carcinogens. Research Triangle Park (NC): US Department of Health and Human Services, Public Health Service, National Institutes of Health, National Institute of Environmental Health Sciences, National Toxicology Program.

[17] Matt, G.E., Quintana, P.J.E., Destaillats, H., Gundel, L.A., Sleiman, M., Singer, B.C. *et al.* (2011). Third-hand tobacco smoke: Global estimate of SHS burden. *Environ. Health Perspect.*, 119: A66–A67.

[18] Sleiman, M. *et al.* (2010). Formation of carcinogens indoors by surface mediated reactions of nicotine with nitrous acid, leading to potential third-hand smoke hazards. *Proc. Natl. Acad. Sci. USA*, 107(15): 6576–6581.

[19] Panchamukhi, P.R., Woollery, T.A. and Nayanatara, S.N. (2008). "Economics of Bidis in India", *In*: Gupta, P.C. and Asma, S. (*eds.*), "Bidi Smoking and Public Health", New Delhi: Ministry of Health and Family Welfare, p. 171.

[20] Giriappa, S. (1987). "Bidi-Rolling in Rural Development", New Delhi: Daya Publishing House.

[21] National Sample Survey Organisation (NSSO) (1998). "Fifth Quinquennial Survey, NSS 50th Round, July 1993 - June 1994", New Delhi: Department of Statistics, Government of India. Available from, *http://www.mospi.gov.in/national_data_bank/pdf/438_final.pdf* (Last accessed on 17 July 2017).

[22] Sarkar, S. and Bhuimali, A. (2005). Disadvantaged Women in Informal Sector (A study of Domestic Help and Bidi Workers). Delhi: Abhijeet Publications.

[23] Morrow, M. and Barraclough, S. (2010). Gender equity and tobacco control: Bringing masculinity into focus. *Global Health Promotion*, 17(1_suppl): 21–8.

[24] Courtenay, W.H. (2000). Constructions of masculinity and their influence on men' swell-being: A theory of gender and health. *Soc. Sci. Med.*, 50: 1385–1401.

[25] Ng, N., Weinehall, L. and Ohman, A. (2007). 'If I don't smoke, I'm not a real man': Indonesian teenage boys' views about smoking. *Health Educ. Res.*, 22(6): 794–804.

[26] World Health Organization (2004). The Millennium Development Goals and tobacco control. Geneva: WHO.

[27] World Health Organization (2008). WHO report on the global tobacco epidemic, 2008: The M power package. Geneva: WHO.

[28] World Health Organization (2002). World report on violence and health. Geneva: WHO.

Subject Index

R

S

T

U

V

W